SCHAUM'S OUTLINE OF

THEORY AND PROBLEMS

of

MARKETING

•

by

HERBERT F. HOLTJE

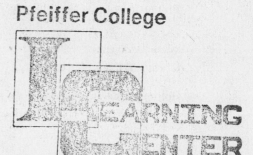
SCHAUM'S OUTLINE SERIES

McGRAW-HILL BOOK COMPANY

New York   St. Louis   San Francisco   Auckland   Bogotá   Guatemala   Hamburg   Johannesburg
Lisbon   London   Madrid   Mexico   Montreal   New Delhi   Panama   Paris
San Juan   São Paulo   Singapore   Sydney   Tokyo   Toronto

HERBERT F. HOLTJE has a B.S. degree in Advertising and Marketing, and an M.A. in Psychology, both from Fairleigh Dickinson University. He is the author of 22 books, including Schaum's Outline of Theory and Problems of *Advertising*. He is president of Tek-Mark, Inc., an advertising and marketing consulting firm.

Schaum's Outline of Theory and Problems of
MARKETING

4 5 6 7 8 9 10 11 12 13 14 15 SH SH 8 7 6

Sponsoring Editor, Harriet Malkin
Editing Supervisor, Denise Schanck
Production Supervisor, Claudia Dukeshire

Library of Congress Cataloging in Publication Data

Holtje, Herbert.
  Schaum's outline of marketing.

  (Schaum's outline series)
  Includes index.
  1. Marketing. 2. Marketing—Examinations, ques-
tions, etc. I. Title.
HF5415.H7498   658.8′002′02   80–14402
ISBN 0-07-029661-8

Preface

This book can be used by itself, as a basic text on marketing, or it can serve as a source of additional information and solved problems that will complement other text materials and classroom instruction. The information is current, and every attempt has been made to present the case studies as they occur in everyday marketing situations.

The outline is organized as follows:

1. The first part of each chapter deals with the material that is basic to the topic being covered. Within this section there are a number of examples that illustrate the basic principles of marketing.

2. A short series of review questions follows. The questions are all based on the material in the first section of the chapter. Answers are provided with each question. This quiz serves two purposes: first, it enables the student to measure what has been learned, and second, it serves as reinforcement. The feedback gained from immediately checking answers enhances the learning process. The section from which each question and answer is drawn is identified, so the student can easily review the material.

3. The solved problems follow the brief review questions. It is important to note that in every case, *the solved problems introduce new material*. These problems are not merely restatements of the material presented earlier in the chapters. However, this new material all builds on subjects which were introduced earlier in the chapter. Presenting new material in this form tends to make the learning dynamic, rather than a static statement of the facts. It presents problems faced by those working in marketing, and it helps students see how professional marketing people solve problems. The student should note that the solved problems, although presented as questions, are not tests of information gained in early parts of the chapters.

4. The midterm and final examinations are drawn directly from all sections of every chapter. No new material is introduced, and the score gained by the student will be a direct indication of the amount of material that has been learned. The questions are typical of those asked in introductory courses given at the college level.

5. There is a glossary at the end of the book. You will find this section helpful both as a study guide and as a working reference.

Herbert F. Holtje

Contents

Chapter *1* **THE MARKETING PROCESS** **1**

1.1   Introduction 1
1.2   The Marketing Concept 1
1.3   The Marketing Mix 2
1.4   The Competitive Climate 2
1.5   The Economic Climate 3
1.6   The Consumer Climate 4
1.7   An Expanded View of the Marketing Concept 4

Chapter *2* **MARKETS** **12**

2.1   Introduction 12
2.2   A Working Definition 12
2.3   Product Differentiation 12
2.4   Market Segmentation 13
2.5   Determining the Characteristics of a Segmented Market 13
2.6   Product Life Cycle and Market Segmentation 14
2.7   Consumer and Industrial Markets 14
2.8   How to Look at a Market 14
2.9   Age Effects in Consumer Markets 15

Chapter *3* **ORGANIZING FOR MARKETING** **21**

3.1   Introduction 21
3.2   Basic Organization 21
3.3   Departmental Integration 21
3.4   Organizing to Suit the Business Environment 22
3.5   Organizing to Suit the Corporate Environment 22
3.6   Planning a Marketing Organization 23
3.7   Marketing Functions 23
3.8   The Functionally-Oriented Marketing Organization 23
3.9   The Product-Oriented Marketing Organization 24
3.10   The Market-Oriented Marketing Organization 26

Chapter *4* **PRODUCT PLANNING** **34**

4.1   Introduction 34
4.2   How Marketing Defines a Product 34
4.3   The Product Life Cycle 35
4.4   The Introductory Stage of the Product Life Cycle 35
4.5   The Growth Stage of the Product Life Cycle 35
4.6   The Maturity Stage of the Product Life Cycle 36

CONTENTS

4.7   The Decline Stage of the Product Life Cycle 36
4.8   The Practical Application of the Product Life Cycle 36
4.9   New Product Development 37
4.10 New Product Failure 37

Chapter 5   PRICING STRATEGY **45**

5.1   Introduction 45
5.2   A Definition of Price 45
5.3   The Goals of Pricing 45
5.4   The Profitability Goals of Pricing 46
5.5   Using Market Share Goals to Establish Prices 46
5.6   Growth vs. Profits 47
5.7   Effects of Distribution on Pricing 47

Chapter 6   DISTRIBUTION SYSTEMS **55**

6.1   Introduction 55
6.2   Distribution Systems Add Value: Time Utility 55
6.3   Distribution Systems Add Value: Place Utility 55
6.4   The Business of Wholesaling 56
6.5   Choosing the Best Channel of Distribution 56
6.6   Multiple Channels of Distribution 57
6.7   Choosing the Most Efficient Methods of Distribution 57
6.8   Exclusive and General Distribution 58
6.9   Intensive and Selective Distribution 58

Midterm Examination **66**

Chapter 7   MARKETING RESEARCH **69**

7.1   Introduction 69
7.2   Market Research Defined 69
7.3   Market Research: For Development and Feedback 69
7.4   Application of the Scientific Method 69
7.5   Defining the Problem 70
7.6   Preliminary Analysis 70
7.7   Conducting an Informal Investigation 71
7.8   Planning the Research Project 71
7.9   Carrying Out the Research Project 72
7.10 Research Interpretation 72

CONTENTS

Chapter 8 MARKET PLANNING AND FORECASTING **80**

8.1 Introduction 80
8.2 Focusing the Marketing Mix 80
8.3 Barriers to Successful Marketing Planning 80
8.4 Anticipating Response to Market Variations 80
8.5 Planning Based on a Composite of Marketing Mixes 81
8.6 Long- and Short-Range Marketing Planning 82
8.7 Marketing and Total Corporate Planning 82
8.8 The Annual Marketing Plan 82
8.9 Market Demand Forecasting 82
8.10 Market Potential and Market Share 83

Chapter 9 CONSUMER BEHAVIOR **90**

9.1 Introduction 90
9.2 Learning Theories of Behavior 90
9.3 Stimulus-Response Theories 90
9.4 Cognitive Learning Theories 90
9.5 The Gestalt Theory of Learning 91
9.6 Psychoanalytical Theories of Learning 91
9.7 Motivation 92
9.8 Perception 92

Chapter 10 ADVERTISING AND SALES PROMOTION **100**

10.1 Introduction 100
10.2 The Promotion Mix 100
10.3 Establishing an Optimum Promotional Mix 101
10.4 The Goals of Promotional Activity 101
10.5 Establishing a Promotional Budget 102
10.6 Evaluating Promotional Effectiveness 103

Chapter 11 THE LEGAL ENVIRONMENT OF MARKETING **113**

11.1 Introduction 113
11.2 A Summary of Major Acts Affecting Marketing 113
11.3 The Sherman Antitrust Act 114
11.4 The Clayton and Robinson-Patman Acts 115

Chapter 12 MARKETING MANAGEMENT AND CONTROL **122**

12.1 Introduction 122
12.2 Market Planning, Management, and Control 122

CONTENTS

12.3   The Basics of Marketing Control 122
12.4   Sources of Marketing Control Information 123
12.5   Using the Sales Forecast as a Measurement Tool 123
12.6   Planning a Marketing Control Report System 123
12.7   Information to Be Included in Market Reports 124
12.8   Determining the Value of a Reporting System 124

Final Examination 133

GLOSSARY 136

INDEX 144

Chapter 1

The Marketing Process

1.1 INTRODUCTION

Reduced to basics, all businesses do two things: they create a product or a service and they market it. Not long ago, the word "sell" would have been used in place of the word "market." However, the difference between these two words is essentially the difference between a modern economy in which its citizens have a choice of products and services that meet specific needs and one in which the people have little or no choice. Today, the type and quality of goods and services are determined by the consumers who will buy and use them. Economists call this want-satisfying concept *utility*. As long as the products satisfy consumer wants economically, they can be said to have utility, and they will continue to be produced. Those that fail to satisfy will not be purchased, and eventually will be forced from the market.

It is the concept of economic utility that has led modern nations and businesses to the system we call *marketing*. The function of marketing is to plan, create, price, promote, and distribute goods and services.

1.2 THE MARKETING CONCEPT

Before World War II, most goods and services were created and sold with very little thought of the customer. An engineer's innovative idea was turned into a product and then handed to a salesperson to sell. In some cases there was a need for the product, but in most it was up to the salespeople to create the need as well as the sales. The emphasis was on the product and the needs of the company that made it.

After the war, peace-time production turned to satisfying consumer wants that had been neglected because of military requirements. Consumers had a lot of catching up to do, and industry scaled up to meet the demands. However, this created a strong buyer's market, and heavy competition meant that the old methods would no longer serve industry very well. Consumers now had a wider choice of products, and manufacturers found that they could profit only if they first determined what was wanted and then made it accordingly. The emphasis had shifted to customer's wants.

In essence, industry recognized and converted to a customer orientation. In a modern marketing system products are not manufactured and handed to salespeople. They are the result of careful examination of what is needed, how it can be made efficiently, and how it can be sold profitably. When all of these criteria can be met, the chances are good that a product will succeed. It is the evaluation and implementation of these criteria that shape modern marketing decisions and provide the best products and services for the consumers.

EXAMPLE 1.

The way in which the pressure of competition led to a consumer-oriented marketing approach is clearly illustrated in the development of the automobile industry. The automobile's rise in popularity began during the 1930s. But this was a period of economic depression as well as an era during which people had to become accustomed to an entirely new mode of transportation. There were many more car manufacturers than there are now, and competition was keen for what little market there was. However, most manufacturers were production oriented, believed they knew best, and designed their cars with little thought of customer wants. For example, Henry Ford, who first mass-produced automobiles, said that customers could have any color they wanted, as long as it was black.

When the war ended and the market for cars expanded, the manufacturers that were successful designed automobiles to meet the requirements of potential buyers. Most of the features we now take for granted are the result of market research that pinpointed what people wanted on their cars. These range from frivolous features such as automatic windows to important improvements such as more efficient engines. In fact, one automobile manufacturer uses this line in its advertising: "You asked for it, you got it." This is the marketing concept in a nutshell.

1.3 THE MARKETING MIX

Not all products can be treated in the same way. Needs for a product can vary with seasons or style changes or a variety of other factors. The success or faliure of a product in the marketplace depends on the manner in which a number of marketing elements, called the *marketing mix,* are blended.

The elements of the marketing mix are as follows.

Product planning. This includes, but is not limited to, the physical attributes of the product. Decisions about packaging design, trademarks, branding, warranties, guarantees, and the anticipated market life of the product are also part of product planning. The product must be developed as it relates to the satisfaction of consumer needs.

Distribution. Distribution involves everything from the physical aspects of getting the product to the customer to the selection of appropriate marketing channels. The channels can include wholesalers, distributors, and retailers if the product is intended for the general consumer. For an industrial product, direct factory salespeople, manufacturers representatives, or distributors in regional locations may be required. Essentially, this phase of the marketing mix is considered to include all intermediaries, regardless of how they are defined. See Chapter 5.

Promotional strategy. This includes personal selling as well as advertising, sales promotion, and indirect selling. Whatever methods are used, it is important that they be blended carefully to produce a unified effort. When money is spent to advertise a product and the sales follow-up is not properly planned and implemented, the money will have been wasted. See Chapter 11.

Pricing. A major part of the marketing mix. Prices must be set at a point where profit is possible, yet be justifiable to the consumer and competitive with similar products offered by competitors. See Chapter 4.

EXAMPLE 2.

Marketing mix tailored to the problem. The marketing mix elements must all be considered when a marketing plan is being developed. Depending on specific conditions, however, some elements may be more important than others. For example, a company planning to sell clothing to people in rural and less accessible areas must give considerable thought to the problems of distribution. A store in a sparsely settled area might be expensive to run, based on the volume of business that could be done. However, selling clothing to these same people by mail involves a distribution system that would probably be cost-effective, whereas the store would lose money. Of course all of the other elements of the marketing mix must be considered, but the pivotal element of success could hinge on the selection of an appropriate channel of distribution.

1.4 THE COMPETITIVE CLIMATE

There is hardly a product or service that doesn't have some competition. In some cases, the market may be flooded with competitors; in others there may be few.

The development of a marketing strategy, then, begins with the decision to compete. The firm must determine the market or markets they will seek and decide just how to compete. Whatever the situation, competition in the marketplace creates a dynamic rather than a steady state. Everything a competitor does has some effect on the market and the other competitors.

EXAMPLE 3.

A classic description of market dynamics can be seen in the gas wars that once took place between rival station owners. Service stations would vie with each other to have the lowest price. They hoped that lower prices would produce higher volume. They didn't realize that volume alone was not enough; the price/volume factor must be considered, regardless of the number of gallons sold. Sooner or later they lost money while pumping unheard of gallonage. But the situation does illustrate in graphic and compressed time terms what can happen in a highly competitive market.

Competition can be *direct,* as when the maker of one television set competes with all others for the same type of set, or it can be indirect, as when a family must decide whether to buy a new TV set or spend the same money on new outdoor furniture. In general, it is difficult for individual manufacturers to attack indirect competition. But when several band together to form a trade association, their collective efforts can have some effect on indirect competition.

EXAMPLE 4.

Companies belonging to a trade association often jointly promote the product they have in common. The Tea Council is made up of a number of companies that compete with each other when the consumer buys tea. But collectively they all must compete with other beverage producers, such as those who sell coffee. Therefore, as a group the Tea Council will spend money to increase the consumption of tea, but each producer will also spend money individually to increase its share of the tea market.

EXAMPLE 5.

Some companies gain market advantage through specialization. Some companies are big enough to compete with others in many markets. Other companies prefer to specialize in one market segment. This segment may be defined by geographic location, consumer age bracket, income levels, etc. However, before any particular segment is selected, it is important to know what the individuals who make up the market want, and what they would be willing to pay for the product or service.

Business consultants are a good example of this type of specialization. When a person has a skill that can be offered to solve a narrow range of problems, the chances are good that he or she will be more competent than a person who claims to be able to do everything. Generally this advantage of specialization can even be recognized in many of the larger consulting firms which handle different types of consulting work. Such firms are generally conglomerations of a number of individuals who were successful in a narrow area, and found it economically advantageous to grow by joining forces with other consultants in related, but noncompetitive fields.

1.5   THE ECONOMIC CLIMATE

Any market planning must take into account the economic climate. However, there is never just one economic climate at any given time. The overall or national picture must be considered as well as that of local regions where the product or service will be marketed. Even during the recent recessions there were areas of the country that were in full production.

In general, our economy is cyclical and follows this pattern: recession, depression, recovery, prosperity. There are those who claim that government controls are such that a depression is now impossible, but it appears that this is more a way of redefining a depression than of actually preventing one.

It might appear that every company should contract its operations during a downturn and expand during periods of relative prosperity, but this is not necessarily true. This kind of decision should be based on an analysis of potential, regardless of the economic conditions. For example, a business which provides retraining services to people who are out of work would probably do well in a recession or depression, and poorly during periods of peak employment.

EXAMPLE 6.

Certain economic conditions require marketing people to do exactly the opposite of what they had been doing to make their firms successful in order to limit product consumption. The term applied to this activity is *demarketing*. Consider the effort the power companies have expended to reduce the demand for electricity in the face of energy shortages. The utilities and their trade associations have gone to considerable expense to produce information that will help power users make the most efficient use of less power. The effect is to limit the consumption of their product, power, but it must be done at a point in the price-volume ratio that still produces a profit.

EXAMPLE 7.

Inflation is perhaps one of the most persistent problems faced by American business, and the government can and does take certain steps to control it. In simple terms, rising prices tend to reduce consumer purchasing power and savings since consumers buy today because they fear higher prices tomorrow. As this happens, fewer purchases are made. This is inflation, and it can occur during any of the four economic cycles. The usual approach to solve the problem involves reduced government expenditures, or increased taxes. Often both measures are adapted at the same time. For the marketer, higher taxes mean even less money available for products and services other than the essentials. When the government decides to reduce its expenditures, those who sell to it lose business. Of course, there is also the possibility of mandated controls, but these, too, have inherent problems. In essence, all of these approaches are used in some combination, and the entire system must be constantly fine-tuned to maintain a safe balance.

1.6   THE CONSUMER CLIMATE

Marketing people must also be able to understand and predict the social and psychological conditions that contribute to marketing success. For example, consumer reaction to shoddy workmanship has resulted in better products. The feelings of frustration and anxiety encountered during periods of national strife have resulted in increased savings, and less spending.

EXAMPLE 8.

Many factors affect consumer behavior. Contemporary psychological theory states that buying behavior is goal oriented. Behavior is initiated when needs create tensions in the individual. This tension leads to activity which satisfies the needs and thus reduces the tension. An individual seeks out a particular goal based on the perception of available alternatives. Usually, people are selective and choose carefully from the brands, ads, and products to which they are exposed. Past experience, attitudes, beliefs, and personality traits contribute to this process so that a final product choice is the result of many factors. The consumer's self-image is one of the most important elements to consider. Automobile and cigarette manufacturers, for example, go to great lengths to advertise their products being used by certain types of people—thus creating an image for the consumer to identify with. One cigarette company stresses the macho image with its ads featuring rugged cowboys, and another makes it plain that only the modern, self-assured woman would smoke the brand.

This activity is called positioning. It is a strategy that concentrates on a specific market segment, rather than using a broader appeal. Products are "positioned" relative to their competitors. The brewer that says its beer is the one beer to have when you're having more than one is trying to attract heavy beer drinkers.

1.7   AN EXPANDED VIEW OF THE MARKETING CONCEPT

It's no longer enough to satisfy the need of customers and to achieve the profit motives of the corporation and its stockholders. Companies must also consider and satisfy the needs of individuals whose lives are affected by the company's activities. This area in known as *social responsibility*. Along with the marketing concept, social responsibility must be taken into consideration in all phases of product planning and corporate growth.

EXAMPLE 9.

Social responsibility takes different forms; one of these is the effort to create products that are ecologically safe. The automobile company that, through careful market research, determines just what the car-buying public wants and produces cars to meet the requirements makes a profit. But, when the same company pollutes the air near its factory with dangerous fumes, it hasn't considered another public it must satisfy—its immediate neighbors.   Many marketing-oriented companies realized this social obligation long before it was mandated, and did what was necessary to solve their problems.   Their approach was similar to that used to sell their products. They first determined what the problem was, then decided how to resolve it.   When they took the appropriate action, they satisfied their neighbors.   Unfortunately, many companies have ignored their social responsibilities, and it has been necessary for the Environmental Protection Agency to mandate the steps that must be taken.

Review Questions

1. Basically, all businesses do two things: they create a product or service and then sell it.   True or false?

    Ans.   True.   See Section 1.1

2. In a marketing-oriented economy, consumers have a wider choice of products and services than they would have under a system which produced goods with little concern for customer needs and wants. True or false?

    Ans.   True.   See Section 1.1

3. When a product satisfies consumer wants economically, it is said to have (*a*) demand, (*b*) utility, (*c*) economy, (*d*) functional application.

    Ans.   (*b*)   See Section 1.1.

4. In terms of goods and services, the function of marketing is to (*a*) plan, (*b*) create, (*c*) price, (*d*) promote, (*e*) distribute, (*f*) all of these.

    Ans.   (*f*)   See Section 1.1.

5. Before World War II, considerable consumer planning went into the development of products and services.   True or false?

    Ans.   False.   See Section 1.2.

6. In a modern marketing system, it is entirely up to salespeople to create a need for products as well as sell them.   True or false?

    Ans.   False.   See Section 1.2.

7. Not all products can be treated in the same way.   The appropriate blending of number of elements called _____ helps insure success.   (*a*) utility, (*b*) the marketing concept, (*c*) the marketing mix, (*d*) market research.

    Ans.   (*c*)   See Section 1.3.

8. The marketing mix includes (*a*) product planning, (*b*) distribution, (*c*) promotion, (*d*) pricing, (*e*) all of these.

    Ans.   (*e*)   See Section 1.3.

9. Product planning is limited strictly to the physical characteristics of the product.   True or false?

    Ans.   False.   See Section 1.3.

10. Distribution includes everything from the physical aspects of moving the product to the marketplace to the selection of appropriate selling channels.   True or false?

    Ans.   True.   See Section 1.3.

11. Promotional strategy includes only advertising and sales promotion.   True or false?

    Ans.   False.   See Section 1.3.

12. Prices must be set at the point where profit is possible but without regard to consumer attitudes and competitive prices.   True or false?

    Ans.   False.   See Section 1.3.

13. All elements of the marketing plan are of equal importance, regardless of individual circumstances. True or false?

Ans. False. See Example 2.

14. When a number of competitors exist within a market, there is a tendency for the economic conditions to remain fairly stable. True or false?

Ans. False. See Section 1.4.

15. Manufacturers of similar products generally try to combat indirect competition through (*a*) price wars, (*b*) overwhelming advertising campaigns, (*c*) price reductions, (*d*) trade association activity.

Ans. (*d*) See Example 4.

16. The development of a marketing strategy begins with the decision to (*a*) find investors, (*b*) compete, (*c*) create an advertising campaign, (*d*) none of these.

Ans. (*b*) See Section 1.4.

17. In general, our economy is cyclical and follows this pattern: recession, depression, recovery, prosperity. True or false?

Ans. True. See Section 1.5.

18. The effect of demarketing is to (*a*) separate markets, (*b*) limit consumption of a product, (*c*) identify secondary markets, (*d*) none of these.

Ans. (*b*) See Example 6.

19. The marketing concept and social responsibility have no relationship to each other. True or false?

Ans. False. See Section 1.7.

20. The choice of a product is, among other things, based on (*a*) past experience, (*b*) attitudes, (*c*) beliefs, (*d*) personality traits, (*e*) all of these.

Ans. (*e*) See Example 8.

Solved Problems

1.1. The marketing concept stands in strong contrast to the sales approach. Describe the major differences between the two points of view.

In a selling orientation, the emphasis is on the product. The product is created with little regard for its utility or value to a customer. However, when a company is marketing oriented, planning begins with the needs of the market. Products are created to satisfy these needs. The marketing-oriented company will not only determine in advance what is needed, it will determine if it can make the product and if the product can be sold profitably. In a sense, the sales-oriented company has internalized its operation, and pays little attention to the needs of the market. The marketing-oriented company begins with the marketplace and then works back through all of its operations to see if it can produce a product for which there is a need and which will produce a profit.

For example, most book publishers now think of themselves in terms of their markets, rather than simply as publishers. Those who publish fiction think of themselves as providing entertainment. Those in the text field think of themselves as suppliers of knowledge. The concept of a book as the publisher sees it is that the content is the end product and the book is the vehicle. When companies reorient their thinking in this way they are often able to serve the needs of their customers better.

1.2. Since the industrial revolution, American business has undergone four distinct stages of development. Production orientation characterized the first stage. How were businesses organized in this period and what were the major characteristics of their operations?

A company which is production oriented is generally under the guidance of executives who are trained in production and engineering. The major thrust of their efforts is to emphasize mass production and to simplify a product line that can sell at low unit costs. The sales department seldom has much voice in management and sales people are expected to sell the output at a profit. Marketing activity is carried on at a very rudimentary level. There is usually a sales department, but marketing research and advertising are seldom considered. As such a company grows, there is often a tendency to expand into specialized markets, and separate divisions often grow from this trend. Advertising is usually begun, but the department responsible for selling is still thought of as the sales department. With few exceptions, this was the way most industry was run until the early 1930s.

1.3. During the Depression of the 1930s, it became apparent that a production orientation would no longer work. Why? What happened to move American industry from the production to the sales stage of development?

During the Depression, people could no longer buy all of the products that were made. Just making a better product was not enough; the emphasis had to be placed on selling. Selling became aggressive, and the sales function within the company began to grow in stature and responsibility. However, there still was little interest in determining what was wanted before a product was made. Also at this time, other activities that had been separate from sales began to be included within the sales department. In some companies, the sales manager became responsible for sales training, product installation and service, market research, and other sales-related activities. The sales phase of development in America lasted until the 1950s. World War II had created huge shortages, and after the war a production orientation was quite practical. However, once industry caught up, a new approach was required; it was at this point that what we know as marketing had its beginnings.

1.4. As companies grow from a sales orientation to a marketing point of view, more attention is paid to customer requirements. Describe this change and its ramifications for the corporation and the economy in general.

When American industry recognized the importance of marketing, the executives in this area were elevated to positions of responsibility greater than those held during the production-oriented phase. Functions that were at one time the responsibility of production, finance, and engineering executives became part of marketing. Because the orientation of the companies had switched to the needs of the customer, it became the responsibility of the marketing person to coordinate all of the other activities within the company in a profitable way. The marketing influence was now being felt at the beginning of the production cycle, rather than at the end of it.

It is interesting to note that at different times executives from other disciplines had greater chances of rising from their middle management specialty to the top. The presidents of many big corporations during the production phase rose from engineering, and this is often true today of companies that begin their life with this orientation. But today many of the chief operating officers of the country's leading companies have risen from the ranks of marketing. It is important to note that even though it is possible to plot the trends of American industry through the production, sales, and marketing stages, not every company is, or starts out with, a marketing orientation. However, sooner or later, even those companies which began with an idea that was created without a marketing orientation, must turn to marketing to survive. This generally occurs when competition becomes difficult for such a company.

1.5. We are now seeing the good and bad effects of a strong emphasis on marketing. In some cases, we see millions spent on products that have little real value, but were produced because marketing people determined that they could be made and sold at a profit. On the other hand, we see the development of products that meet very real needs and solve pressing problems. Obviously the marketing and other earlier phases had their drawbacks. Some say that the next trend, consumerism, will give us the best of marketing thinking with few of the problems. What should the goals of consumerism be?

The goal of marketing will always be to make a profit for the corporation, but these goals are now being tempered by a concern for human values as well as profits. There appears to be a trend from materialism to humanism, and companies that take this change seriously will have to pay more attention to long-range, rather than short-range, goals. In a sense, marketing people will be more concerned with the delivery of a quality of life rather than the products that characterize a materialistic society.

1.6. To some, the marketing concept was the answer to all sales problems. Why would you disagree with this and how would you view marketing as but another step in the continuing evolution of business?

In general, there are two main classes of variables with which a marketing executive must deal. The internal variables can, to some extent, be controlled and shaped to conform to company's marketing plans and its overall strategy for growth. The external variables are, in general, not controllable. They can be reacted to and often guided, but outright control of all external influences is next to impossible. The degree to which a marketing plan succeeds is determined by the speed and flexibliity with which a company can react to changes outside of its direct influence. If marketing managers are able to predict the direction and extent of these outside changes, they will be in a good position to profit in a competitive market. And, if marketing people can make use of the variables which can be controlled, there will be a better chance for growth and profits.

1.7. Some marketing executives are referred to as "bottom liners." This implies a pragmatic attitude that reflects itself in purely economic decisions. Discuss why this alone is insufficient to plan a marketing strategy and what other major factors should be included.

A knowledge of economic factors such as concentration of customers, income levels, and national and local economic conditions is important, but a knowledge of the social and behavioral aspects of the market is also important. As people rise in terms of income, their tastes change and they respond to different influences. When a person is able to afford only the necessities, buying decisions are made mainly for practical reasons. Which product costs more? What is the real value of one purchase over another? But as discretionary income levels rise, consumers make choices that are no longer strictly utilitarian. Other factors such as traditions and socioeconomic backgrounds affect these decisions. The marketer must have at least a working knowledge of the influences that affect decisions in the market he or she serves. Further, the marketer must understand the motivations behind the selection of one product over another under these varying circumstances.

1.8. The buying public is not the only force with which a marketer must contend. Local and federal governments are playing an increasing role in business. How has this occurred, and what are the implications?

In general, Americans have voted for more and more controls over society as well as the economy. Government planning has had strong effects in many areas. For example, legislation which has mandated a cleaner environment has caused hardship for some and unexpected profits for others. It is too soon to know just what the outcome of the activity will be in economic terms, but there can be no doubt that some of the pollution-control laws were long overdue. The company which marketed pollution-control equipment could view this legislation in very positive terms, but the company which found itself spending large sums of money to prevent its equipment from polluting the environment suffered. Without arguing for or against the enactment of pollution control laws, it can be stated that an astute marketer who could predict the trends would be in an excellent economic position.

Similar situations exist for other areas of government activity. Government intervention appears to be a strong trend in our economy, and the company that senses the political climate and relates its marketing efforts to the trends will be ahead of those who hope that government will just "go away."

1.9. When business is criticized, the comments are very often aimed at deceptive and misleading advertising as well as questionable selling tactics. What is the greatest force controlling these practices?

Even though considerable government legislation has been enacted to protect the consumer, there still are many companies and individuals providing less than the value promised in the products and services they offer. In the long run, those who intentionally mislead the public often find that their own greed is the cause of their downfall. In the meantime, however, it is possible for them to cause much harm. Consumer groups and strong government action are helping to keep this activity to a minimum, but the best way to solve the problem is to insure that consumers know and understand everything about the products they buy. The shabby marketers are responding to a market—those who can be fooled. If consumers understood the products, the sales contracts, and the promises made by the manufacturers, there would not be an environment in which shady operators could work. Consumer groups and government agencies are trying to solve the problem by such consumer education.

1.10. Competition is seldom limited to a direct substitute for a particular product. What other aspects of competition must be kept in mind by marketing people?

A direct substitute is definitely considered competitive, but only if it can be sold at a lower price, or possesses another characteristic which is important to the buyer. For example, it is often possible for a company to sell a product which is almost identical to that made by another manufacturer for a higher price. If delivery time is important, a customer may be willing to pay a higher price just to insure delivery. Therefore, it is important for the marketing executive to consider availability as well as price in the competitive picture. Often, the production of substitutes creates competition. For example, until a few years ago glass companies made all of the bottles used to deliver liquids such as milk, juice, soda, and liquor. Now many of these containers are made by people who never made anything of glass—plastics manufacturers. However, in the turnabout that often occurs in such situations, some of the glass companies have either entered the plastic business themselves, or have acquired plastics companies just to regain this lost market.

1.11. Making a good product is important. But without the right distribution system, even the best product can fail. Discuss this concept.

Even when a product is created to meet a specific need of a certain segment of the population, unless the distribution system is effective, there will be marketing problems. Perhaps the most obvious examples of this can be seen in advertising for products in magazines that don't reach the right readers. For example, advertising monogrammed bowling shirts in a literary magazine would be a waste of money. Trying to sell expensive clothes in discount stores would be equally useless. A direct sale approach, door-to-door, for books on investment opportunities would succeed in some neighborhoods, but fail in others. The point is this: The delivery system is just as important as the concept of the product itself and the need it satisfies.

1.12. Marketing is most successful when the goals set specify the means by which they will be achieved. What is wrong with a goal which states that the company must capture such-and-such market and maximize profits?

These goals are too vague. To be effective, goals must be specific; there should be provisions by which progress and success can be evaluated. Specific goals such as a twenty-five percent increase are more specific, but lack the precision needed to put them into action and evaluate results. If the twenty-five percent increase is to be achieved by adding twelve new distributors, and the distributors are all given specific dollar or unit sales quotas, the goals and the means to achieve them are clear.

1.13. Apart from specific market-oriented goals, what else must be given serious consideration when establishing a marketing plan?

The goals of the corporation must be carefully integrated with the marketing goals. If marketing says that, through its efforts, it can increase sales by twelve percent, this may not be enough in terms of the debt obligations of the company and the factors of inflation.   If the corporation requires a higher increase, marketing must try to see how its own as well as the corporate goals can be met.

1.14.   Marketing planning is of little value without the establishment of marketing policies. Discuss this concept.

A marketing policy sets up basic rules.   For example, a manufacturer selling through commission agents may establish a discount policy of different percentages based on sales volume.   This policy, when incorporated in a marketing program, establishes the operating rules.   It allows management to plan for manufacturing as well as pricing and all of the other variables.   If there were no established discount schedule, and every agent were given different terms, it would be all but impossible to plan effectively.   However, it should be noted that such policies need not be adhered to when conditions indicate that there should be a change.   Considering the example of the agent's discount, some companies find that they can open a territory or bolster lagging sales by temporarily relaxing the policy.   When the goal has been accomplished, the company can return to an enforcement of the general policy.

1.15.   Profits are the goal of marketing, but they are not the sole basis on which a marketing program should be evaluated.   What are some of the other considerations?

Profits are what keep a company in business, but it is possible to make a profit in only a small area of business.   For example, a company marketing products nationally may make a profit, but on analysis find that this profit comes from one small area.   Further analysis might show that if the other territories were closed, the cost of sales would be greatly reduced and result in a much higher profit.   The same could be true of individual salesmen or commission sales agents.   It could also be shown that advertising might have cost too much for the results it produced.   An evaluation of the effectiveness of a marketing program only begins with the balance sheet.

1.16.   Suppose that an engineer in your company has developed a product which seems interesting and exciting to everyone.   What would be the first step you would take before deciding to add it to the company's product line?

It would be necessary to determine if there is a market for the product.   This situation parallels that of the production-oriented economy discussed earlier.   However, it is important to note that just because a product is conceived without assurance of a good market does not necessarily mean that it cannot succeed.

1.17.   Assuming the product in the previous problem was found to have an adequate market, what might be the next step?

The next step would be a purely marketing decision.   The company considering the product would have to determine whether or not the product would coordinate with existing products and whether it had appeal for the markets already being served.   This is not necessarily a pass-fail point, however.   If it could be shown that the product had sufficient potential, even though present distribution was inadequate, it might be wise to establish a new distribution system just for one product.

1.18.   Assuming that the product can be sold by the company to the markets it already serves, what would be the next step in the decision process?

It would be necessary to determine whether the product could be made within the company's existing production capabilities.   Again, this is not a hard and fast rule.   If anticipated sales warranted it, the company might elect to build the proper facilities or find a source of manufacture outside the plant.

1.19.   Having progressed this far, what would be the next step in the evaluation of the potential for the new product?

It would have to be shown that all of the previous problems could be solved economically.   An economic analysis would have to be made showing if and when the product would become profitable and what the total investment would have to be.

1.20.   Are there any other barriers to the development of this product that should be considered?

All legal aspects such as patent infringements and copyrights would have to be investigated.

Chapter 2

Markets

2.1 INTRODUCTION

The term *market* is used in many ways, even within the business community. There are stock markets and retail markets, as well as other places where products are sold or traded. In general, the word means a place where sellers and buyers meet for the purpose of satisfying their respective needs. The place need not necessarily be a physical location, such as a store. If you think of a market as being made of collective demand for a product or service that is being met or could be met by producers, you will be using the word in a way in which most business people use it.

EXAMPLE 1.

The *demand* for a product is often affected by its price, as is seen in the history of the electronic calculator. In order for a market to exist, there must be demand. That is, there must be a need for a product or a service. However, this is only the beginning. If the need cannot be fulfilled with the right product or service for a price that satisfies the buyer and insures the seller a profit, the market will not come into being.

When electronic calculators were first introduced, there was a demand for them from every quarter. But because of relatively high prices, few were sold to students. However, now that they can be made and sold for less than the cost of a slide rule, the market has become huge. Demand and price are such that nearly every student now has an inexpensive calculator that would have sold for several hundred dollars a few years ago.

2.2 A WORKING DEFINITION

The term market will be used throughout this book in a way that can be summed up as follows:
A market is people or businesses that have purchasing power and the willingness and authority to buy.

For the purposes of this book, the word *need* will not be limited to the traditional definition which restricts its usage to necessities such as food and clothing. Needs, in marketing terms, include acquired tastes such as the desire for caviar. Think, then, of a need as a lack of something useful, whether it is based on an acquired taste or the satisfaction of a basic requirement for life.

2.3 PRODUCT DIFFERENTIATION

When there is a need that can be satisfied by only one producer, there is seldom any incentive for the producer to improve the product or service. However, as competition enters the field, producers often capture a share of someone else's market or hold on to what they have by modifying the product to increase its utility to the customer. In marketing terms, this is *product differentiation*. That is, a producer attempts to compete by enhancing the product as it relates to consumer needs.

EXAMPLE 2.

The automobile industry is, perhaps, the most obvious example of product differentiation. Auto manufacturers go to great lengths to make their cars different, or at least to make them appear different. Annual style changes are one example of this activity. The industry is geared to high volume annual sales, and such an approach is one way to encourage consumers to trade in their cars more frequently. For that certain segment of the market interested in mechanical aspects, auto makers produce models called performance cars. Those who drive them will argue endlessly about the relative merits of such features as carburation systems. The promotion of these points dominates the advertising for such autos.

12

2.4   MARKET SEGMENTATION

There are often a number of submarkets for the same or a slightly modified product.   New markets can be tapped by incorporating minor product changes, or by applying a slightly different marketing technique to the same product.   Each submarket tends to be a homogeneous grouping which is easily reached because of characteristics its members have in common.   Note that *market segmentation* is a customer-oriented concept.   It is a marketing tool that had little relevance during the production-oriented period of our industrial history.

EXAMPLE 3.

Marketing people talk of marketing segmentation, and advertising people, when called upon to promote the products, think of the "rifle" approach, rather than the "shotgun" technique.   That is, the single shot is aimed at a specific target market, rather than scattering shots for every market.   A segmented market often requires a variety of marketing programs.   For example, in the springtime, the airlines and Florida hotels push hard to attract vacationing college students.   Their marketing approach used at this time of year is entirely different from the one used to fill the same planes and hotels with families during the other seasons.   The planes are the same and the hotels are the same, but the same marketing approach would not work for both groups.   Segmentation techniques like this help to maximize the distribution of the product.

EXAMPLE 4.

Some of the specific benefits to be gained when different markets are approached by segmentation are cited below.

1. Products and services can be created that specifically match the needs of different markets.

2. Promotional money and efforts are put to their most efficient use.   The strongest appeals can be made to each market, rather than using one or two appeals with limited value for all groups.

3. Advertising media can be used much more effectively.   If timing is important, the program can be more effective and cost-efficient than if all markets had to be reached at the same time with the same message.

2.5   DETERMINING THE CHARACTERISTICS OF A SEGMENTED MARKET

To gain the most benefit from a segmented market, information about the buyers in each segment must be accessible, measurable, and subject to evaluation.

Access.   Reliable data about the buying habits of potential customer segments must be readily available to the seller.   The seller must be familiar with information sources such as trade associations, consumer reports, and market research techniques (See Chapter 6).   The seller must also know that the market segment itself is accessible (i.e., that it can be reached).

Measurement.   The seller needs to know that individual buying habits in the intended segment represent quantifiable trends.

EXAMPLE 5.

A certain segment of the amateur photography market is willing to spend considerable sums of money for good equipment.   The manufacturer of a top-of-the-line camera who wants to try to reach this market might first consult the Photo Trades Association to determine amateurs' buying habits and purchasing trends.   The manufacturer might also undertake a survey of the stores it supplies.   See Chapter 6.

In contrast, real estate buyers represent one of the most active and lucrative markets in the country. However, until a person contacts a broker there is little chance of knowing of his or her interest.   And when the contact is made, no broker is going to tell another, so the accessibility of those who are thinking about the purchase of real estate remains hidden until they actually approach a broker.

These two situations show that while any readily accessible market represents a good possibility for the effective use of market segmentation techniques the measurement criterion is equally important in making the appropriate decision.

Evaluation.   Once the market segment data is accumulated, it must be subjected to economic analysis in terms of projected sales volume and cost of sales.   The bottom line is *profitability*; this is what determines whether or not a decision to implement market segmentation techniques is viable.

EXAMPLE 6.

The importance of profitability is clearly illustrated in the following description of market segmentation. A manufacturer of valves may see several markets for one of its products. One may be a large volume market found in the air systems of large and small industrial plants. The other may be found in the air systems used in analytical laboratories. Both are entirely different markets for the identical product. However, in this case the cost of promoting to the lab market separately may be too high in comparison with the resulting sales to make market segmentation profitable.

2.6   PRODUCT LIFE CYCLE AND MARKET SEGMENTATION

Most products go through a distinct life cycle. That is, if the product represents a new idea, its initial sales are high. As soon as competition enters the field, there will be a scramble to protect the market. Product differentiation (see Section 2.3) helps competitors gain access; sooner or later a number of producers become very competitive for the existing market. Also, as needs and lifestyles change, the demand for a product will change. Thus, the four stages of the product life cycle are: introduction, growth, maturity, decline. Steps taken to segment a market must consider all of these variables. See Chapter 4.

2.7   CONSUMER AND INDUSTRIAL MARKETS

It is possible to differentiate in broad terms between the two major markets—the *consumer market* and the *industrial market*. In general, consumers buy products which will be used by themselves and/or their families for personal and household applications. The industrial market is composed of buyers who purchase products for use in their businesses, for inclusion in the products they make, or for resale. Products sold to industry for use in the manufacture of other products are often referred to as *O.E.M.* (Original Equipment Market) *products*.

EXAMPLE 7.

There are many cases in which the same products can be used by both consumer and industrial markets. But to be successful, manufacturers must segment the markets and treat them differently. A manufacturer of wood screws, for example, might sell some of its output to furniture manufacturers and some to hardware stores for use by the home craftsman. The home craftsman would probably not use more than a few hundred screws a year, but a furniture factory might use thousands. To sell to the hobbyist, it is often best to concentrate on attractive packaging which will catch the attention of the buyer in a store that might also offer the screws of competitive manufacturers. However, the buyer in a manufacturing plant is less interested in the things that attract a consumer and probably wants to know more about the quality of the screws, the price, quantity discounts, and availability. It's obvious that an approach that uses one appeal to capture both markets would fail.

2.8   HOW TO LOOK AT A MARKET

The importance of understanding the basic characteristics of a market before any marketing plans are developed was clearly shown in the preceding sections. Once general market trends are identified, the buying patterns of individuals within the market must be analyzed. In an industrial market, for example, the point of view of the persons making the buying decisions (be they engineers or purchasing agents) is a major determinant of the type of marketing strategy designed. A consumer market can be characterized by a knowledge of age factors, personal interests, and income levels, among other things. This basic information is extremely relevant to the marketer and should be supported by current quantitative data. If one particular industry is in a slump, it might not pay to promote in it. If one segment of a consumer market is currently spending money, and the product is suitable for this market segment, it might indicate the possibility of success.

EXAMPLE 8.

The clothing industry is a prime example of how changes in consumer demand affect business operations. Those who continued to manufacture double-knit clothing after the trend had peaked lost their shirts (pun intended). But those who first anticipated the demand, predicted the reduced interest, and got out before their inventories piled up were making sound use of marketing data.

2.9 AGE EFFECTS IN CONSUMER MARKETS

Consumer markets can be and often are segmented effectively by age groups. While this is the case, current marketing attention seems to be focused on the youth market. There are several economic reasons for this: (1) younger people still living with their parents can influence some of the purchases made by the family, (2) parents spend considerable amounts on their children, (3) young people themselves have considerable purchasing power, and (4) young people tend to have a wide variety of needs which, in many cases, must be satisfied.

EXAMPLE 9.

The contrast in buying habits between younger and older consumers is easily illustrated. For example, those who market home furnishings concentrate on young couples who are just starting out. Older married people do buy furniture, but not in the quantities bought by younger people just starting to furnish their homes.

Mature adults represent a significant, albeit more sporadic, market. They are often willing to commit larger sums for items such as housing, major appliances, and automobiles than their younger relatives can afford. Even though such individual purchases amount to significant sums, these consumers are not considered as active a market as their juniors. When children have left home and financial responsibilities have been reduced, older people often consider such purchases as summer homes and recreational items, such as boats, that would have been impossible during their children's school years.

Review Questions

1. A market may be thought of as a collective demand for a product or service that is or could be met economically by producers. True or false?

   Ans. True. See Section 2.1.

2. In order for a market to exist, there must be (a) demand, (b) magazines in which to advertise, (c) transportation facilities for the product, (d) none of these.

   Ans. (a) See Example 1.

3. A market is made up only of people who have needs that they want to satisfy. True or false?

   Ans. False. See Section 2.2.

4. In marketing terms, the word *need* is limited strictly to such essentials as food and shelter. True or false?

   Ans. False. See Section 2.2.

5. One of the main incentives for product differentiation is (a) raw material shortage, (b) new technology, (c) competition, (d) economic stagnation.

   Ans. (c) See Section 2.3.

6. New markets for existing products can often be tapped by (a) making slight product changes, (b) a different marketing approach, (c) neither of these, (d) both of these.

   Ans. (d) See Section 2.4.

7. Submarkets tend to be (a) heterogeneous, (b) homogeneous, (c) difficult to reach, (d) a last resort when it has been found difficult to reach the entire market.

   Ans. (b) See Section 2.4.

8. The advertising analogy of market segmentation is (*a*) the shotgun approach, (*b*) the rifle approach, (*c*) a saturation campaign, (*d*) none of these.

   Ans. (*b*) See Example 3.

9. Market segmentation often allows the producer to make the most efficient use of promotional dollars. True or false?

   Ans. True. See Example 4.

10. When approaching a segmented market, it is possible to zero in on the most effective sales appeals. True or false?

   Ans. True. See Example 4.

11. To gain the most effect from market segmentation, it is important that information relating to buyers be (*a*) accessible, (*b*) measureable, (*c*) capable of analysis, (*d*) all of these.

   Ans. (*d*) See Section 2.5.

12. The more precisely a market can be segmented, the greater will be the profit potential in all cases. True or false?

   Ans. False. See Example 6.

13. When competition enters the market, the product life cycle for the originator of the product enters the _____ stage.   (*a*) defensive, (*b*) phase-out, (*c*) discount, (*d*) competitive.

   Ans. (*d*) See Section 2.6.

14. Lifestyle changes seldom effect the market viability of a product. True or false?

   Ans. False. See Section 2.6.

15. There are no fundamental differences between the consumer and the industrial markets. True or false?

   Ans. False. See Section 2.7.

16. The Original Equipment Market is (*a*) any market for new products, (*b*) made up of products that will be used in the manufacture of other products, (*c*) a collectors market, (*d*) limited to automotive industries.

   Ans. (*b*) See Section 2.7.

17. When the same product can be used by consumer and industrial markets, it's smart to save promotional money by treating both markets in the same way. True or false?

   Ans. False. See Example 7.

18. Understanding the composition of individuals within a given market is a basic step in the development of a successful marketing plan. True or false?

   Ans. True. See Section 2.8.

19. To approach the understanding of a consumer market, one should have a knowledge of (*a*) age factors, (*b*) personal interests, (*c*) income levels, (*d*) all of these.

   Ans. (*d*) See Section 2.8.

20. Older adults do not represent a significant market for many products or services. True or false?

   Ans. False. See Example 9.

Solved Problems

2.1.   Apart from the obvious social benefits, increased opportunities for and reduced discrimination against women have led to significant marketing opportunities for some companies. Discuss this point and give some examples.

The stereotyped buying behavior which had limited women's purchasing participation to goods such as food and household items is rapidly disappearing. Women today are taking the initiative in many decisions that were traditionally in the male domain. For example, more women are concerned with the technical advantages offered by different automobiles than they were in the past. Astute marketers have recognized and accepted this trend and now present their messages so that the female market will not be offended by sexist overtones and other image-related biases.

2.2. Planning a marketing strategy based on sex or age only can be a mistake. Not all middle age men are interested in bowling nor do all nonworking women respond to advertising on soap operas. Suggest a better way to plan a marketing program that would still incorporate the factors of sex and age.

Sociologists and marketing people often think of people in terms of a family life cycle. During the bachelor stage both men and women have different needs and interests than do their contemporaries who are married and have children. As young marrieds, their needs and interests change and, from a marketing point of view, they respond to different products and services than they would have before they were married. In the next stage, the couples have children, and some marketing people tend to differentiate between those with younger and those with older dependent children. This is a logical distinction when you think of the expenses parents have with children in college compared with their expenses during the children's younger years. Later, when the children leave home, the term "empty nest" is used. At this point, adults are often likely to spend more heavily on themselves than they did when they were educating their children. The last stage is characterized by older, but now in some cases single individuals who may be working or retired. If you think of people you know in each of these stages, you can see how they represent entirely different markets for a variety of products and services.

2.3. Why is it dangerous to plan a marketing program strictly on the basis of annual income?

Although two persons may earn the same income, their tastes may differ widely. For example, it is not uncommon for a first class machinist to make as much money as a manufacturing executive. A college professor and a carpenter may make the same amount of money. Few carpenters would be interested in a book of art reproductions, and probably not many professors would respond to a promotion for hand tools. The point is this: There must be a common point of interest within a particular market. A description of income level alone is not sufficient information on which to base a program.

2.4. Over one hundred years ago Ernst Engel, a German statistician, postulated that three things occur as family income increases. What are these three factors? Do they hold true today? What are the marketing implications?

Engel stated that as family income increases, a smaller percentage would be used for food. He also stated that the percentage spent on housing, running the household, and clothing would remain constant. Third, he postulated that the percentage spent on other things, such as recreation and education, would increase. In general terms, Engel's Law is true today. Apart from its value to theoretical economists, Engel's Law is valuable as a rough guide for marketing people. Knowing where individuals belong in terms of the three factors, a marketing person can plan a program that will either avoid the pitfalls or take advantage of specific situations.

2.5. Markets for industrial products tend to be geographically concentrated. For example, Ohio has a heavy concentration of industry which relies on machine shop operations. Texas is a major center for petroleum and petrochemical processing operations. Discuss some of the obvious advantages of such concentrations to a marketer.

Perhaps the most significant benefit is that it permits effective concentration of direct selling efforts. With major prospects and customers located in proximity to each other, sales people spend less time traveling from one location to another. Areas of heavy industrial concentration also encourage manufacturers to establish local warehousing and distribution systems; these not only save money for owners, but also enable products to be provided more quickly than is possible in areas of less concentration.

2.6.   What are Standard Industrial Classification codes? How are they helpful for the marketer?

The S.I.C. codes were adopted a number of years ago by government and industry to aid in analyzing industrial economic performance and to help predict trends for future activity. There are ten main industry groupings, listed by 2-digit codes. Three- and four-digit codes are available to provide further differentiation when needed. The main headings of 2-digit codes are:

01–09	Agriculture, forestry, fishing
10–14	Mining
15–19	Contract construction
20–39	Manufacturing
40–49	Transportation and public utilities
50–59	Wholesale and retail trade
60–67	Finance, insurance, and real estate
70–89	Services
90–93	Government, federal, state, local, and international
99	Other

S.I.C. codes are an invaluable aid for the marketer because they present a clear picture of potential customers in specific marketing areas.

2.7.   The concept of Zero Population Growth has far-reaching implications for marketing people. Explain the concept.

Zero Population Growth is technically defined as that point at which the number of live births is equal to the number of deaths. The point is thought to be attainable when there are between 60 to 70 births for every thousand women of childbearing age (between ages 15 and 44).

2.8.   It has been claimed that Zero Population Growth has been reached, yet the total number of Americans is greater every year. What is the cause of this?

Even though the approximate number of births and deaths may balance, we now have a greater life expectancy than we had in the past. There are also more women in the childbearing years now. In addition to these two factors, immigration also swells the population. It is estimated that even if the ZPG ratio is held, we will not reach a constant population until late in the twenty-first century.

2.9.   Why is it important for marketing people to understand population trends?

Careful economic planning will prevent companies from overproducing products in the face of a declining demand that results from a steady population state. In addition to the obvious economies for the producers, proper planning will also prevent overutilization of diminishing natural resources.

2.10.   By 1980, it is expected that 64% of the American population will be high school graduates. By the same year, 13.7% of the population is expected to have college degrees, and approximately 25% will have had some college work. What are the implications of these trends for marketing people?

It has been shown that better educated people tend to be more discriminating in their choice of products and more critical of advertising claims. Interest in fashion increases, and taste level rises. Therefore, both products and the claims for them must be more carefully planned. As the level of education rises, interests change. When compared with other segments of the population, college educated people tend to be more interested in the arts, travel, and other cultural activities. Those who produce products and services for these people will have greater opportunities if they plan their products and strategies carefully.

2.11. Marketers of products and services often find it profitable to segment their markets in terms of ethnic or cultural heritage. This is, perhaps, most obvious in the marketing of foods. Foreign language newspapers serve as advertising media in many cases. What is one major problem a marketer who is not a member of the ethnic segment he or she plans to serve might face?

Perhaps the most serious marketing mistake that can be made is to assume that all members within an ethnic or cultural group are homogeneous in their tastes, needs, and attitudes. Northern blacks have interests and needs which can be dramatically different from those of Southern blacks. Within groups with a common national origin, there may be differences which are great enough to spell failure for a poorly planned marketing program.

2.12. In recent years, marketers have been able to move from a traditionally masculine to a feminine market for the same product with relative ease. Cigarettes, clothing, and even safety razors are common examples. Can you think of a product that still has mainly masculine appeal, but which often requires a woman's approval for purchase? How might you go about marketing such a product to gain female interest?

Pleasure boats are seldom bought by women, but when a married man considers such a purchase, his wife's approval is often sought. Research has shown that when this is the case, women are primarily interested in safety, comfort, and styling of the craft. Because the main motivation for the purchase of a boat often begins with the husband in a family purchasing situation, the main thrust of the campaign should be aimed at him. But the astute marketer will include evidence of the boat's safety and will highlight the styling and comfort features so that when the two discuss the purchase, the facts that influence the woman's opinion will be emphasized.

2.13. Industrial products are often bought by purchasing specialists, many of whom are technically trained as well as experienced at locating sources and negotiating for the best terms. How do such people differ from those who would be encountered in the market for a consumer product? How would the marketing approaches to individual consumers and industry differ?

The industrial purchasing agent buys products for use by the company that employs him or her. Price, delivery, and product quality are often the prime purchasing considerations. The consumer often thinks of the same factors, but is usually more influenced by emotional considerations. Those selling to industrial markets generally try to avoid emotional appeals, high pressure selling, exaggerated claims, and promises that cannot be fulfilled. Long-term buying patterns in industry are based on confidence, not on the one-shot appeals that are so common and often successful in the marketing of some consumer products.

2.14. Not all markets can be defined in terms of the products they buy or use. They can be described in terms of services which they need and consume. Accountants, lawyers, advertising agencies, and consulting engineers are only a few of the types of services which are marketed today. Discuss the similarities and differences you might encounter between marketing a service and a tangible product.

From a marketing point of view, services and products should have their beginnings rooted in the needs of the individuals to whom they will be sold. Here, there is little difference between the marketing of services and products. However, it is usually possible to show tangible proof of the benefit of competing products. The potential buyer can often test competitive products before he or she makes a purchasing decision. However, in the marketing of services, about the only real evidence a company can offer is its record of work done for others. In other words, it is difficult to differentiate between the claims of one service organization over another. Service is personal; it is the interaction of people. In the final analysis, it is the quality of this interaction that either spells success or failure for the marketing effort of a service organization.

2.15. In certain service industries, management must contend with more than the traditional factors of competition and other economic forces.   Airlines, broadcasting, and banking, for example, are under close government control.   What are the implications of this control for marketing people?

Government control tends to reduce competition, or at least soften its intensity.   It also has a tendency to reduce the marketing options that might otherwise be available.   Because of these conditions, a major role of marketing is to try to anticipate regulatory decisions and to act in a way that will be in the best interest of the company, yet conform to the regulations.

2.16. Because the buying of industrial products tends to be based on an analysis of such points as quality, price, and delivery, some people feel that advertising and personal selling have little value.   What is wrong with this thinking?

Actually, advertising and personal selling are very important and it is just the repositioning of these efforts that is significant in the industrial buying cycle.   The astute manufacturer knows that the final decision depends heavily on quality, price, and delivery, but he also knows that before a sale can be made, he must be on the bidder's list in order to be considered.   Therefore, he tries to make sure that his advertising and sales calls are timed well enough ahead of the need for and the actual selection of a vendor to insure a place on the bidder's list.   This timing is what insures that he will be in the running when the selection is to be made.   If the buyer is unaware of a manufacturer's products, the manufacturer will not even be in on the preliminary buying stages.   And if several products meet all of the specifications, then the crucial factor is the selling job.   The reputation of the company, the integrity of the salespeople, and the ability of the advertising to inform and persuade all help to influence the decision.

2.17. Briefly discuss the five major ways in which markets can be segmented.

   (1) A market can be segmented in terms of demographic data.   This includes geographic area, family make-up and size, education, occupation, income, ethnic origin, race, property ownership, and marital status.

   (2) Behavioral traits are also helpful when defining a market.   Some behavioral characteristics that are important are experience with a product, consumption levels, brand loyalty, social class characteristics, social and fraternal affiliations, and religion.

   (3) Physical characteristics such as sex, age, and condition of health are important.   Physical differences such as baldness, height, and weight are points on which a market can be segmented.

   (4) Characteristics such as intelligence, personality, hobbies, political bias, and acquired traits (such as the desire for fresh breath as a social reaction rather than for health reasons) are also valuable information for the marketer.

   (5) Marketing conditions, such as methods of distribution and levels of competition, may also be used to segment a market.

2.18. What is the ultimate market?   What are the problems you would have reaching it?

The ultimate market is the individual.   If you had one product that could be bought by one person, your problem would be simple.   But markets must be defined in terms of the characteristics that a number of people have in common.   In essence, this is one of the jobs of marketing research— the descriptions of group characteristics that can be used to help market a product.   Obviously, if it were necessary to determine the specific characteristics of every individual, and to sell individually, marketing would indeed be a difficult and expensive proposition.

Chapter 3

Organizing for Marketing

3.1 INTRODUCTION

Markets of any type are seldom static. Planning the phaseout of a product in a declining market can require as much effort as the development of plans to capture a share of a rapidly growing market. Therefore, it is important to strive for a marketing organization that is flexible enough to adapt to changing market situations. The department must also be able to respond to changing conditions within the company. For example, a product may be selling well, but no longer be profitable. Marketing must decide whether the product should be kept as a loss leader or dropped entirely from the product line.

Marketing organizations that seem to be most effective are staffed by people with sound theoretical grounding as well as the ability to deal with real business problems.

EXAMPLE 1.

There may be a strong inclination on the part of a newly formed marketing organization to copy its rivals' structures. One of the most common mistakes made in organizing for marketing is to assume that another company has a good organization simply because it is successful. Adapting a marketing department to the model created by another company does not allow for the problems that the other company might have. Every company should analyze its own needs and create a unique marketing department that is fully able to work with its own problems.

3.2 BASIC ORGANIZATION

A marketing department should be organized around the needs of current and potential customers. In a sense, this is building an organization from the bottom up. It is also necessary to work from the top down, in terms of staff. However, if the structuring starts from the bottom by defining the work to be done, the company will be in a better position to select the people most able to handle the jobs.

EXAMPLE 2.

In today's economy, complete product lines are often acquired from other companies through a merger. When such a line and all the customers are acquired, it is generally possible to build a good department from the bottom up, as described. All the needs and problems are known, and it's simply a matter of staffing to implement well-defined objectives. Obviously, building a department from scratch when the product is new and the market is unknown requires considerable experimental work.

3.3 DEPARTMENTAL INTEGRATION

It is imperative that all departments within a company work together if the company is to prosper. There is a tendency in some companies to downplay departments that do not have profit responsibility and to overemphasize those which contribute to the bottom line. This causes the total organization to become inefficient and promotes harmful interdepartmental rivalries.

If, for example, purchasing makes a mistake and buys high, all of the marketing efforts could be wasted when profits are calculated. However, if the two departments had kept in touch with each other, this problem could have been avoided.

All departments must be marketing oriented. This does't mean that all departments must be subordinate to marketing, but it does mean that all departments must think in terms of their customers and their needs and wants.

EXAMPLE 3.

Commitment to the marketing concept should involve the entire company. Even though a marketing department within a given company may engage in considerable research to determine the needs and wants of its customers and prospects, a lot of effort can be wasted if this philosophy doesn't exist in the engineering department. When development engineers are allowed to create without any guidance, they will often work on what interests them most, and not on products that will meet the needs of the company's customers. Often these interests can be channeled effectively without the need for interdepartmental skirmishes. But all must keep in mind that the goal is to satisfy customer needs and to make a profit.

3.4   ORGANIZING TO SUIT THE BUSINESS ENVIRONMENT

No two marketing departments will be the same. However, when planning a department, it is important to clearly understand the nature of the business environment in which the department will function.

EXAMPLE 4.

The difference between industrial and consumer oriented organization is examined in this example. The marketing organization of an industrial company would, relatively speaking, pay less attention to the advertising function than would a consumer product marketing department. Some consumer products depend so heavily on advertising that this function dominates the organizational considerations. In contrast, an industrial product marketing department might tend to organize around a strong sales and distribution format.

EXAMPLE 5.

The objectives of the marketing organization determine the distribution system it develops. A company making products sold directly to retailers has different marketing requirements than a company which sells its products to a few wholesalers who then sell to the retail trade. The former might employ its own field sales force. The latter might elect to use independent manufacturers' agents.

3.5   ORGANIZING TO SUIT THE CORPORATE ENVIRONMENT

Even though a well-organized marketing department is developed around the needs of customers, it cannot operate in a vacuum, and it must also relate to the internal organization of the corporation. The basic corporate philosophy, whether specifically stated or implicit in the activity of top management, must be considered. Such things as whether the company stresses new products or works its existing lines must be considered in any organizational planning. And, of course, people must be considered. Not only is it important to have people with the skills to do the job, but they must be able to interact personally as a working unit. The decision must be made to promote from within the company or to seek others outside the company to fill vacancies.

EXAMPLE 6.

Direct selling is another method used by companies to fill the consumers' needs. A company which sells consumer products only through the mail is, perhaps, a good example of an organization that is strongly marketing oriented. Such companies usually have their own lists of people who have in the past bought products from them through the mail. Since the best prospect in most businesses is one who is already satisfied with a company's product or service, direct marketing people spend much of their time determining their customers' needs, and in either buying or developing products which will fit their marketing format and sell at a reasonable profit. In this case, the corporate philosophy *is* the marketing philosophy.

In other companies, such as those which are technology oriented, there is often less of this emphasis. Top management often rises through the engineering ranks, and even though they may subscribe to the marketing concept, their orientation is still engineering and production.

3.6   PLANNING A MARKETING ORGANIZATION

The following steps are most often taken in the original planning or in the reorganization of a marketing department:

(1) The objectives of the department are defined.   This begins with an analysis of the company's business as well as the policies it has used to achieve its present goals.

(2) A long range departmental organization plan is created.   Simply stated, this plan should tell what the organization will look like at some point in the future, assuming the product is successful and meets the goals that have been set for it.

(3) A working plan for the department is created.   This plan would include descriptions of the people and processes needed to accomplish the marketing goals.   It should also include specific steps to be taken to adapt to the changes that will occur as the department expands and takes on greater responsibility.   This planning is often done in sequenced phases.   This allows for a periodic review and analysis to keep the department oriented toward its goals.

(4) Implementation of the plan is the final step.   If planning and control are spelled out carefully, implementation generally goes more smoothly than if the plans are less structured.

3.7   MARKETING FUNCTIONS

In a sense, a one-person marketing department may do everything that is handled by many people in a large department of a giant corporation.   The basic functions to be included depend on the needs of the company, its markets, and a variety of other factors. See Example 7.

EXAMPLE 7.

These are some factors to consider when organizing a marketing department:

- The establishment of operating policies and goals
- The identification of markets
- An evaluation of market share, both for the company and its competitors
- Sales forecasting
- The development of new products
- The establishment of distribution systems
- The development of short- and long-range marketing plans
- The establishment and management of pricing policies
- Development of training plans and criteria
- The management of internal sales and order processing
- The management of sales, based on budgets and forecasting

3.8   THE FUNCTIONALLY ORIENTED MARKETING ORGANIZATION

Within a functionally oriented marketing department, all marketing activities for all of the products are carried out by a single group.   Advertising, sales, sales promotion, market research, product planning, etc., are all included under the aegis of one marketing director.   This is, perhaps, the simplest form of marketing organization, and it is useful for large as well as small companies.   It can be especially effective when the company has a limited number of products that are sold to only a few markets.   Often, as a business grows, the functional orientation becomes cumbersome, and gives way to a product orientation.   See Section 3.10.

EXAMPLE 8.

A typical functionally integrated marketing organization might take the structure shown in Fig. 3-1.

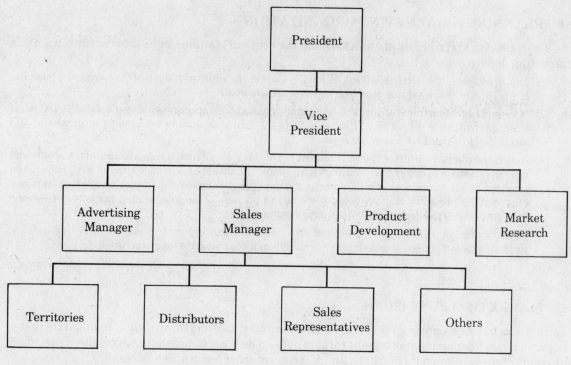

Fig. 3-1

3.9 THE PRODUCT-ORIENTED MARKETING ORGANIZATION

When a company has many different products, it is often advisable to organize the marketing department along product lines.   This allows each product to receive the attention and support that a functionally oriented department with many products is incapable of giving.   There are a number of ways to establish a product-oriented department; a few of them are described in the following examples.

EXAMPLE 9.

The *product marketing group* establishes individual product marketing units for separate products, while all other departments within the company remain centralized. The step is often taken when total divisionalization is not practical.   However, the concept does allow for individualized efforts where they are needed for each product line.   See Fig. 3-2.

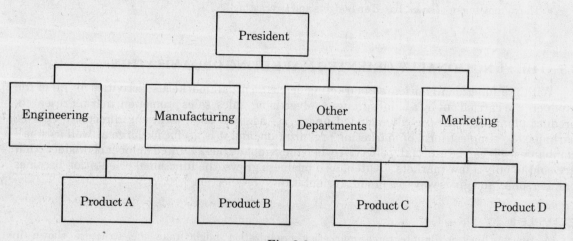

Fig. 3-2

EXAMPLE 10.

Product divisions are, in essence, self-contained operating units within the corporation. When the business aspects of each product are quite different from the others, and the company can sustain the organization, this system is often chosen. See Fig. 3-3.

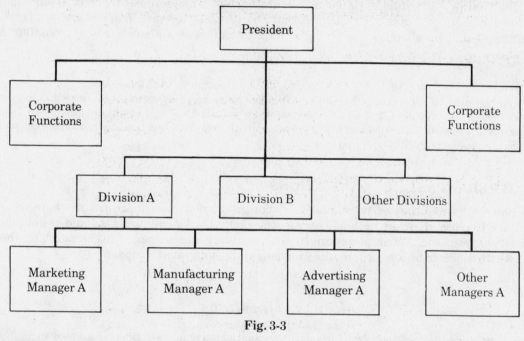

Fig. 3-3

EXAMPLE 11.

The *product manager* concept is relatively new, and is, perhaps, one of the more flexible and effective ways of marketing consumer goods. Product managers are less likely to be found in industrial companies.

In most companies using this concept, the product manager is responsible for coordinating and managing virtually everything that relates to the success of the product. The product manager concept evolved, in part, as a result of the increasing responsibilities that had been assigned to marketing managers. The product manager is a generalist, although it is likely that he or she rose through the marketing ranks. The product manager is often assigned the responsibility of developing and recommending the annual marketing plan as well as managing it once it has been approved by corporate management. See Fig. 3-4.

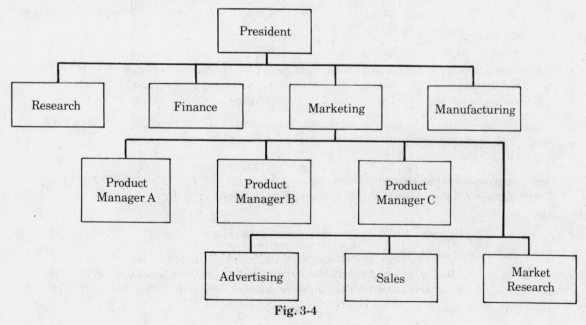

Fig. 3-4

3.10   THE MARKET-ORIENTED MARKETING ORGANIZATION

Companies which serve different markets, even though the same products may find their way into each marketplace, often organize for marketing according to the markets served. When the markets are differentiated and large enough, this can be a practical approach. Companies which have taken it recognize that the problems of each market are sufficiently different, and that an effective marketing program requires specialists working in individual fields.

EXAMPLE 12.

The *market-oriented* organization has proved to be effective for large chemical companies with multi-use products. The same chemical that can be used to clean industrial boilers might be useable by home handypersons to remove grease from hand tools. The approach to each market is best served by such market orientation.

3.11   OTHER TYPES OF ORGANIZATIONS

Do not assume that the types of marketing organizations described and illustrated here are the only ones. In truth, there are probably very few marketing organizations that could be described with textbook precision. Most marketing organizations are an amalgam of different approaches, each of which seems to be practical for the problems of the individual company.

Review Questions

1. Marketing organizations should be (*a*) static systems, (*b*) dynamic systems, (*c*) isolated from other departments, (*d*) none of these.

    Ans. (*b*) See Introduction.

2. An understanding of marketing theory is of little value to the working marketing person. True or false?

    Ans. False. See Introduction.

3. A fast and safe way to build an effective marketing organization is to imitate the department of another company which has been notably successful. True or false?

    Ans. False. See Example 1.

4. A marketing organization should be developed around the needs of (*a*) present customers, (*b*) prospective customers, (*c*) neither of these, (*d*) both of these.

    Ans. (*d*) See Section 3.2.

5. It is always necessary to build a marketing department from the top down, and never from the bottom up. True or false?

    Ans. False. See Section 3.2.

6. Corporate departments which do not have profit responsibility should never be allowed to work with those which have such responsibility. True or false?

    Ans. False. See Section 3.3.

7. Organizing a marketing department requires (*a*) a definition of department objectives, (*b*) long- and short-range planning, (*c*) a working plan plus implementation, (*d*) all of these.

    Ans. (*d*) See Section 3.6.

8. All corporate departments should think in marketing terms. True or false?

    Ans. True. See Section 3.3.

9. An industrial product marketing department might tend to organize around (*a*) strong sales and distribution, (*b*) an elaborate advertising department, (*c*) television production, (*d*) public relations.

    Ans. (*a*) See Example 4.

10. The functions to be included in a marketing department depend, in part, on the size of the company as well as the products being made.   True or false?

    Ans.   True.   See Section 3.8.

11. Which of the following should be included in the functions of a marketing organization? (*a*) The establishment of policy, (*b*) the development of new products, (*c*) the identification of markets, (*d*) all of these.

    Ans.   (*d*)   See Example 7.

12. Within a functionally oriented department, the marketing functions are carried out by a number of different product managers.   True or false?

    Ans.   False.   See Section 3.8.

13. The functionally oriented marketing department is (*a*) the simplest form, (*b*) the most complex form, (*c*) being replaced by research departments, (*d*) not practical for industrial companies.

    Ans.   (*a*)   See Section 3.8.

14. Within a functionally organized marketing department, which functions are under the direction of the marketing director?   (*a*) advertising, (*b*) sales, (*c*) marketing research, (*d*) all of these.

    Ans.   (*d*)   See Section 3.8.

15. When a growing company reaches the point where the product lines are too complex for a functionally oriented marketing department, it will often turn to (*a*) its advertising agency, (*b*) the director of research, (*c*) a product orientation, (*d*) consulting marketing managers.

    Ans.   (*c*)   See Section 3.9.

16. The product marketing group concept represents a situation in which there are individual marketing units for separate products.   True or false?

    Ans.   True.   See Example 9.

17. A company that establishes product marketing groups always decentralizes the other departments within the company to serve each group.   True or false?

    Ans.   False.   See Section 3.9.

18. Product divisions are (*a*) segmented product lines, (*b*) alternatives to market segmentation, (*c*) self-contained operating units within a corporation, (*d*) companies that were acquired from other companies.

    Ans.   (*c*)   See Example 10.

19. The product manager is usually on the lower levels of the department and often reports to the advertising manager.   True or false?

    Ans.   False.   See Example 11.

20. When a company organizes by markets served, the markets are usually (*a*) differentiated and large, (*b*) homogeneous and small, (*c*) always difficult to reach, (*d*) new and untested.

    Ans.   (*a*)   See Section 3.10.

Solved Problems

3.1.   It is generally held that the success of the product manager concept is largely due to the total business management orientation that is brought to bear on a product or brand. What aspects of a general business background would be most helpful for a product manager?

   The ability to determine the needs of the market, the capabilities of the company, the strategy of the competition, and the strengths and weakness of the product are only the beginning of the product manager's task.   Once the product is deemed viable, the product manager must be in a position to plan a practical strategy.   Such a strategy includes a definition of the company's objectives, identification of the customers, creation of product policy, and an identification of benefits that can be used in advertising and selling. After this, the product manager must be able to assemble a working program which would include advertising, sales promotion, product improvement, packaging, pricing, and distribution. Once the program gets underway, it is important for the product manager to monitor the results and fine-tune the system to insure highest profits. All during the implementation of the program, the manager should be monitoring results with an eye for next year's program.

3.2. Not everyone is suited to the role of product manager. What are some of the characteristics that would be important for success in the job?

The product manager must be able to identify very strongly with the product. For example, it might be as difficult for a non-athlete to run an effective sports equipment program as it would be for a non-technical person to plan for a scientific product.

It is very important for a product manager to be able to pick out the factors that will have the greatest impact and to concentrate on them. A product manager is always involved in many things and attention paid to problems with small payoffs will hinder the program.

The successful product manager must be able to command the cooperation and respect of many people. In a sense, he or she is running a company within a company, and without full cooperation, success can be limited.

3.3. Product managers are usually given some profit responsibility for the products under their control. What are some of the factors that often adversely affect profits?

If any department on which the product manager depends for information errs, profitability can be affected. For example, if the production department gives a low estimate of the cost of production, the planned-for profits could evaporate. Purchasing people might not be able to buy the raw material at the price quoted when the product manager was developing his or her plan.

Profits can be eroded by so many factors that product managers seldom have full profit responsibility for their products. Their responsibility is usually defined in terms of guidance for all the aspects of the operation that ultimately bear on profitability.

3.4. Why is it desirable for a product manager to have some financial knowledge and experience?

A business is an economic system, and one of the ways of describing progress or the lack of it is by using financial terms and data. Since the ultimate goal is profits, it is important for a product manager to understand the financial underpinnings as well as the dynamics of money movement as it relates to marketing. The product manager may not need to be able to run a set of books, but he or she should be able to read and interpret a financial statement.

3.5. In some companies, product managers spend most of their time working with the sales force. Think about the orientation of the two departments, and describe one of the problems a product manager faces when working with professional salespeople.

The product manager thinks in terms of products and profits. The salesperson thinks in terms of sales. Often, to build volume, salespeople will shave prices and make special deals that have the effect of reducing profits. The salesperson who thinks in terms of volume seldom is faced with the problem of net profit, as is the product manager. The salesperson often thinks of the future business that will develop as a result of special pricing, and may not be aware of the margin that must be made to stay in business. Since the product manager is acutely aware of this, it is often the area of greatest conflict.

3.6. Under what circumstances might a product manager devote considerable time to the research and development department within the company?

When a product line is new and still being improved, the chances are that the product manager will spend considerable time with the research and development department. Input from the field may indicate that certain changes would enhance the chances for success. The product manager will interface this information with research and development so that the product can be modified to meet the needs of the market.   Both departments must understand each other's problems, capabilities, and limitations.

When the product line is mature, and little more is planned or expected of it, the manager will spend more time in the other areas that contribute most to profits.

3.7.   Describe how the orientation of a market manager differs from that of a product manager.

The product manager is product oriented.   Because his or her responsibility is defined specifically in terms of relations with other departments within the company as well as the market, the market orientation is seldom as intense as it is for the person who is concerned with a specific category of customer.   The latter individual is the market manager.   For example, a company that produces valves that can be used as components in other products as well as by contractors might separate the sales by markets.   One market manager might serve the OEM (original equipment market) where the products are purchased for inclusion in other products.   The other market manager would have the responsibility for end-user markets.   The market manager generally feels a stronger orientation to the market, while the product manager is more company and product oriented.

3.8.   Under what circumstances is the marketing manager concept most effective?

Managers for specific markets can be most effective when the products of the firm are sold to a number of very different markets.   It is usually difficult for one manager to be sufficiently aware of the needs and conditions of a number of disparate markets.   Also, in rapidly expanding fields, the marketing manager, since he or she is a specialist, can be very effective in anticipating changes in customer needs.   Armed with this information, the company can modify its products to meet the new needs or develop entirely different products.   In many areas of high technology, the marketing manager system has proven to be especially effective.   When the manufacturer of a complex product must do more than simply sell and ship, the marketing manager can be very helpful.   Translating customer needs into solutions offered by the products being marketed is a job that benefits from the orientation of a marketing manager system.

3.9.   Those who favor the concept of the marketing manager over the product manager usually argue one point.   State it.

Advertising and sales programs, if they are to be successful, should be developed in terms of the potential customer's needs and wants.   The ads should stress what the product can do for the user, rather than emphasize other points.   This is the traditional difference between features and benefits. Those who favor the marketing manager system feel that this orientation is based on a knowledge of the market, and therefore is benefit, or customer oriented.   The product manager is believed to be more product and company oriented.   There is some validity to the statement, but it can only be considered in specific cases.   Some product managers could be much more customer oriented than some market managers.   However, it's important to note the difference and to be aware of it in case such problems should arise.

3.10.   As companies and their product lines expand, the needs for specialization within the marketing department also grows.   The *marketing planning manager* is often one of the specialists added.   Write a brief job description for this position.

Job description: Marketing Planning Manager

(1) Develop short- and long-range plans, including marketing strategies, departmental policies, and procedures for interfacing organization with the other corporate departments.

(2) Work with the sales and advertising managers, develop plans and programs to be implemented by these departments.

(3) Work closely with all other corporate departments, insure that each departmental plan dovetails with and contributes to corporate goals.

(4) Prepare sales forecasts based on, among other things, an analysis of economic trends, market potentials, competitive activity, and the goals set by top management.

Note that the duties of the marketing planning manager vary, depending on the structure of the corporation and the specific marketing job to be done. Although there can be differences between the work done by a person working for a company with a single line, the differences are often more in emphasis rather than in the type of work.

3.11. One of the functions of a marketing department is to organize and monitor the activity of a sales department. No two sales departments are or can be alike, but in general, there are a few guiding principles that can be used to insure that the work of the department is effective. What are the major factors to consider when organizing a sales department?

Here, perhaps, is where the marketing concept becomes most important. To insure a customer orientation, the sales department should be organized from the bottom up. The word bottom doesn't imply the low end of a ranking scale, but the view that the customer is most important. When it is known what the customers and prospects are like, what they want, and what they need, executives are in a better position to start building a sales department. People can be hired who can do the work from a customer point of view. It is often very difficult for an individual executive, who may be quite set in his or her ways, to switch the orientation to meet the requirements of the market.

Multilevel sales organizations should be avoided. When there is an endless chain of responsibility, communication is not only slowed, but the message is often distorted by the time it reaches the right people. Such an organization cannot move as quickly as one with fewer levels. It is very important to grant authority commensurate with the responsibility given to members of the sales department. When a salesperson must act decisively, the authority to do so can often make the difference between sale and no sale.

Salespeople often complain about the nonselling work they are expected to do. Market research people want them to gather data in the field, regional managers want reams of reports, and the sales manager often insists on using a productive salesperson to train a junior. All of this limits the effectiveness of the sales organization. Therefore, when organizing a sales department, it is important to assign such nonsales work to other people within the organization, allowing the sales people to do what they should do best—sell.

Ancillary services must be provided. Sales training, order processing, and other functions must be planned and set up to run smoothly and to act as a bridge between the salespeople in the field and those to whom they report within the company.

Perhaps the most important job cannot be specified in direct terms. Organizing a sales department is usually thought of in the present tense. The department and the work to be done is envisioned in terms of today and the systems and people are assembled to form a working department. If the salespeople do their job well, the company will grow concomittantly, and the sales department must be flexible enough to adapt to changing company and marketing situations. It is difficult to plan for change in specific terms, but if everyone involved is aware that change is inevitable, and that it usually leads to growth, it is seldom difficult to get the cooperation that is needed.

3.12. For a sales department to be effective, it must first identify its markets and then determine the potential that exists. Explain why these steps must be taken early in the organization of a sales department.

The markets may exist in different places. For example, a company selling to the aerospace industry would be ill advised to open sales offices only in major industrial centers. The manufacturers of aircraft are, in some cases, not found in what may be thought of as major industrial centers. They may be the largest employer in an area, but the area may not support other industry, and therefore not be considered an industrial center.

If an area cannot produce sufficient business, the cost of selling may be too high, relative to profit. When a company can estimate the annual volume they might expect from an area, it is possible to create a plan which would include an estimate for the cost of selling. Obviously, where a larger market exists, more can be budgeted for sales expenses, and vice versa.

3.13. The organization of a sales department should be based on an estimated share of the market. Define this concept and explain why it must be estimated when organizing for sales.

When there is only one company making one product, and all who want it can afford to buy it, the company has a 100% share of the market. However, this situation seldom exists. Most producers who sell a competitive product know what the total market is for all of the producers. It is then a relatively simple matter to determine their share of market as well as the shares of other producers. Because market share objectives are more readily accessible and useable as a measure against which to view sales efforts, market share figures are often used as goals for a sales force. For example, rather than project that the sales force is to sell 1000 more units next year, the sales manager may state the goal as a 10% increase in market share. As the market share increases, it often becomes more difficult for competitors to take away business.

The market share is, of course, translated to the individual salespeople in terms of quotas, or goals described in other ways.

3.14. A description of the sales job must meet the conditions of the market. Describe some of the factors that should be considered when formulating this job description.

Apart from the factors of personal compatibility and qualifications, sales jobs can be defined in terms of the required frequency of sales calls. Those selling heavy industrial machinery will visit a prospect many more times than would an individual calling in a territory of a large number of wholesalers dealing in inexpensive retail items. It is important to know, on the average, how much time must be spent with individual accounts. Technical products often require much longer visits than is required for the sale of products with well understood functions. When these factors are known and understood, the related sales expense can be determined. Then, based on the volume of business that has been estimated, it can be determined if a salesperson will be able to produce enough sales to make a profit for the company. There are, of course, other points that must be considered, such as physical distance and time between calls. If a salesperson must spend a day driving from one customer to another, the cost of this activity must be included when the cost of sales is computed.

3.15. What are some of the factors to consider when planning the size of the sales force?

Once the territory potential has been determined, and the characteristics of the person who would be successful are defined, it becomes necessary to determine just how many people will be needed to make the most productive use of each territory. This depends mainly on the size of the territory and the concentration of the prospects. In some major cities, it is not uncommon for people selling products, such as office supplies, to be assigned to only one building. Consider the number of businesses that are located in the metropolitan skyscrapers, such as New York's World Trade Center, and you can see that a city territory can be defined vertically as well as horizontally. Another basis for determining the number of salespeople is the share of market the company wants to acquire. At first, the company may be willing to have more salespeople in a territory, in essence sacrificing profits to secure customers. When the desired market share is achieved, such a company will often thin out the territory to an economically practical level by transferring some salespeople to other areas.

3.16. Sales departments, like marketing departments, can be organized in a number of ways. In general, they are set up either by market specialization or according to the products sold. What decisions must be made when selecting either of these forms of organization?

The decision to organize along market lines is usually made when the same, or quite similar, products must be sold to very different markets. When this type of organization is selected, those selling each market should be experts who are able to relate to the problems faced in each field. A company which makes hand tools that can be used by hobbyists as well as professional builders would probably find it difficult to use the same sales force in both markets. The needs and problems of each market are quite different; those selling to each should be familiar with them and able to offer specific solutions.

When a company makes a number of products which differ significantly from each other, it is often most practical to organize the sales department along product lines. In this case, the salespeople become experts in the products, and can relate to the customers in a more sales-effective way.

3.17. Advertising is one of the other functions included in the marketing department. How should it be positioned within the marketing organization?

The relative importance of advertising to the total marketing effort must be established first. In a company that sells its products only through the mail and uses no salespeople at all, the role of advertising is central.   In some industrial companies where advertising is considered only in terms of its effect on the corporate image, and revenues depend mainly on the efforts of direct salespeople, the advertising function is minor.   Unfortunately, it is easy to downplay the role of advertising in some companies, particularly those industrial organizations where technology is important.   It is often difficult, if not impossible, to measure the contribution advertising makes to sales.   However, in many cases when advertising programs have been discontinued, it has been shown that sales have dropped off.   Hence, even though bottom-line figures are not available, the pragmatic view is that advertising works and does contribute to sales.

3.18.   Is it always wise to have only one advertising department in a company?

The same thinking can be applied to this problem that relates to the organization of a marketing department.   In a multiproduct, or multimarket company, it is often wise to establish several advertising operations and staff them with the specialists needed to be most effective.   For example, a company making pharmaceuticals may advertise to the professional (doctors) market with one product and directly to the consumer with another.   In such a case different departments are established to insure the best thinking for both markets.

3.19.   Advertising, not unlike other functions within a company, is often subject to the scrutiny and control of people outside the department.   What are the problems inherent in this situation?   Who should be responsible for advertising?   How should this responsibility be defined?

The creation of advertising is a subjective effort.   But, to be most effective, the creative efforts should be based on sound marketing information and plans.   Unfortunately, it often occurs that those in the company without specific advertising training think in terms of clever campaigns alone and neglect the important points such as the benefits to be presented to the potential customer.   To insure that advertising is the result of the best efforts of all involved, individual responsibilities should be defined carefully.   For example, if the product is a technical one, the responsibility of the engineering department might be limited to the technical accuracy of advertising statements. Responsibility for the sales strategy in the copy and art belong to the advertising manager.   It is he or she who is responsible for translating product features into benefits that will move people to buy.   (See Chapter 10 for a complete discussion of advertising and its role within the marketing organization.)

3.20.   A marketing department can be staffed by drawing upon people already working for the company or the jobs can be filled by recruiting from outside the company.   What are some of the advantages of promoting from within the organization?

Promoting from within is an excellent way to build company loyalty and morale.   And there is often less risk when an employee of the company is given a new assignment.   The strengths and weaknesses of the individual are already known; it is difficult to have this kind of information about an outsider.

Usually the person who is promoted from within can learn the job more quickly than one brought in from the outside.   Since such a person already knows the company and its policies, the job is mainly one of adapting to the new situation.

If the company has established a good executive development program, promotion from within can be an excellent source of people for the marketing department.   However, companies that spend little or no time in such training often find that promotions from within do not work out as well as they expected.

From the point of view of economics, it often costs less to promote from within than to bring in outside people.   A person interested in changing jobs often does so to improve his or her earnings, and may want more in terms of salary and benefits than a person promoted from within who is seeking a long-term career with one company.

3.21.   What are some of the disadvantages of promoting from within?

Promoting from within reduces the possibility of finding the best possible person for the job. The insider may be capable, but the job may require an outstanding individual.   It is possible to promote a person to a position beyond his or her level of competence.   Many an excellent field salesperson has been rewarded with the sales manager's job, only to find that selling and managing are two entirely different things.

Internal promotions tend to check the flow of new ideas.   When all jobs are filled by promotions from within, the ideas they have can be stale.   Outsiders often offer a fresh point of view and can bring an unfettered mind to solve problems that may have been insoluble by those who have spent most of their working life with the company.   Remember, this is not always the case.   There are companies which promote from within almost exclusively; however, they often stress creative effort and are usually willing to use consultants to supply that outside point of view they feel may be missing.

3.22.   What are some of the advantages of hiring people from the outside?

It may be necessary to hire from the outside simply because people with the required skills do not exist within the company.   This often occurs when a company wants to develop a product and finds no one within the company with the experience to do the job.   It has occurred that entire marketing and research and development departments have been acquired in this manner.   But the best reason for hiring outsiders is simply that they usually provide fresh ways of looking at problems.   They may not be hampered by the restrictions within the company that have already made it difficult for present employees to solve existing problems.

3.23.   What are some of the disadvantages of hiring from the outside?

New people, no matter how well recommended they may be, are untried under the working conditions of the company.   It usually takes quite a while before it is known whether or not the right decision has been made.

When new people are given jobs that others within the company expected to fill, friction and morale problems can develop.   When the only alternative is to hire from the outside, problems of disgruntled employees should be anticipated and solved before they have serious effects.

Chapter 4

Product Planning

4.1 INTRODUCTION

The task of creating a product that will meet the needs of a market and produce a profit for the company is not easy. On the surface it may seem that all that is required is good marketing information and the capability to produce and distribute the product. But this is not the case. The needs and tastes of the market are in constant flux and the effects of competition can make a product in the development stage obsolete before it ever enters the market.

Many products being sold today will not be available in a few years because of market dynamics. And many contemporary products were not even being considered a few years ago. Apart from styling changes that effect the markets for products such as clothing and automobiles, changing technology also has a dramatic effect. Ten years ago few people thought that the miniature electronic calculators that were being sold for several hundred dollars would ever make the slide rule obsolete. Now it is possible to buy a calculator for under ten dollars that will do more than a slide rule, do it with greater precision and actually cost less than the slide rule. As a result, the slide rule is a product of the past. It should be noted that product planning includes not only activities to expand product use, but often the effort needed for an efficient and economical phase-out of a product.

4.2 HOW MARKETING DEFINES A PRODUCT

A product is more than the sum of its physical characteristics. To describe a camera in terms of its body, lens, and accessories does nothing more than place it in a familiar frame of reference. However, when a person considers the purchase of a camera, he or she thinks of what it will do, and what benefits can be derived. To some, the camera is a tool for making a lasting record of a growing family. For others, the camera is a vehicle for self-expression.

For marketing purposes, we can define a product as *something tangible, or a service, which satisfies a customer need.*

EXAMPLE 1.

Redefining the word "new" is a favorite of advertising people. Many new products are not new products at all, but simply new to the line of the company that is advertising and selling them. However, from a marketing point of view, the concept of a new product can be defined in several ways.

(1) A truly new product is one which never existed before. Drugs that cure disease where no cure was known are new products. The automobile was a new product in its time.

(2) Significant innovations which can eventually replace original products can, for marketing purposes, be thought of as new products. Plasterboard was an adaptive replacement for the handplastered wall. Color television is an adaptation of the black and white set. Much of the technical innovation common in the development and manufacture of scientific instruments can be viewed in this way. For example, virtually all read-out devices were once analog (dials or meters). Now most equipment is designed and produced with digital systems.

(3) When a firm wants to penetrate a market, it may find that the best way to do it is with a product that is not innovative, but quite similar to those already being made and sold by others. In this case, the new entry must have some significant feature that differentiates it from the other products. This is often done by finding a way to produce a product comparable to the competition's, but making and selling it for less.

EXAMPLE 2.

Product planning is also based on factors other than needs.   Needs are not always specific and definable in terms that make it easy to plan a marketing program.   Where the utility for a product, such as goods and clothing, is well established, another element must be considered.   Apart from pure utility (warmth, durability, etc.), people look for other things in the clothing they buy.   Some seek status and buy clothing which boldly proclaims the logo (signature) of the designer.   Even though this is an acquired need, it is still valid in terms of product planning.

4.3   THE PRODUCT LIFE CYCLE

Not unlike people, products pass through cycles which begin with birth and progress to death.   Not all products go through all of the stages, and the product life cycle may last a few weeks or extend for many years.   The proportionate amount of time in each phase of the cycle also varies.   But, from a planning point of view, it is important to recognize the steps through which the product will pass and then plan for each accordingly.   The four stages of the product life cycle are the *introductory, growth, maturity* and *decline* stages (see Sections 4.4–4.6).

4.4   THE INTRODUCTORY STAGE OF THE PRODUCT LIFE CYCLE

In the introductory stage, the product is unknown, and considerable effort and money are usually expended to familiarize potential customers with it.   The promotion may be aimed directly at customers, and may also be tailored to motivate wholesalers and retailers who would handle the product.   It is not uncommon for the product to sustain losses during this period, but if the planning and forecasting prove accurate, future profits will more than make up for early losses.

EXAMPLE 3.

Projected expenses are an important aspect of long-range planning.   When a new series of books, such as those developed on specific topics for well-defined markets, is introduced, a publisher will often spend millions of dollars before any profits are made.   However, such early expenses are included in long-range planning, and later sales will not only offset the early losses, but produce the profit needed.

4.5   THE GROWTH STAGE OF THE PRODUCT LIFE CYCLE

During the growth stage, the investment made in the introductory stage should begin to pay off.   Customers will buy again if the product is a repeat sale item.   Satisfied users will tell others and the cumulative effect of all the advertising and sales promotion will have its effect.

It is during this stage that profits will be highest.   By this time development costs have been recovered, the results of the promotion are paying off and it is not necessary to combat serious competitors.   When competitors do enter the picture, increased promotional spending will tend to reduce profits.

It is at this point that innovators usually begin to attract competitors.   Other companies see the potential, and depending on their own capabilities, will develop competitive products and enter the market.   For this reason, when a truly new product is introduced, it should be done with the best effort possible.   The company should try to secure the market firmly for itself before competitors begin to nibble away at it.   Think of the early diet foods that started the trend a number of years ago.   How many of them are still in existence?

EXAMPLE 4.

Innovation and high standards are important in product planning.   The first electric typewriters were a curiosity, but now there is hardly a typewriter manufacturer that doesn't make them.   During the growth stage, I.B.M., the innovator, was besieged by the entry of many competitors. But it has maintained its position by steady innovation and strict adherence to high quality standards.

4.6 THE MATURITY STAGE OF THE PRODUCT LIFE CYCLE

When a product reaches *maturity,* there are generally a number of competitors, and the market is saturated. Each company tries to increase its share of the market at the expense of its competitors; this is often done by price cutting. The differences between the competitive products often become trivial, and much promotional money and effort is spent emphasizing these minor points.

In this stage, sales will peak. The combined efforts of all competitors will saturate the market. However, the time factors vary considerably. Some products will peak in a short period of time and others will take much longer. Even after 50 or more years, automobiles are still in the growth stage. New uses, new types, and an expanding population are mainly responsible for this particular condition.

At some point in this stage, supply will exceed demand, and price cutting will increase revenue for those who practice it. However, this tactic seldom leads to long-term increased profits. Price reductions are only successful when they enlarge the market.

If the product has a finite life, the marketing emphasis will shift to replacement sales. At this point manufacturers may seek to gain replacement sales for products made by competitors by claiming their products are superior and will last longer.

EXAMPLE 5.

Competition in the maturity stage of the product is shown in this example. Laundry powders can be used to illustrate the maturity stage of the product life cycle. A number of years ago, competition for these products accelerated in proportion to the sale of automatic washers. When a number of producers were competing with each other, each began to introduce smaller and smaller innovations in an attempt to set their product apart from the others. Those who could afford to continue to compete and had products with market acceptance made it. How many of those early cleaning preparations are still on the market?

4.7 THE DECLINE STAGE OF THE PRODUCT LIFE CYCLE

As new innovations are introduced and consumer buying habits shift, an absolute *decline* in the sales made by all of the competitors often occurs. In a sense, the market is contracting. Sales drop, profits shrink, and producers generally begin to stop making the product. If the need still exists, but at a diminished level, those who can afford to stick it out as others leave the field may be able to hold onto their market share profitably.

EXAMPLE 6.

Products that disappear as a result of style changes provide dramatic and time-telescoped examples of the final stage of the product life cycle. Consider the Nehru jacket—the coat that buttoned all the way up the front and had a mandarin collar. When it first appeared, it seemed that everyone had or wanted one. Many clothing manufacturers, each with their own slightly differentiated version, jumped into the market. The decline came quickly. In fact, it was only a year later that there was a return to the traditional jacket, but with somewhat wider lapels. Any manufacturer who failed to recognize the product life cycle of the Nehru jacket and continued to produce it was probably stuck with unsalable inventory.

4.8 THE PRACTICAL APPLICATION OF THE PRODUCT LIFE CYCLE

Apart from its theoretical use for economists, the product life cycle provides a framework on which all product planning should be based. Historical data exists that can help companies plan their products through the life cycle.   If nothing else, understanding the product life cycle may prevent a company from beating a dead horse.   Any company that persisted in making tube-type radios as the semiconductors became popular probably had no idea that the life of a product really is finite.

Product life cycles are getting shorter and shorter.   This is the result, in part, of the accelerated rate of technological change as well as the competitve influences that characterize the free-enterprise system.   The implication for industry is that those with new products must attempt to make the most of them in the early stages, when the profit potential is greatest.   It is also important to consider the product life cycle in all planning to know when innovations will be important as well as to recognize when it is no longer profitable to continue manufacture.

EXAMPLE 7.

Short product life cycle is illustrated in this example.   Double-knit fabrics were hailed as the answer to a lot of clothing problems.   And they were for a while.   But the life of the product was short.   Anyone who banked on a longer life than the fabric probably ran into considerable difficulty.

4.9   NEW PRODUCT DEVELOPMENT

Some companies maintain departments specifically for the purpose of developing new products.   In others, representatives from various departments make up a committee that is responsible for new products.   Whatever method of organization is chosen, it is important that new product development receive the full support of top management.

No two companies are alike in the way they approach the development of new products.   However, there are a few basic steps which all must take, regardless of the organization and the formal corporate structure.   Beginning with the review of ideas and concepts that seem, on the surface, to be practical for the company, those charged with new product development then move on to actual development work on those products which seem most practical.

After a prototype of the product has been produced, the marketing mix is created and matched with the facilities and goals of the company.   If the product successfully passes this stage, the next step is usually a test market analysis.   To do this, a limited production of the product is advertised and sold in a specific area.   An analysis of sales and an estimate of the cost required to market the product fully are usually the final step.   If the product passes all the tests, it usually goes into full-scale production and marketing.

It is important to note that the test market phase of new product development is usually the first exposure for the product.   If the product has a short life cycle and will immediately invite imitators, the company must plan to capture a significant market share as quickly as possible.

When it is necessary to recover development costs quickly, a firm will often choose a relatively high price for the product.   The feeling is that they can sell fewer at a high price and "skim the cream" of the market.   Such a policy is set with the understanding that competitors will enter the market soon with a lower price, forcing a price reduction.   Such a policy recognizes that it is easier to lower a price than it is to raise it.

4.10   NEW PRODUCT FAILURE

It has been estimated that 80% or more new products fail.   The rejection rate is high mainly because the cost of succeeding steps gets higher and the risks become greater the closer the product gets to the go-no-go point.   The cost to test market a consumer product that will be sold by mass merchandising can go into the millions.   A decision to test the product or use the same money for advertising a product which is already successful is often made on the conservative side.   In other words, those products that do get to the test market stage are reasonably sure of success.

Review Questions

1. Markets are, in general, fairly stable, and it is seldom necessary to plan for change.   True or false?

    Ans.   False.   See Section 4.1.

2. Product planning is only concerned with the development of a product, and never with the phasing out.   True or false?

    Ans.   False.   See Section 4.1.

3. A product is something tangible, or a service which (*a*) is always test-marketed, (*b*) satisfies a customer need, (*c*) is at the mature stage of development, (*d*) goes through all stages of the life cycle.

    Ans.   (*b*)   See Section 4.2.

4. A new product, from a marketing point of view, can be (*a*) truly new, (*b*) a modification of an existing product, (*c*) the same as a competitive product, but priced lower, (*d*) all of these.

    Ans.   (*d*)   See Example 1.

5. Needs are always specific and definable and never represent anything but pure utility as far as products and marketing are concerned.   True or false?

    Ans.   False.   See Example 2.

6. The product life cycle is predictable and all products go through each stage, regardless of the market conditions.   True or false?

    Ans.   False.   See Section 4.3.

7. In the introductory stage of the product life cycle, promotion may be directed at (*a*) the prospects, (*b*) wholesalers, (*c*) retailers, (*d*) all of these.

    Ans.   (*d*)   See Section 4.4.

8. During the introductory stage, the company introducing a new product often (*a*) makes large profits, (*b*) breaks even, (*c*) sustains considerable financial losses, (*d*) doesn't care whether it makes or loses a lot of money.

    Ans.   (*c*)   See Section 4.4.

9. The investment made in a product during the introductory stage should begin to pay off in the (*a*) growth stage, (*b*) the maturity stage, (*c*) the declining stage, (*d*) competitive stage.

    Ans.   (*a*)   See Section 4.5.

10. Competitors usually jump in when the product they plan to copy is in (*a*) the introductory stage, (*b*) the growth stage, (*c*) the maturity stage, (*d*) the decline stage.

    Ans.   (*b*)   See Section 4.5.

11. When a truly new product is introduced, the best protective strategy for the company to use is to secure the market before any competitors can make inroads.   True or false?

    Ans.   True.   See Section 4.5.

12. During the maturity stage of the product life cycle, companies often try to increase their share of a market by cutting prices.   True or false?

    Ans.   True.   See Section 4.6.

13. The differences between competitive products in the maturity stage of the product life cycle are often (*a*) great, (*b*) no different than they were during the introductory and growth stages, (*c*) trivial, (*d*) of considerable consequence, as seen in product advertising.

    Ans.   (*c*)   See Section 4.6.

14. During the maturity stage, when supply exceeds demand, competitors often turn to (*a*) higher prices, (*b*) lower prices, (*c*) no price changes, (*d*) none of these.

    Ans.   (*b*)   See Section 4.6.

15. During the declining stage of the product life cycle (*a*) sales drop off, (*b*) profits shrink, (*c*) producers stop making the product, (*d*) all of these.

Ans. (*d*)   See Section 4.7.

16. The only value of the product life cycle is found in its use in theoretical economics.   True or false?

Ans. False.   See Section 4.8.

17. Understanding the product life cycle may prevent a company from continuing to market products for which the need is diminishing.   True or false?

Ans. True.   See Section 4.8.

18. An accelerated rate of technological change as well as competitive influences seems to be responsible for a shortening of the product life cycle.   True or false?

Ans. True.   See Section 4.8.

19. When the product life cycle is shortened, it is important to (*a*) make the most of the early stages, (*b*) concentrate on the maturity stage, (*c*) skip the maturity stage, (*d*) prevent the product from reaching the decline stage.

Ans. (*a*)   See Section 4.8.

20. A new product often becomes vulnerable to competition as early as the test marketing stage.   True or false?

Ans. True.   See Section 4.9.

Solved Problems

4.1.   Not only does a firm go through a number of stages as it develops and markets products, but the consumers follow a somewhat predictable route to the adoption or rejection of a product.   Discuss these stages.

During the first stage, the prospect is *aware* of the product but seldom has sufficient information to make the decision to buy or reject the product.   If there is sufficient *interest,* the prospect will seek to discover more about the product.   Ads are read more carefully, and information may be sought from those who have bought and used the product.   At this point, the prospect will begin to think about the product seriously—to *evaluate* it in terms of whether it will do what is promised and whether or not the same money spent on other purchases might be the better decision.

If the evaluation phase turns out positive, a *trial* is next in the process.   If the product requires a small investment, the consequences of the expenditure are minimal, but if the cost is high, the prospect will seek to confirm his decision in other ways.   For example, it is possible to take a test drive in a car before such an expensive purchase is made.   If the test is successful, the product is purchased; if not, it is rejected.

For the marketing person, it is important to know and understand these phases.   A prospect who is at the evaluation stage may lose interest if it becomes difficult to try the product.   The trial offer is a very practical way to turn prospects into customers.

4.2.   New product planning should include some estimate of how the product will be accepted and adopted by the market.   Marketing people talk of the diffusion process when they discuss this aspect of planning.   Describe this concept and its implications.

Although the adoption of each new product is different from that of any other, there are some general characteristics which the marketing person can use for basic planning.   When a new product is first introduced, only a few people, relatively speaking, will adopt it at first.   When it becomes apparent that the product is valuable, more and more people will adopt it.   The rate of adoption then drops off as the number of potential customers is reduced.

The early adopters of new products are often referred to as the innovators.   The next group, those who are usually influenced by the innovators, are called the early adopters.   They are followed by the early majority, a group which is usually about the same size as the late majority. The laggards follow. Figure 4-1 provides a general description of the process from introduction to saturation.

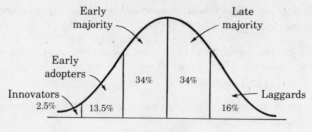

Fig. 4-1

4.3.   A company rarely makes and sells only one product. Discuss several of the reasons why it is practical for a company to have a broad line of products.

With rare exceptions, a company with a single product has placed automatic limitations on its growth. If the product is seasonal, it is often good practice either to develop uses for the product in other seasons, or to utilize existing facilities to make products that can be sold in the off-seasons. Antifreeze was once a seasonal and regional product. However, now antifreeze with its engine protecting qualities is put in automobile engine cooling systems all year.

Seldom is a firm's capability used at its most economical level with a single product. Equipment, people, and time can be turned to good advantage when additional products can make use of them. It is this need to optimize resources that leads many companies to product line expansions. Because most products respond to the product life cycle, it is important to have new products in the early stages as older ones are phasing out. Because of the overlap, the line is expanded, rather than appearing to be a serial introduction and phase-out of products.

To take advantage of related selling possibilities, many companies offer products which complement those already on the market. Those who make razors also make blades. Those who make shampoo also make hair conditioners. Name a few companies that have built huge product lines on this concept alone.

4.4.   Even though only a fraction of the new product ideas presented to a company ever become commercial successes, it is important to stimulate the steady production of ideas. Discuss several ways this can be done.

Apart from those companies that have organized for new product development by staffing departments specifically for the task, there are several practical ways to keep the flow of ideas coming. It is not difficult to imagine that many good ideas come from the company's customers. If we are to take the marketing concept seriously, then it is important to take seriously the ideas for products that customers would like to have. However, even though they are, in a sense, marketing oriented, they should still be subjected to the same rigorous evaluation as ideas from other sources.

Looking to the product line of a competitor for ideas is neither dishonest nor poor business. If you can see how to make the product better, or sell it for a lower price, you should be able to get a share of the market. After all, this is the competitive process that advocates of the free-enterprise system point to when they state that the consumer benefits more from this system than any other. Company employees, those not normally charged with the development of new products, can also be a good source of new product ideas. Often a company will establish a system which rewards employees for their ideas. Some are paid for outright, and others arrange for royalties when the product is sold.

There are outside specialists who do nothing but develop products for manufacturers. Some work on special assignment, and others, on their own, create products that they then place with manufacturers.

More often than not, all of these avenues are used. It is important that a system for processing of ideas be established and working, or those with the ideas will lose interest.

4.5.   Why is a preliminary screening process important when dealing with new product ideas?

Working with new product ideas is usually an exciting job, and there is a tendency to be carried away with enthusiasm.   When this happens, and the new ideas are passed on to the next stages of review and development, it could mean the commitment of significant amounts of money.   When considerable money is spent on numerous ideas, there is often a lack of funds when it comes to actually working with the products that have genuine potential.   Those working with new product ideas within the company often find it most practical to establish a set of complete and fairly rigid criteria with which to evaluate new product ideas.   Such decision rules should, however, be flexible enough to allow the unusual idea which does not conform to the parameters, but shows promise, to be further evaluated.

4.6.   Compatibility with the existing line and the ability to make the product with existing facilities are, of course, major considerations for a new product idea.   In addition, what business aspects must be considered?

An assessment of market potential is, perhaps, one of the most important business tests a new product idea must pass.   Such an analysis should also be able to provide a rough picture of the product life cycle in order for the financial people to project investment requirements and income potentials.   The product should also be compared with its competitors, both in terms of the benefits it offers to users and in relation to the profit structure.   This analysis, done before a prototype of the product is developed, is usually referred to as *concept testing*.

4.7.   Once the concept testing has proven out, an actual product is usually developed and subjected to limited testing.   Why does it occasionally occur that the finished prototype varies considerably from the product as it was originally envisioned?

Once a product is in the development stage, a number of different individuals become involved. At this point, their ideas begin to reflect new and better ways of making the product.   Often these ideas are incorporated in the prototype until it bears little resemblance to the original idea.   This may be unnerving for the individual who conceived the product, but the collective input, if carefully controlled and channeled to be most productive, can often transform a good idea into a great one.   It is very important for those involved with the development of new products to watch for a psychological problem that can hamper progress.   This problem has been given a name and an acronym, the N.I.H. Factor.   N.I.H. stands for *Not Invented Here*.   Some people, for personal reasons, find it difficult to accept the ideas of others.   If it wasn't invented *Here*, it can't be very good is the translation.

4.8.   When a big investment is involved in the introduction of a new product, planning a test marketing program is wise.   What is test marketing, and what can be expected when such a program is carried out?

Prior to the introduction of a new product to its entire market, only limited input on it has been received—from those who have been involved with its development and possibly from a few outsiders whose opinions might have been sought.   Such limited experience represents an important safeguard in fields where competition is strong and competitors are prone to trying to beat others to the market.   But limited exposure under any circumstances does nothing to give the marketer an indication of what the real world will be like.

The test market is a controlled sample of the real world.   The area chosen is based on characteristics deemed representative of what the entire market will be like when the product is ready for total marketing.   The characteristics of consumers as they relate to the product are important, but it is just as important to get a feel for the advertising media that will be used as well as for the viability of the selling organizations.   Therefore, test markets are chosen very carefully.   If any one of the choices is wrong, and the results point to a go, millions could be lost.   And, if a poorly planned test market rejects a product that might have been successful, the loss in potential profits could be considerable.   Test marketing is a very sensitive business that requires considerable skill and experience on the part of everyone involved.

4.9.   There are times when the crucial test marketing stage is bypassed, and the company goes directly into production and national marketing. Can you think of several reasons for such a decision?

Even though a test market may be selected that is geographically remote from the company's major competitors, a test market program will draw attention to itself via the marketing grapevine. When this occurs, two things can happen. The competitor, in order to make the test market results difficult to interpret, may institute a special sale of its own product. Under such circumstances, normal market conditions will be disrupted, making it difficult for the company with the new product to get reliable information on which to base further decisions.

In addition, competitors may see that the product is one they can make and sell themselves. A test market situation gives competitors a chance to introduce a new product of their own. Many new products have been preempted this way.

4.10.   If the test marketing project is successful, what is the next step?

The next step is commercialization. If the company that has taken the product through test marketing is on the ball, it will have most of the systems and procedures ready for a full-scale national marketing program. This includes an advertising program, a distribution system, and a selling organization that take the product to the consumer. Of course, other company functions must be primed and ready as well. Service, credit, and repair are but a few of the departments that must be keyed in.

4.11.   Even though a product may have reached the stage of decline, a company may elect to keep it. In the face of economic loss on the product, why is this often a wise decision?

Sometimes an unprofitable product is part of a line, and those who buy it also buy other products in the line. In such cases, the unprofitable product may be continued in order to keep the customers for the other products. Manufacturers of industrial components often find themselves in this position and respond to advice that is based strictly on accounting. However, when the unprofitable *lines* are dropped, the customers often take *all* of their business elsewhere. Even though the company may recognize its mistake, getting such lost business back is usually quite difficult even if the unprofitable product is reinstated.

4.12.   Not all product planning pertains to products that will be manufactured by the company that will market them. In some cases, a company may choose to buy an existing product just to market it. Describe some of the circumstances under which this might be done.

A manufacturer with a line of products that is incomplete may elect to buy the remaining products from other manufacturers in order to complete its line. Industrial manufacturers who need products to complement their lines, but are unable for any number of reasons to manufacture them, may turn to other manufacturers for the missing products. For example, a manufacturer of valves may buy accessory products, such as couplings and fittings, from another company in order to have a full line.

In many cases, the full line is very important. Purchasing agents find it convenient to deal with one company, rather than many, when they are buying related products. This practice can reduce paperwork, time spent talking with vendors, and may even reduce costs if the manufacturer provides incentives to buy more of its line.

A clothing manufacturer may elect to contract with others to produce complementary garments for the line it manufactures. The outside purchases would be branded by the company marketing the entire line.

In most cases, the company that elects to buy products outside to fill out a line will impose stringent quality and delivery requirements on its suppliers. The products bought must be up to the standards of those manufactured by the company marketing the products.

4.13.   The decision to make or buy is not a simple one. What are some of the questions a company must have answered when deciding what to do?

Perhaps the most often asked question is that of economics—is it more economical to make or buy. If the product can be made on existing machinery, and production time is available, it is usually more economical to make the product. But, if the decision to make the product involves plant investment, new machinery, and an expanded staff, it may be better to buy outside. Of course, the bottom line of this situation will always boil down to profitability. Even though millions may be involved in capital investment, if it will be more profitable to make the product in-house, the decision will probably go that way. And, there is the risk involved in depending on an outside supplier. Because the manufacturer who is buying the product has little control over the operations of the supplier, the buy decision can be perilous. If the supplier becomes unable to continue in business, there will be no product; considerable time may have been lost that could have been better spent earlier in developing in-house capabilities. If any secret processes are involved in the manufacture, an outside supplier will have to know them in order to produce the product. This, obviously, poses potential problems.

4.14. When a customer perceives a particular brand as satisfying, he or she tends to continue purchasing the brand, rather than to investigate a new brand. This is an advantage to the customer because it speeds up shopping, but what benefits accrue to the marketer as a result of such behavior?

Once a customer is satisfied with a product and buys repeatedly by brand, the marketer can spend less on promotion. The brand identification and product satisfaction will tend to maintain a steady level of sales. Direct selling costs can be reduced for the same reasons.

4.15. The use of brand names can help a marketer expand the sale of its products by segmenting the market. What are the advantages of this approach? How can it be used?

People buy products for different reasons. Many times, one product will meet the needs of several groups, but because of varied interests and background it might be difficult to advertise and sell to them with the same approach. When such a segmented market is encountered, one of the best ways to benefit from it is to create different brands of the same product. Some industrial cleaners and household cleaners are similar, but it would be difficult to sell the two markets the same product with the same advertising and sales campaign. Therefore, a different brand is created that can be advertised to meet the requirements of each. There are times, too, when a manufacturer may make a product that is sold to several competing retailers. It would be impossible to sell them the same brand, so private labels are created to solve the problem. Some prepared food products fall into this category.

4.16. A good brand name can enhance the corporate image. How can this be used profitably by the company?

Once a brand name has acquired a good reputation, it is often easier and less expensive to introduce a new product under the banner. Customers are already satisfied with the products that carry the brand name and expect that the new product will provide the same satisfaction as the other products.

4.17. Not all products can be branded successfully. What conditions should exist if a new brand is to succeed?

The introduction of a brand can be expensive. Therefore, there should be a large enough market to support the brand introduction, and the demand should be strong enough for the price of the product to support the additional promotional costs. Many branded products can be mass produced. As demand increases, production economies possible in mass production should increase the profit margin and allow the company to recapture its introductory costs.

Whether the brand is to be high end, or an economy version, it should represent the best product for the price. It is important that the quality be maintained. Any variations will send customers to other brands, and such defectors are almost impossible to get back. There should be no question of the brand when it is seen. The package design should be distinctive enough so that it stands out and makes it easy for the customer, who is already predisposed to purchase, to find it in a crowded store.

Dealer support for a brand is important. If the product is a retail food item, the dealer's cooperation in placing the product in an advantageous place should be secured.

4.18.   Product planning for a branded product aims at customer brand insistence. Differentiate this term from brand preference and brand recognition.

Brand recognition is simply the recall of the brand. It is a measure of the effect of promotion more than anything else. Actually, the attitudes toward the product could be negative as well as positive. All that it indicates is that some percentage of a sample recognizes the brand. Nothing is stated about product use.

The condition of *brand preference* describes consumer behavior in which the branded product is selected over others. In a sense, this is a habitual selection, and it is a condition that marketers aim for because it tends to stabilize a regular segment of the buying population. With a certain segment of the market preferring a product, promotion money does not have to be spent to retain old customers; it can be dedicated to market expansion, or for other marketing activities. With a condition of *brand insistence,* customers will accept no substitute. They simply will not buy the product unless they can have the brand they want.

4.19.   Much criticism has been leveled at planned obsolescence by consumer groups. Apart from that planning which intentionally sets out to make a product that will not last, what are the positive aspects of this concept both for manufacturers and consumers?

Technological improvements often make products obsolete. When these improvements offer something that is genuinely better or more effective than the existing product, the resulting obsolescence benefits both the consumer and the manufacturer. Built-in light meters and automatic exposure controls in modern cameras have reduced the need for an external light meter for all but the professional and the serious advanced amateur. However, the same light-measuring technology has now been incorporated within the camera, and for most camera owners the processes of making good pictures without requiring extensive effort is a real possibility.

In some cases, technological advances are held in abeyance until the demand for the current model of the product decreases. When this point is reached, the manufacturers introduce the modified product and take up the slack in the declining market.

It should be noted that when products are designed to wear out in a period shorter than they would normally, the manufacturer is doing no one a service. It is this activity that is criticized, and not the obsolescence of a product by making it better. Even though many consumer groups deservedly criticize manufacturers for this behavior, few of them note the most obvious example of the practice. It exists in the clothing industry where every year there is a new fashion. Last year's clothes may not be worn out, but this industry creates a psychological obsolescence, rather than a real obsolescence, to insure their annual market.

Chapter 5

Pricing Strategy

5.1 INTRODUCTION

Pricing, one of the elements of the marketing mix, is considered by many economic theoreticians as well as practical marketing people to be the most important activity in the free-enterprise system. It has a direct effect on wages, investment, interest, and profits. Flaws in pricing tend to reflect flaws in the entire economic system; this seems to be most evident during periods of inflation.

Apart from the need to insure a corporate profit the company must see to it that its pricing policies do not cause problems for the economy in general. Only a few corporations may be large enough to influence the economy directly by their pricing decisions, but when they and many smaller companies ignore the restraints necessary in rational pricing, the economy can suffer. In this sense, the price for a unit of labor has the same effect as the price for a product.

5.2 A DEFINITION OF PRICE

Prior to the development of a monetary system, early cultures bartered item for item. A handful of grain might have been exchanged for an arrow. Each item had certain value, or practical utility, to each individual. When each person had a need for something that was possessed by the other, and the utility of each seemed equivalent, the items were traded. Such barter systems still exist, not only in primitive cultures, but in many modern, economically sophisticated countries.

The introduction of money as a bargaining medium provided a base line against which products and services could be evaluated and sold. A monetary system offers a simpler way to facilitate the sale and acquisition of goods and services.

EXAMPLE 1.

In contrast to the barter system, when money is used, a tradable item which another might want is not required in order to negotiate for a product or service. Money has value itself, and can be applied to the purchase of anything. The system provides flexibility. Consider the problems a person might have if he or she wanted to trade a vacation for two cows. The resort owner might not be interested in the cows, but with money he or she can buy anything that might be needed.

However, in some areas of even the most modern countries the barter system still functions well. In rural America, individuals with special skills, such as that of shoeing horses, will trade their work for the product of the skills of another, such as crops. Such simple transactions represent an understanding of the utility of each product and service and serve to facilitate a practical exchange. Even though neither party may have stated the price in terms of monetary units, a price for each was implied before the agreement to swap was made.

5.3 THE GOALS OF PRICING

Pricing decisions must be based on a number of considerations. Implicit in all business pricing decisions is the profit goal. Even though the pricing of a product in the early stages may be such that profit is small or nonexistent, the decision includes an anticipation of sufficient future profits to make up for the loss.

In general, three factors must be taken into account when making pricing decisions: *profitability, volume,* and *social considerations.*

5.4   THE PROFITABILITY GOALS OF PRICING

Traditionally, pricing decisions are made in the following manner:

Profits = total revenues less all expenses
Total revenue = price times the number sold

When using the *profit maximization* approach, price is increased to the point where a decrease in the number of items sold is noted, and profits begin to drop. For example, a 10% increase in price may reduce the number sold by only 4%. Even though there may be fewer items sold, it may still be profitable for the firm to charge the higher price. The loss in volume is offset by higher profits. To make this system work, the increased total revenue must be just balanced by an increase in total cost. Such a system is easier for a small company to manage than a large one with many products. But for both, the dynamics of the market make it a system which requires constant attention and fine-tuning.

Most modern firms, however, establish their pricing in terms of a system of *target returns.* That is, they set short- and long-range goals, usually stated as a percentage of sales or investment, that will cover expenses, and allow for a reasonable profit. When such a system is used, a goal exists, and all effort is aimed at achieving it. Such goal setting helps implement departmental and personal goals within the corporation, and such cooperative activity is often more effective than the system of pricing to the point of diminishing returns.

EXAMPLE 2.

There are benefits to be derived from using the target return system. The target return concept not only provides benchmarks by which management can evaluate progress, but also has a built-in safety feature. When competing firms that operate under profit maximization pricing set their prices to meet the optimum price-volume level, the possibility of a price war exists. Each firm is seeking to build a larger volume and is often willing to accept a lower profit. When a critical point is reached, the price-cutting warfare will take place. However, when prices are established on the more rational target return basis, there is less chance that this instability will occur.

5.5   USING MARKET SHARE GOALS TO ESTABLISH PRICES

Many firms set their prices in response to their goal of obtaining a certain share of the market. When market share is used as the basis for pricing strategy, the goals are measureable and provide management with objective criteria by which to evaluate progress. And because there is evidence for higher profitability as share of market increases, such goals allow management to make fairly long-range predictions which are difficult to formulate when other pricing strategies are used. When a firm sets out to "own" a certain share of the market, it is less likely to suffer competitive attacks than if the goals had been set to simply maximize profits.

EXAMPLE 3.

Pricing is an important aspect of the attempt to capture a share of the market. Whether the market and the product are new, or the company is dealing in an existing market with a number of competitors, the effort to seek a certain market share should be predicated on room for growth within the market. Capturing a share of the market can be accomplished by setting the prices below that of the competitors. It may not be necessary to set prices lower for all buyers; aiming at a target market may be all that is required. It is most practical to look for a market segment where the competitors are especially vulnerable. This vulnerability can exist in high price differentials or in other situations such as delivery and quality problems. It is also possible to set prices below only a few of the competitors, rather than below all of them. Of course, it should be determined in advance whether such competitors have the ability to retaliate.

The results of these actions are likely to lower the gross margin (money which is available to cover selling costs, business management and to provide a profit after these expenses have been paid). However, it is also quite possible that the increased volume will result in lower production costs, resulting in an even greater profit.

5.6 GROWTH VS. PROFITS

Ever-increasing sales volume does not necessarily bear a direct relationship to increased profits. Depending on a number of variables, it is possible for profits to diminish after a certain point in increasing sales. Savings made in volume buying of raw materials and increased utilization of existing facilities may be offset by the company's need to subcontract some of its work, for example; such costs could actually cut into profits. Therefore, the final determination for pricing should be made in terms of profits, rather than volume.

EXAMPLE 4.

Profit and volume are important areas of interest to the sales representatives. Many salespeople are volume-oriented. They incorrectly assume that increased sales always equal increased profits. However, many companies base sales salary increases and bonuses on increased profits, rather than on increased volume. When volume is important, salespeople will sell "anybody." That is, they are willing to sell to poor credit risks, just to increase their volume. But, when profit is the main consideration, their efforts will be directed at buyers who will not only buy in volume, but also pay their bills.

5.7 EFFECTS OF DISTRIBUTION ON PRICING

Products are often sold through wholesalers and/or retailers. A company must incorporate the profits of middlemen into the prices it sets.

Criticism is sometimes leveled at intermediaries (often referred to as middlemen), charging that they do little but add to prices paid by consumers. However, intermediaries bring the product to market, whether they are wholesalers selling to retailers, or retailers selling to consumers. There are, of course, times when these organizations do little and collect much, but for the most part they serve a useful function.

EXAMPLE 5.

Pricing for direct sale also involves an accounting of the cost of selling. If a company were to sell its product directly to the consumer, it would have to employ its own salespeople to do the job. The expense of doing this might be equal to or greater than that added by an intermediary. This is the cost of selling, and must be considered no matter how it is distributed. Even mail order companies which advertise "eliminate the middleman," have selling costs that are reflected in the final price. The costs of postage, printing, and handling of mail order catalogs can be as much or more than might be encountered if intermediaries were used and the product were sold in retail stores.

Review Questions

1. Prices have a direct effect on (*a*) wages, (*b*) investments and interest, (*c*) profits, (*d*) all of these.

   Ans. (*d*) See Section 5.1.

2. Economists seldom consider prices to be very important in general economic terms. True or false?

   Ans. False. See Section 5.1.

3. The barter system has been completely replaced by a monetary system in which money is the unit of exchange. True or false?

   Ans. False. See Section 5.2.

4. Money has an advantage over the barter system because it can serve as a substitute for the value of an item. True or false?

   Ans. True. See Example 1.

5. In a barter system, the value of the items to be traded must have utility for each participant. When money is used, this utility can be defined in terms other than the practical value of the items. True or false?

   Ans. True. See Example 1.

6. Implicit in the goal of all business pricing decisions is (*a*) profitability, (*b*) volume, (*c*) social considerations, (*d*) all of these.

   Ans. (*d*) See Section 5.3.

7. A firm may decide to forego profit at some point, but long-range planning must include sufficient profit to make up for this loss as well as to sustain continued profitability. True or false?

   Ans. True. See Section 5.3.

8. Profits equal (*a*) total revenues less expenses, (*b*) total revenue less returned merchandise, (*c*) total revenues plus discounts, (*d*) total revenues less federal taxes.

   Ans. (*a*) See Section 5.4.

9. Total revenue equals (*a*) price times the number made, (*b*) price times the number shipped to retailers, (*c*) price times the number sold, (*d*) price times profit.

   Ans. (*c*) See Section 5.4.

10. When a firm uses profit maximization to set prices, prices are raised to the point where a disproportionate decrease in volume is noted. True or false?

    Ans. True. See Section 5.4.

11. To make the profit maximization system of pricing work, increased total revenue must be balanced by a like increase in total cost. True or false?

    Ans. True. See Section 5.4.

12. Most modern firms establish their pricing by a system of target returns. True or false?

    Ans. True. See Section 5.4.

13. When long- and short-range goals are set as a percentage of sales or investment, the system is called (*a*) profit maximization, (*b*) profit stabilization, (*c*) target marketing, (*d*) target returns.

    Ans. (*d*) See Section 5.4.

14. The pricing system of target returns has the added effect of helping to (*a*) set departmental goals, (*b*) simplify accounting, (*c*) reduce taxes, (*d*) provide dynamic market information.

    Ans. (*a*) See Section 5.4.

15. The target return system provides benchmarks by which management can evaluate progress. True or false?

    Ans. True. See Example 2.

16. Firms which price according to the target returns concept are much more likely to find themselves in a price war than those which use the profit maximization system. True or false?

    Ans. False. See Example 2.

17. When a market share projection is used as the basis for establishing a pricing strategy, there are seldom any objective criteria by which management can evaluate progress. True or false?

    Ans. False. See Section 5.5.

18. When setting prices in order to obtain a share of the market, the firm must: (*a*) file with the government, (*b*) seek permission from the stockholders, (*c*) determine if there is room for growth in the market, (*d*) determine if all the competitors' products are in a declining phase.

    Ans. (*c*) See Example 3.

19. When using market share to establish prices, it is always necessary to price below every other producer. True or false?

    Ans. False. See Example 3.

20. A steadily increasing sales volume bears a direct and positive correlation with profits.   True or false?

   Ans.   False.   See Section 5.6.

21. When a product is to be sold through intermediaries, the price must (*a*) be reduced, (*b*) be doubled, (*c*) reflect the profit to be made by the wholesaler, (*d*) be negotiated with each individual wholesaler.

   Ans.   (*c*)   See Section 5.7.

Solved Problems

5.1.   Most product pricing is based on the concept of list price.   What is the list price?   How does it differ from the market price?

   The *list price* is the quoted price, or the price stated to a potential buyer.   The *market price* is the actual price paid by the buyer after any discounts are granted.   In some instances, when bills are paid immediately, eliminating a period of waiting, the seller will offer a cash discount.   When products are bought in quantity, it is common for the seller to offer increasing rates of discount as the quantity increases.

   For example, suppose an automotive battery is listed by a wholesaler at $25.   The wholesaler offers a 10% discount for purchases of 2 to 10 units, and a 2% discount for payment in 10 days or less.

   List price of battery: $25.00
   Retailer buys 10: $250 less $25 (10%) = $225.00
   Discount for prompt payment: $225 less $4.50 (2%) = $220.50 (market price)

   Trade discounts are offered to other business people who will provide a function in the marketing chain.   For example, publishers offer discounts that average 40% to bookstore operators.   The bookstore operator will sell at list, and the 40% represents his or her profit.

5.2.   Explain how the cash discount works.   What is the business reasoning for it?

   Cash discounts are usually offered on a predetermined period, such as 10 days.   If a company offered a 2% discount for payment within this period, the invoice would state, 2/10, net 30, which means the buyer can take the discount if payment is made within ten days of the invoice, but otherwise the entire amount is due in 30 days.   It should be noted that all customers must be offered the same privilege.   Discrimination by the seller is grounds for legal action.

   The cash discount was originally conceived to improve cash flow, or the liquidity position of the seller.   It is also used to reduce the costs associated with the collection of money.

5.3.   How is it possible to give a buyer an effectively lower price on a product, yet not change the list price?

   If the product being sold is a replacement for another product and the seller is willing to take the customer's old item, such as an automobile, in trade, the seller will offer a trade-in allowance.   In some cases, the traded-in item will be refurbished and sold as a used item, but in others it will have only scrap value.   However, the trade-in does allow the seller maneuvering room when the list price cannot be altered.

   For example, suppose a new car is offered at $9,500 by a dealer to a person with a car to trade-in.   If the dealer figures that the used car has resale potential and offers a $1000 trade-in, the price paid by the purchaser will be $8,500 with the trade-in.

5.4.   What pricing strategy is used by manufacturers of consumer goods to motivate dealers to advertise the products locally?

   Manufacturers who sell through retailers often offer a *promotion allowance*.   That is, when proof of local advertising is presented to the manufacturer, a discount or rebate will be given to the retailer.   Such activity is called *cooperative advertising*.

5.5. Although there is little evidence that it works in all cases, some products have been shown to sell better at the highest price when tested at several price levels.   Why?

Products that have a prestige quality, and those which are advertised to convey this impression, can often be sold more profitably at higher prices than would normally be expected.   Luxury automobiles do, in some cases, cost more to make, but the cost added to the price often exceeds the added cost by a considerable margin.   People who are status conscious will pay the price.   In some cases, however, if the price were lowered, fewer of the products might be sold.   It would appear that the psychological value of a product is directly proportional to its price and not to its actual value in terms of cost of materials and construction.

Those who sell products through the mail have an excellent opportunity to determine price early in the marketing program.   They can mail to a sample of the population they plan to try to sell to, and vary the price in different mailing pieces.   If all of the variables are controlled, this kind of test can provide direct evidence of the appropriate price before all of the advertising money is spent on the entire mailing.   Often, a prestige product will sell best for the highest price.

5.6. Why is $5.95 a more popular price for some products than $6.00?   The difference is only a nickel!

Odd pricing, such as 99¢ rather than $1.00, was originally a device to force clerks to make change, helping in the store's cash control.   When this practice started, the difference of a few pennies was more significant than it is today, but the psychological difference of a few cents, coupled with the habit of seeing such prices, still makes the concept practical for marketers making pricing decisions.

5.7. Describe the concept of unit pricing.

Using this approach, all products are priced according to some standard unit, i.e., pounds, feet, quarts, etc.   All labeling must contain the unit price as well as the price for the item.   Assume that the price for a pound of butter is $1.00, but the package being sold contains two pounds.   The unit price of $1 per pound must be displayed along with the $2 price of the package.

5.8. Apart from the basics of recovering costs and earning a profit, what other factors should be considered when determining the price of a product or service?

Pricing decisions should also include consideration of competitive reactions.   Will a lower price trigger a round of profit-reducing, price-cutting activity by competitors?   Will an initially high price entice competitors to enter the market with lower prices?   In other words, pricing decisions involve much more than an accountant's analysis based strictly on costs and profit margins.

5.9. The pricing of a new product is especially tricky.   The initial price may be the sole determinant of whether or not the product will be successful.   It would appear that a company introducing a new product should try for the lowest possible price in order to capture the market.   However, the opposite is often done intentionally.   What is this pricing policy called?   What is the reasoning behind it?

When a marketer deliberately chooses to price a product higher than it would ordinarily, the technique is referred to as *skimming*.   It should be remembered that new products are costly to develop; this tactic represents an effort to recover development costs as quickly as possible.   The system, derived from skimming the cream, assumes that enough of the product will be sold at the high price to recover the investment before competitors jump in with lower prices.   At that point, the company that introduced the product can reduce its price and fight it out with its competitors.   With the company's costs recovered, the situation is now one of ordinary price competition, but with no heavy developmental costs to pay off.   It is easier to lower a price than to raise it; such reductions often help to expand the market.

5.10. New products can also be introduced at prices which reverse the skimming technique. What is this system called?   What is its rationale?

The technique used when the initial price of a new product is deliberately set lower than it should be to achieve the best profit position, is called *penetration pricing*.   The theory here is that the low price will garner a large share of the market quickly and that those who buy the product will remain loyal when the price is later raised.   Generally, this technique is most effective with branded products where promotion is aimed at building brand loyalty.   However, the point at which the price is raised must be carefully calculated.   If the price increase comes too soon after the introduction at the lower price, brand loyalty may not be strong enough.   The amount of the raise must also be carefully planned.   It is often better to raise the price in several smaller steps rather than in one big step.

Penetration pricing offers a decided advantage because it discourages competition from entering the field.   However, it is important for the company to be sure that it will be financially able to sustain itself at the reduced price until the price can be increased to a more profitable level.

5.11. Why would a marketing manager set a price exactly equal to the amount charged by a competitor?

On the surface, there would seem to be no advantage to this, but it does allow the person who follows the competition considerable flexibility when dealing with the other variables that affect sales.   For one thing, price does not have to be considered.

The company that follows its competition usually has plans to attack the competitor on another front.   For example, a saturation advertising campaign might be mounted.   Or, special discounts could be offered to motivate the dealers to sell the product, despite the fact that both carry the same list price.   Since dealers make additional money in the form of trade discounts, or on special purchase arrangements, this strategy is often effective.

5.12. What is loss leader pricing?   Where is this technique used most effectively?

The loss leader is a product which is priced very low in order to attract customers.   Normally, the technique is most effective in retail stores where many items are sold.   The plan is to get customers into the store to purchase the loss leader, and to recapture the loss on that item through the volume buying of other items.   Food stores in competitive areas often use this technique.

5.13. How do customers perceive the quality of a product as it relates to the price charged? What are the implications of this phenomenon for marketing people?

Within limits, people tend to attribute superior qualities to products that are more expensive than those for which the price is less.   However, consumers tend to have upper and lower limits which define what they will pay for "quality" and for "budget" items.   When such limits can be determined by marketing research, prices at whichever end of the range is to be used can be tested prior to national marketing.   Many products are promoted as quality items in order to maintain the higher price, but the marketer must know the product and the market to which the product is directed.   Such purchasing often boils down to a matter of status maintenance, and unless the personal characteristics of the individuals are known, a quality appeal, along with a higher price, may fail.

5.14. Retailers generally price the products they sell on a mark-up system.   Describe the two ways this can be handled, and explain why one is preferred over the other.

The simplest way a retailer can determine the price at which a product will be sold is to add a mark-up to the price he or she paid for the product.   Thus, a retailer might buy an item for $5.00 and add a mark-up of $2.50.   Since mark-ups are generally computed as percentages, this mark-up would be 50% of cost.   This system is workable, but one that is more commonly used is based on the selling price.   Using the same figures, the $7.50 price would now be thought of as a 33.3% mark-up based on the selling price.   This system is somewhat more popular because the mark-up percentage based on the selling price is usually close to the gross margin, and is thus a figure more easily related to standard accounting procedures. The businessman who is conversant with accounting terms will, therefore, prefer to work with this system, rather than to simply mark up the cost of the product.

5.15. Is it important for a businessperson to strive for the highest possible mark-up at all times?

Seeking to get the highest mark-up can lead to trouble when there is aggressive competition in the area. It may be possible to get an 80% or 90% mark-up, but the volume of business may be low if a competitor has only a 10% or 20% mark-up and the volume necessary to make a better profit. The keys are volume and overhead. With low costs and high volume, the lower mark-up may return a better profit than a high mark-up alone.

Discount stores have proven this. Operating in low rent locations without elaborate stores, they have shown that a small mark-up and high volume can lead to significant profits. The point is this: It's not the high mark-up that is always most important, it's the bottom line—profits.

5.16. Pricing decisions must include the consideration of shipping costs. F.O.B. point-of-production is one widely used method. What is this system? What are its implications for competitors located outside the geographical area of the producer?

When the selling price is quoted F.O.B. point of origin, the buyer is expected to pay all freight charges. The seller assumes the cost to put the freight "on board," but the balance of the transportation charges are assumed by the buyer. Note that title passes to the buyer once the merchandise is loaded, and appropriate insurance should be carried by the buyer to protect the merchandise.

This system makes it difficult for a competitor located at some distance to compete with a company that is closer to the market. The freight charges raise the cost of goods bought; the cost of buying from a more distant manufacturer may become prohibitive because of shipping charges.

5.17. Under the uniform delivered pricing system, the inequities of the F.O.B. method of pricing are eliminated. How does this system work?

Using *the uniform delivered pricing system*, the same price is quoted to any buyer, regardless of the geographical location. This system is used primarily in industries where transportation costs are a small percentage of the total price of the products bought. To make the system work, the seller averages shipping costs in order to be able to quote the uniform price. In effect, the buyers closer to the factory pay some of the costs to ship the products to distant locations.

Retailers who make local free deliveries also use this system. They estimate their cost to operate a delivery service and add an appropriate mark-up to their prices to cover the related expense.

5.18. Zone-delivered pricing is a way to compensate for the inequities of the uniform delivered pricing system. How does this system operate?

Under *zone-delivered pricing*, a series of zones, each with its own freight charge, are established, usually as a series of rings which spread geographically from the point of shipment. The farther the zone from the factory, the higher the freight charge. In a sense, this is really a series of uniform delivered zones. Freight quoted as "slightly higher west of the Rockies," or "East of the Mississippi," is a good example of a zone-delivered pricing system.

5.19. In the later stages of the product life cycle, it is often wise to reduce prices for a product. This decision, to be effective in retaining a share of the market, must be perfectly timed. What are some of the indicators to look for when this decision is to be made?

Price reductions should be considered:

(1) When there is a weakening in brand preference, and the brand seems to be unable to retain a certain sales level at an existing price.

(2) When the physical variations between all the competitors' products have narrowed, and product differences become trivial. The makers of television sets and calculators experi-

enced this as their products became somewhat standardized, and the essential differences between the products became negligible.

(3) When market saturation is observed.   This is often difficult to define in meaningful terms; however, one type of strong evidence is the ratio of replacement sales to new equipment sales.

(4) When a market begins to be flooded with private label competitors.

5.20. Not all pricing situations can be handled with a pre-established system.   For example, contractors who bid on large and complex jobs must develop their prices individually for every situation.   On what are these bids usually based?   What is one of the major pitfalls for the bidder?

Before any estimating and bidding can take place, all costs must be assembled.   Bids for work, such as construction, are based on costs plus charges to cover overhead and profit.   Industries in which bidding is required have widely varying cost-estimating problems, not only at the time of the bidding, but at the time the contract is finally awarded.   If a bidder's costs and expenses increase substantially once a job is quoted, the contract may no longer be profitable when it is awarded.

Because companies using this system will ask several competitors to provide bids for the work, it is necessary to watch costs as well as the overhead and profit figures closely.   When bidders quote the same overhead and profit figures on every job, regardless of the competition, they usually end up getting fewer contracts.   Pricing for bid must include consideration of the history of bids offered by the competitors for earlier work as well as just how much a competitor might want the job.   There are times when a company will bid low to get the job, but make no provision for profit.   Such bidding is done occasionally to keep people and equipment working.   Costs are covered, but no profit is realized.   Obviously, this is an extraordinary measure, but it is important to know if a competitive bidder is in this situation.

5.21. Prices are often based on costs plus a desired profit.   Suppose that a small furniture manufacturer who anticipates profits at 20% of cost has the following costs associated with producing and selling 100 chairs: labor and materials, $10,000; other expenses (rent, depreciation, management wages, etc.), $3,000.

Using the cost plus profit method, compute the selling price of one chair.   What is the major drawback of the cost plus pricing system?

Labor and materials	$10,000
Other expenses	3,000
Total cost	13,000
Anticipated profit	2,600
Cost plus profit	15,600

Selling price is determined by dividing the cost-plus-profit figure by the number of chairs to be made.

$$\frac{\$15,600}{100} = \$156.00$$

Profit per chair = $26.00

The selling price, determined by a basic cost-plus method is $156.   However, there are different types of costs and not all of them act alike as output increases or decreases.   If the manufacturer sold only 84 of the 100 chairs that were produced, the costs would remain the same, but the profits would be reduced to almost nothing. $84 \times 156 = \$13,104$.   This is only $104 above cost, hardly worth the effort.

However, it should be noted that this is a much simplified example of cost-plus pricing, and when more sophisticated methods are used, it can be an effective pricing system.   Advanced methods provide cost variations that relate to output expansion or contraction.

The figures used here illustrate full-cost pricing.   The system uses all relevant variable costs to establish the price of the product, as well as an allocation of the fixed costs that cannot be attributed to the item being priced.   The major weakness of the system is that it does not consider demand for the product or the effects of competition. It could be that no one would be willing to pay the price as calculated. Also, any attempt to allocate fixed expenses (overhead) is arbitrary and often impractical.

5.22. The problem of arbitrary allocation of fixed expenses when cost-plus pricing is used can be overcome by using a system called incremental cost pricing. Use the income statement for a small manufacturer given below to explain this system.

Sales (1000 units @ $90)		$90,000
Expenses		
Variable	$40,000	
Fixed	35,000	75,000
Net profit		$15,000

Incremental cost pricing attempts to use only costs which are directly attributable to a specific output. If the company got an inquiry for an additional 500 items, how low could it price the product to be competitive? Using the full cost approach, it would divide its total expenses by its output of 100 units. The full cost price would be $75, a profitless figure. Any markup of this figure would provide a profit, but the system would be arbitrary and probably uneconomical because of the lack of profit planning. Assuming that it is possible to charge variable cost at $40 per unit, profits can be increased using an incremental method. Fixed overhead remains the same. This is how the income statement would look using an incremental approach:

Sales (1000 units @ $90		
+ 500 units @ $45)		$112,500
Expenses		
Variable (1500 × $40)	$60,000	
Fixed	35,000	95,000
Net profit		$ 17,500

Note that using this system allows the company to quote a very competitive price, yet still make a profit. It is assumed that selling to this one customer at a much lower price will not effect pricing to its existing market.

5.23. What is a *mark-up*? A *mark-on*? What are the problems inherent in pricing systems that use these approaches?

Mark-up is an amount added to cost to determine the selling price. The mark-on is a mark-up based on cost. Both can be expressed as percentages.

$$\text{Mark-up (\%)} = \frac{\text{Amount added to cost}}{\text{Price}}$$

$$\text{Mark-on (\%)} = \frac{\text{Amount added to cost}}{\text{Cost}}$$

Suppose a retailer sells an item for $1.00 that costs him $0.65. The mark-up would be $0.35. This is a mark-up percentage of 35% (0.35/1.00). The mark-on percentage would be 53.8% (0.35/0.65).

The use of traditional mark-ups often leads to inertia in an industry. Industries which use this approach, regardless of fluctuations in demand, tend to stagnate.

Chapter 6

Distribution Systems

6.1 INTRODUCTION

Making a good product or providing a superior service is seldom enough to insure a business success. Apart from local businesses, such as retail bakeries, which make and sell their products in the same place, it is necessary to develop ways to get the products to those who will buy them.

It is a mistake to think of distribution as a high cost factor. A well-planned and carefully run distribution system adds value to the products or services at every point from the producer to the consumer.

The problems that must be solved include planning appropriate strategies, selecting efficient channels of distribution, and managing the actual physical movement of products from where they are made to where they will be sold.

6.2 DISTRIBUTION SYSTEMS ADD VALUE: TIME UTILITY

Few products today are made on a job-order production basis. Most products are produced in the quantities manufacturers believe they can sell and then are released through appropriate marketing channels. This is known as *speculative production*. While the word speculative implies an intuitive approach, such decisions are generally made on the basis of considerable marketing research.

EXAMPLE 1.

The relation of speculative production to product availability is clearly seen in the clothing industry which relies heavily on speculative production. Garments are completed many months in advance of the season, and are often in the retail stores a season ahead of when they will be worn. It is this availability of a product when it is needed and wanted that distribution contributes to the marketing cycle.

EXAMPLE 2.

A manufacturer's ability to deliver the product on time has far-reaching effects and the concept of time utility is not limited to consumer goods. For example, manufacturers who supply the automobile industry with parts must be sure that the products they make are at the assembly lines when they are needed. A poorly coordinated distribution system might result in new cars being late in the showrooms. In a competitive market such as this, where products are dated, the loss of even a week or two of selling time could seriously endanger profits.

6.3 DISTRIBUTION SYSTEMS ADD VALUE: PLACE UTILITY

A product has no value to a potential customer unless it is available for purchase at a convenient place. Companies servicing consumer markets concentrate on distribution systems that place products in retail stores, catalog showrooms, mail order houses, or other places where consumers are most likely to seek them. Manufacturers of industrial products often use independent distributors who specialize in reaching particular markets.

EXAMPLE 3.

The manufacturer of industrial products sells to the distributor at a discount, and the distributor then sells at list price in order to make a profit. Industrial distributors most often stock products made by a number of different manufacturers, but all bear some relationship to each other in terms of the people and companies that use them.   For example, distributors who sell to chemical processing plants might stock valves, fittings, gauges, regulators, and other controls, each made by a different company.   The distributors tend to specialize in order to make their selling efforts most efficient.   If they were to sell to several diverse industries, separate sales forces, each with the skills appropriate to the particular industry, might be required for optimal effectiveness.   Thus, product concentration in distribution benefits both the buyer and the seller.

6.4   THE BUSINESS OF WHOLESALING

A *wholesaler* is a person or company that buys from a manufacturer, but does not sell to the ultimate user of the product.   The industrial wholesaler may buy from a manufacturer and sell to another manufacturer who will use the product as part of another product.   In the case of consumer products, the wholesaler will buy from the manufacturer and resell to the retailer who, in turn, will sell to the ultimate consumer.

Because the wholesaler will perform some of the costly marketing functions that would have been handled by the manufacturer if sales were made directly, the manufacturer sells goods to the wholesaler at a significant discount.   The wholesaler provides not only the selling activity, but also warehousing and delivery to local locations.

Note that the wholesaler is an intermediary; the terms *distributor* and *jobber* are also used to describe this business activity.   The term distributor is more commonly used in the sale of industrial products, while the term jobber is often used by those who handle consumer goods.

EXAMPLE 4.

The retailer who advertises products at wholesale prices may, indeed, be selling at that price level, but if the customers for the products are end users, he cannot be considered a wholesaler.   In other words, the customer and not the price level determines the description that should be used.

There are some companies that sell their product directly to the consumer as well as to wholesalers but these activities are usually separate.   For example, some manufacturers own their retail outlets and advertise that their merchandise is sold at wholesale prices.   They can do this because they have eliminated the independent intermediary.   However, the same company may sell products to wholesalers serving retailers in noncompetitive areas.   Thus, they serve both markets.

6.5   CHOOSING THE BEST CHANNEL OF DISTRIBUTION

There are no easy answers to the question of choosing the best distribution channel.   The decision must be made to maximize sales at a profit level determined by the manufacturer, and it is important to recognize that changes in business can affect the choice of distribution channel at any time.   A company that had found it best to sell through wholesalers (see Section 6.4) may find after a few years that the discounts are eating too much of the profits and that company-employed salespeople might be the better way.   It is for this reason that every marketing manager must keep in touch with all the trends and costs involved, not only in the marketing system that is being used, but in alternative systems that might be used at a lower cost.

EXAMPLE 5.

Direct sale is the marketing system in which the manufacturer sells the product directly to the user.   It is the simplest system and is most often seen in companies that sell to industrial users.   Company-salaried salespeople sell directly to those who will use the products.   This kind of system is rare in the consumer field.

EXAMPLE 6.

The work of a wholesaler may be augmented by a company's own sales representatives.   Generally, smaller companies reach their markets through wholesalers who then sell to retailers or industrial users.   However, it is not uncommon for such companies to also employ salespeople who call on the retailer or the industrial user to perform merchandising work.   These salespeople augment the work of the wholesaler, but do not actually make any of the sales.

EXAMPLE 7.

Another way for companies to market their products is to use manufacturers' representatives. This system is usually used by smaller manufacturers with markets that are geographically large. *Manufacturers' representatives* (or agents) are individuals or companies who sell the manufacturers' products, but do not buy the product themselves for resale. They never take title to the products and are usually paid by the manufacturer after the customer pays for the merchandise. Agents can be used to call on wholesalers who then sell to either retailers or industrial users. The manufacturers' agent also frequently calls directly on industrial users.

6.6 MULTIPLE CHANNELS OF DISTRIBUTION

When a product can be used in several different markets, it is usually best to establish a different distribution system for each market. There is seldom a true economy in using one system of distribution for several markets. For example, many food processors have different channels for reaching each of the markets for a product. One distribution system may include manufacturers' agents who sell to wholesalers who then sell to the retailer. Another, aimed at industrial food buyers, may use manufacturers' agents directly and eliminate the wholesaler. The point is this: Each channel must be tailored so that it is the most efficient and profitable for the market being served.

6.7 CHOOSING THE MOST EFFICIENT METHODS OF DISTRIBUTION

It is important to understand that a distribution decision has the same financial effect as any other capital investment decision within the corporation. Because profit maximization is the final criterion, the selection of a channel of distribution should be based on an estimate of the rate of return of investment in each of the possible channels.

The factors which must be considered when selecting a system of distribution are described below. Each is illustrated by an example.

(1) *Market characteristics, including customer buying habits, geographic location, and prevailing industry practices.*

EXAMPLE 8.

Buyers of consumer products seldom buy directly from the manufacturer, but those who purchase industrial equipment often deal directly with factory salespeople. In industries with widespread markets, the use of intermediaries is often important. Companies which are located in the same area as their customers will often sell directly by means of their own salespeople.

(2) *The nature of the product.*

EXAMPLE 9.

The product itself has a lot to do with the selection of a system of distribution. Industrial supplies and replacement parts may pass through many hands before reaching the user. From the manufacturer to manufacturers' agents to wholesalers and then to the customer is a common chain. In contrast, perishable food usually has a very short distribution chain. In fact, rather than ship food great distances, some manufacturers maintain regional processing plants to shorten the distribution channel. As a rule, products which require regular service and may involve complicated installation reach the market by way of very short distribution chains. In fact, such products are often sold directly by the manufacturer to the user. If regional warehousing is required, companies that make these products often elect to set up and staff their own facilities, rather than use independent intermediaries.

(3) *The nature of the company.*

EXAMPLE 10.

When a company's financial position makes it inadvisable to support its own distribution system, the company turns to outside distributors. These distributors buy the products in quantity at a discount, creating fewer credit and collection problems than would occur if the company sold directly to the user.

Companies that are in a strong capital position often choose to handle distribution themselves, although this is not always the best approach.   The need for a certain amount of control often motivates a company to handle its own distribution.   Highly technical products which require special engineering attention are often sold directly, the company being reluctant to entrust technical sales to an outside organization.

(4) *The general business climate.*

EXAMPLE 11.

Changes in the business climate often force companies to change their approach to distribution drastically.   With the advent of discount stores which sell products of lesser quality for less money, manufacturers had to try different methods to insure their markets.   In some cases, direct selling door-to-door was tried; in others, special merchandising systems were offered to existing retail outlets.

6.8   EXCLUSIVE AND GENERAL DISTRIBUTION

Some products benefit from the use of *exclusive distributors*. These are wholesalers or retailers who are the sole source of a product within a specific geographical territory.   In most cases, those who are given these exclusive territories are also assigned specific sales goals.   If the goals are not met, the exclusive arrangements can be terminated and given to another company.   Exclusive dealerships, such as those given to automobile dealers, are usually provided with considerable merchandising help from the manufacturer.   In such protected territories, the distributor or retailer does not have to concentrate on competing with others selling products of the same company.   All its efforts can be spent selling against direct competitors.   Exclusive territories are not illegal, but there are a number of problems that can arise from these arrangements which result in violations of Federal and State statutes.   See Chapter 11 for a detailed description of the legal problems of marketing.

6.9   INTENSIVE AND SELECTIVE DISTRIBUTION

Those who make convenience goods often try to provide saturation coverage of their prime markets. Candy, cigarettes, and chewing gum are examples of products that are sold simultaneously in such places as food, general, candy, and department stores in the same area. In order for *intensive distribution* to be effective, regional warehousing is mandatory. Regular shipments to sellers of the products must be made, and this would be impossible from one distant location.

The opposite approach, *selective distribution*, is used when the manufacturer wants to limit marketing costs as well as establish solid relationships with its dealers. To be most effective, however, the manufacturer must select its dealers carefully. With limited distribution, a weak dealer can seriously reduce sales. Not only are sales lower than they would be with a better dealer, but the relationship often prevents the manufacturer from reaping the potential of the area with a more effective dealer.

Review Questions

1. Build a better mousetrap and the public will beat a path to your door. This is an automatic guarantee of success. True or false?

   Ans. False. See Section 6.1.

2. A distribution problem that is often encountered is (*a*) planning an appropriate distribution strategy, (*b*) selecting efficient distribution channels, (*c*) managing the actual physical distribution, (*d*) all of these.

   Ans. (*d*) See Section 6.1.

3. The term used to describe the way most mass-produced products are made is (*a*) job-order production, (*b*) speculative production, (*c*) limited production, (*d*) none of these.

   Ans. (*b*) See Section 6.2.

4. A well-planned distribution system will insure that the products are available at the precise time they are needed. True or false?

   Ans. True. See Example 1.

5. A distribution system actually adds value to a product by assuring that it is delivered to the point at which a need for it exists. True or false?

   Ans. True. See Section 6.3.

6. Industrial distributors seldom take title to the goods they sell, and manufacturers' representatives always take title. True or false?

   Ans. False. See Example 3 and Example 7.

7. Distributors tend to specialize in certain product areas because (*a*) limited franchises force them to do so, (*b*) the interests of the principles are best served by specialization, (*c*) they can make the most efficient use of their sales force, (*d*) it makes it easier for their warehousing operations.

   Ans. (*c*) See Example 3.

8. Wholesalers take title to goods sold to them by manufacturers and then sell to other wholesalers or to retailers. True or false?

   Ans. True. See Section 6.4.

9. A wholesaler is an intermediary and can also be called (*a*) distributor, (*b*) jobber, (*c*) neither of these, (*d*) both of these.

   Ans. (*d*) See Section 6.4.

10. If a retailer sells to the ultimate consumer at wholesale prices, he or she is technically a wholesaler. True or false?

    Ans. False. See Example 4.

11. Once a channel of distribution is established and working, it should never be changed. True or false?

    Ans. False. See Section 6.5.

12. A marketing system in which the manufacturer sells directly to the user is most often seen in (*a*) retail markets, (*b*) industrial markets, (*c*) both of these, (*d*) neither of these.

    Ans. (*b*) See Example 5.

13. Significant discounts are offered by manufacturers to wholesalers because the wholesaler often undertakes much of the marketing effort. True or false?

    Ans. True. See Section 6.4.

14. Manufacturers who sell through wholesalers often also employ their own field representatives to (*a*) keep tabs on the distributor salespeople, (*b*) augment the work of the distributor, but not take any orders directly, (*c*) perform all of the market research needed by the manufacturer, (*d*) fill in for distributor salespeople when they are sick or on vacation.

    Ans. (*b*) See Example 6.

15. Manufacturers' agents call on (a) end users, (b) distributors, (c) jobbers, (d) all of these.

Ans. (d) See Example 7.

16. Multiple channels of distribution are used by a manufacturer when the same, or similar, products are to be sold to different markets. True or false?

Ans. True. See Section 6.6.

17. Industries with widespread markets usually find it more efficient to use some form of intermediary to insure adequate distribution. True or false?

Ans. True. See Example 8.

18. Products which require service and complicated installation are best sold by a long chain of distribution. True or false?

Ans. False. See Example 9.

19. Companies in a strong capital position often choose to use independent distributors, rather than to handle the distribution themselves. True or false?

Ans. False. See Example 10.

20. The argument most often used to justify the appointment of exclusive distributors is that they will not have to compete with others nearby selling the identical product and can concentrate on overcoming the efforts of competing products. True or false?

Ans. True. See Section 6.8.

Solved Problems

6.1. In recent years, the problems encountered by small and medium-sized firms, operating independently of each other, have been greatly reduced by institutional changes in distribution that have been characterized as vertical marketing systems. Describe some of the dominant systems that have emerged and tell how they have helped to eliminate the older, inefficient, and effort-duplicating marketing systems.

Perhaps the most important contribution made by vertical marketing systems is an economy of scale. By coordinating efforts and eliminating much duplication of marketing services, vertical marketing systems can accomplish more with less effort and less cost. There are three basic types of vertical marketing systems, as follows:

(1) *Corporate vertical marketing* system is one in which both the production facilities and the marketing organization are owned and managed by the same company. Several clothing manufacturers in the United States not only make clothing, but also operate the retail outlets in which they are sold. Corporate vertical marketing systems can be observed just about everywhere, and they can exist whether the manufacturer owns only one outlet through which its products are sold, or a national distribution organization.

(2) *Administrative vertical marketing* systems are those in which the manufacturer is so dominant in the field that it can dictate policy to retailers in matters such as pricing, display and local advertising. Consider the case of local appliance retailers in your area whose advertising and sales promotion seem to be dominated by a single brand. In most cases, this indicates the dominance of a strong manufacturer that was able to administer a vertical marketing system.

(3) In a *contractual vertical marketing* system, independent organizations, such as producers, wholesalers, and retailers, work together, most often by specific contract, to achieve the size and power they need to compete. There are three different ways that a contractual system can be organized: wholesalers sponsor a retail chain, retailers form cooperatives, and manufacturers sell company franchises.

Of the three approaches to vertical marketing the most popular, at least in the retail field, has been the contractual system. This can be seen in the rapid expansion of many different types of franchises.

6.2.   Wholesalers are often blamed for increasing the cost paid by the consumer for products they handle.   In some cases there may be validity to this claim, but when an efficient system is established, functions performed by the wholesaler contribute to the utility of the product.   Discuss this point in terms of product availability.

Both the wholesaler and the retailer buy and store goods for their customers so that they are available when needed.   The customer of the wholesaler is the retailer; the end user buys from the retailer.   Both customers are served when local stocks are available, and the product does not have to be shipped from a distant factory.   Because the wholesaler buys in large quantities from the manufacturer, the price to the retailer is lower and can be priced correspondingly lower for the retail customer.   Also, the wholesaler is able to ship smaller quantities for shorter distances at freight savings, compared with what the freight costs would be for the same shipment made at a greater distance by the manufacturer if the product were being shipped directly to the retailer.

6.3.   What other economies can the wholesaler, or other middleman, provide to keep costs to the ultimate customer down?

Wholesalers usually represent and stock the products of a number of different companies.   Because the wholesalers specialize in types of products and customers served, they can spread the costs of sales over a number of different lines.   If each individual manufacturer were to sell with its own salespeople to the same customers, the cost of selling could be prohibitively high.   Each wholesale salesperson can sell the products of a number of manufacturers on a single call.

6.4.   The wholesaler also serves as a source of credit for the retailer.   Describe how this helps the retailer earn a higher return on investment.

Many wholesalers will permit their retailer customers to buy products on credit.   This eliminates the amount of cash that retailers must tie up in inventory, and allows them to pay for the merchandise as cash is produced through sales.   This is a practical application of the *principle of leverage,* in which a smaller investment inflates the return on investment.   If, for example, a retailer has stock valued at $100,000, profits of $10,000 will create a 10% return on investment.   However, if the retailer paid only $80,000 for the merchandise, utilizing credit offered by the wholesaler for the balance, the same $10,000 profit now becomes a 12.5% return on investment.

6.5.   The middleman can never be eliminated.   Is this statement true?

An independent middleman can be eliminated, but someone else must do the job.   For example, if a manufacturer cuts out the wholesalers who used to supply retailers, another system must be established to handle the distribution function.   The manufacturer may take over by establishing factory-owned and operated regional warehouses, or retailers may band together to undertake the wholesale function.   Either group may be able to do the job more efficiently and for less money, but simply eliminating the independent middleman will not in and of itself be reflected in lower prices to the consumer.

6.6.   Why do certain manufacturers prefer to handle their own marketing from manufacture through wholesaling and retailing?

This decision is usually made because of specific product characteristics.   Some food producers feel that they need control over the delivery of perishable products, and therefore establish their own direct channels.   When a product is complex and requires elaborate installation and/or regular servicing, some manufacturers feel that their needs and the requirements of the customers using the products are best served by factory-owned and operated marketing channels.   Most industrial products are sold directly to the users because of this last consideration.

6.7.   Describe the role played by the full-function wholesaler.

Full-function merchant wholesalers take possession of and title to the goods they handle.   They maintain stocks of merchandise in convenient locations, making it possible for their retailer customers to get goods on short notice, thus reducing the need for the retailer to carry a heavy inventory.   In general, full-function merchant wholesalers are most active in fields where the retailers to whom they sell such as drug and grocery stores carry large quantities of relatively inexpensive merchandise.   In industrial markets, such organizations are called industrial distributors.

6.8.   What are the functions of the drop shipper in industry?

A drop shipper is strictly a sales organization that takes orders from customers, and then forwards them to the manufacturers for direct shipment to the customers.   The drop shipper may take title to the merchandise, but never physically handles it.   In general, the drop shipper operates in fields where products are bulky and are often sold in very large lots.   Perhaps the most valuable service performed by the drop shipper is that of assembling a complete line of products needed by its customers.   For example, if a retail lumber yard needs oak flooring, pine shelving, and plaster lath, the drop shipper would work with several individual sources of each, and put together a single order for its customer.   All of the wood would be shipped directly to the customer by the different mills that produced it.

6.9.   Agents and brokers do, on occasion, take possession of the merchandise they sell, but never take title to it.   Describe five distinct types of agents and brokers.

(1) *Commission merchants* act for the producer of the merchandise and are given an agreed-upon fee when goods are sold.   Usually the commission merchant is given considerable latitude by the producer of the merchandise in sales arrangements.   This form of marketing organization is most often used by producers of agricultural products where prices fluctuate because of supply and demand of the product on a day-to-day basis.

(2) *Auction companies* bring buyers and sellers together in one central location.   Potential buyers are given the opportunity to inspect the goods before the actual auction begins.   The auction company will charge the seller an agreed-upon commission based on the sale price.   Auction companies exist in such diverse fields as art, antiques, livestock, automobiles, and agriculture.

(3) *Brokers* are intermediaries whose main responsibility is to bring together buyers and sellers.   They are usually very well versed in market conditions and can provide information for both parties.   Brokers can work for either the buyer or the seller, but do not physically handle the merchandise being sold.   Most brokers represent the seller by initiating the sale, and then leaving it up to the seller to accept or reject the buyer's offer.

Brokers are most active in the fields where products come on the market for only limited periods of time.   For example, food brokers handle specific forms of produce in season, and then may not see the parties they brought together until the next season.   Usually the producer will tell the broker the price being sought and the broker will review the market and prevailing prices.   When price sought and market price are in line, the broker generally leaves the final negotiations to the seller and the buyer.   Brokers earn their living by taking small commissions from the parties that engage them.   Real estate brokers usually represent the seller, but unlike other brokers often take a very active part in the negotiation of the sale.

(4) *Selling agents* are most often found in fields characterized by small, underfinanced, production-oriented companies.   Usually they take responsibility for the total marketing effort of the firms they represent.   They are almost always given full authority over pricing decisions and promotional expenditures.   In many cases they provide financial help to the manufacturers they represent.   The production-oriented companies that often use selling agents are, because of their efforts, able to concentrate on what they know best— manufacturing.

(5) *The manufacturers' agent* is a company or an individual working for several companies which make related, but non-competitive, products. Agents, or manufacturers' representatives as they are also called, receive a commission on the products they sell. They generally have limited and well-defined geographical territories; it is not uncommon for a manufacturer to cover the entire country by using a network of independent manufacturers' agents. The agent is able to keep selling costs down by representing several companies that sell to the same people, making each sales call very productive. For example, an agent might represent a company that makes pipe, another that makes valves and yet another that makes pipe fittings. The individuals in industry who need these products are usually happy to see agents because they can learn about a number of products in which they are interested during a single sales call.

6.10. Many companies do not use middlemen at all. To cover a large territory, they may open either a sales branch or a sales office. Distinguish between these two marketing operations.

The sales branch of a company usually stocks its complete product line, and also serves as headquarters for the salespeople who cover the territory. Order processing and shipping are handled directly by the sales branch. In contrast, a sales office is simply an operating point for company salespeople. Sales offices are generally placed strategically in areas of the greatest business concentrations. Even though the merchandise may be shipped from a distant location, buyers often like to be able to deal directly with company salespeople when they need the products. In the case of a company which makes and sells technical products, service and installation people may also be located at regional sales offices to meet customers' technical requirements.

6.11. Most people think of a store, whether it is small and local or large and national, when they think of retailing. This is only part of the retailing picture. What other marketing institutions are part of the retail world?

Any activity involved in the sale of products and services to the ultimate consumer is within the field of retailing. This includes mail-order, telephone, direct mail, television, and door-to-door sales. It also includes vending machine sales.

6.12. Most retailers in the United States are classified as single, or limited-line, stores. Describe this concept and some if its benefits for the consumer.

Single and limited-line retailers concentrate on a narrow product line but provide a wide selection from which the customer can choose. The current popularity of home electronics has given rise to a number of chains that sell anything fitting this description. From citizen band radios to television sets and now to home computers, these companies center their sales and promotional activities on a narrow target market. There are even furniture stores that specialize in styles of furniture, such as colonial, and others that concentrate on one type, such as bedroom furniture. Because such retailers tend to carry more of the type of product in which they specialize than a general merchandise store would, the customer is given a wider choice and is saved the effort of going from one store to another in order to see everything that is available. Thus, the limited-line store competes with larger stores by offering a wide selection of a narrow line of merchandise.

6.13. How would you differentiate a specialty store from a limited-line store?

The limited-line store carries one type of product in depth, as described in Problem 6.12. The specialty store carries only a portion of a single line of products. Specialty stores stock their merchandise in depth in order to provide a wide selection for their customers. A store selling only women's summer wear would be classed as a specialty store as would one selling only mens' ties, and even a meat market.

6.14.   A supermarket is defined as a large departmentalized retail store in which food as well as nonfood products are sold.   Because competition between the major chains is so intensive, the stores operate on very thin profit margins.   Cite one of the most effective ways a supermarket can increase sales and profits.

Early in the development of the supermarket, it was noted that a large percentage of the items bought by shoppers were not on their shopping lists.   These items were bought on impulse.   Therefore, each chain tries through in-store displays and other sales promotion approaches to induce shoppers to buy more than they intended when they wrote their shopping lists.   Many of the items bought on impulse are the nonfood items now found in supermarkets.   They are particularly important because many of them carry a higher profit margin than food products.

6.15.   Describe the structure and operating methods of a department store.

As the name implies, a department store is a group of limited-line specialty stores gathered under one roof.   Even though it is often a large retailer handling an extensive number of products, it is unlike other retail stores that may have the same breadth of merchandise.   The overall operation is coordinated by one person or a committee, but management, merchandising, and product selection in each department are left to the individual in charge.

Because the success of each department depends to a large extent on the selection of available merchandise, the person running each department is traditionally called the *buyer*.   Buyers are, in a sense, employed entrepreneurs.   That is, they have all the responsibility of an individual running an independent specialty store.   However, the departments can join forces to buy services (such as advertising) and merchandise (that will be offered in more than one department in the store) collectively.   Compared with discount stores which offer nothing but the merchandise they display, department stores may have as many as half of their employees working in such areas as gift wrapping, credit activities, and other service functions.   Department stores usually do an extensive credit business; in contrast, the discount type of retail organizations seldom offers credit, other than through the major national credit organizations.

6.16.   What is the major difference between a department store and a discount store?

Generally, both offer the same merchandise, but because the discount stores have eliminated most of the services offered by the department stores, they are able to sell their merchandise at lower prices.   Credit, sales assistance, and delivery are only some of the services that have been eliminated by the discount stores.

Early discount stores often operated by selling to specific groups, such as the employees of nearby companies.   Often, early discounters did not stock merchandise in any depth, and took orders which were filled directly by the manufacturer.   Now, however, the discount stores are stocking merchandise in some depth and may offer some of the services they eliminated earlier in order to keep their prices below those of the department stores.   As this is happening, discount prices are getting higher.   But having already established a large base of regular customers, these changes are often welcome because prices remain lower than those in an ordinary retail store; the discounter is able to do this by limiting other services.   The most noticeable feature of the discount stores, other than those which carry major appliances and other big items, is the cash-and-carry policy.

6.17.   House-to-house, or door-to-door, selling is well known in America.   Describe the types of products that are most easily and productively adapted to this type of selling.   Are prices of products sold house-to-house low because there is no need to invest in large and elaborate retail locations?

Products which have a repeat sale potential, such as cosmetics and cleaning materials, are sold effectively by the house-to-house method.   Once a customer has been gained, the sales person simply stops at his or her house on a regular schedule to take orders and deliver products.

In order of importance, these products are marketed effectively by door-to-door selling: cosmetics, educational materials (encyclopedias, magazines), household appliances (vacuums, pots and pans), and cleaning agents.   Avon Cosmetics has been very successful because of its personal approach of helping the customer decide which products will be most beneficial.

Actually, products sold door-to-door carry a high mark-up.   Door-to-door selling is quite expensive.   Usually a large number of people are called on before a sale is made.   There is a high turnover in salespeople which results in high training expenses.   Commissions to salespeople of 50% are not uncommon on products such as vacuum cleaners.

6.18.   Even though mail-order selling accounts for only one percent of all retail sales, it is still a very important marketing system.   How are mail-order sales most often developed?

Mail-order selling began in the late nineteenth century, and was effective because it brought products to people who lived in rural America, where few stores of any kind existed.   Since then it has expanded and is a practical method of selling all kinds of merchandise.   General merchandise is still sold effectively to remote areas by mail, but other organizations which have limited but widely scattered customers can make use of the technique.   Those selling hobby supplies who would find it difficult to support retail store locations, for example, make effective use of mail-order selling.   Orders are solicited by direct mail, by television and radio advertising, by telephone, and by advertising in magazines and newspapers.   A relatively recent approach to mass merchandising combines the benefits of mail order with an ability to sell many products without a direct stock back-up.   This is exemplified by catalog showrooms.   Some of these organizations carry a limited stock of some items, but for the most part the merchandise is shipped from a central warehouse after it has been selected and ordered in the catalog showroom.

6.19.   Even though automatic vending machines account for 20% of candy bar sales, their use is limited.   Describe the problems associated with automated vending.

The most important limiting factor of automated vending is that the merchandise which can be sold is limited to convenience items such as candy, cigarettes, and soda.   The items must be standardized in terms of size and weight in order to be used in the machines.   In addition, due to almost constant mechanical problems and the high costs of operation, vending machine prices are often higher than those for the same items when sold in conventional retail stores.   For example, cigarettes are always higher in price.

6.20.   Describe the computerized checkout system now being introduced in retailing.

When a computerized checkout system is used, each product is stamped with an identifying mark within the Universal Product Code.   At the check-out counter, a scanner reads it electronically and accesses a computer for the current price.   The system is especially appealing to stores selling merchandise with prices which vary from day to day.   Under the conventional system, prices must be changed manually on a day-to-day basis.   Consider the problems associated with such a manual system in food store chains in a highly competitive market.   As one chain changed its prices, another might re-mark all merchandise in all stores by hand in order to beat the competition.   Using the computerized check-out system, only the central data bank must be changed.   When the product with its identifying code is exposed to the electronic scanner, the correct price is read, regardless of where and how many stores are in the chain.   Another advantage that accrues to the retailer is that, as products are sold, inventory changes are recorded automatically and instantly.   When stock levels run low, the computer issues a warning, and stock can be replenished to meet current, rather than anticipated, demand.

This system is practical, but very expensive.   In addition, consumers fear that they will be taken advantage of by retailers because prices may no longer be marked on the products.

Midterm Examination

The questions in this test will help you estimate how well you have mastered the material in the first six chapters of this outline.

1. What is the marketing concept? Contrast the concept with pre-World War II selling strategies.

   In essence, the marketing concept is a business system which recognizes and emphasizes consumer needs in the development and selling of products and services. Prior to World War II, products were developed for reasons that were more suited to the needs of the company than to those of the people who would use them. When such products were created, it was necessary for advertising and the sales force to create the need for the product as well as sell it. Sound consumer research is the basis for the marketing concept. When such research turns up a need that can be fulfilled by a product or service that can be developed by a company, its chances of success are much greater than they would have been under the old system. Also, the marketing orientation results in more and better products for the consumer.

2. What are the four elements of the marketing mix? How do they interact with each other?

   Product planning, distribution, promotional strategy, and pricing are elements of the marketing mix that must be considered when a marketing plan is being developed. Depending upon specific conditions, however, some elements may be more important than others. For example, a company selling large machines to industry usually pays considerable attention to product planning. Pricing would probably be of less importance as would promotional strategy.

3. In order for a market to exist, there must be demand. Discuss this concept.

   There must be a need for a product or a service. However, this is only the beginning. If the need cannot be fulfilled with the right product or service for a price that satisfies the buyer and insures a profit for the seller, the market will not come into being.

4. Define product differentiation.

   When there is a need that can be satisfied by only one producer, there is seldom any incentive for the producer to improve the product or service. However, as competition enters the field, producers often capture a share of someone else's market or hold on to what they have by modifying the product in a way that increases its utility to the customer. In marketing terms, this is product differentiation. In essence, a producer attempts to compete by enhancing the product as it relates to consumer needs.

5. Define market segmentation. Give an example.

   There are often a number of submarkets for the same or a slightly modified product. New markets can be tapped by incorporating minor product changes, or by applying a slightly different marketing technique to the same product. Each submarket tends to be a homogeneous grouping which is easily reached because of characteristics its members have in common.

   Market segmentation is a customer-oriented concept. It is a business tool that had little relevance during the production-oriented period of our industrial history. For example, books can be published as hardcover or in paperback. Libraries seldom buy paperbacks, but it is not especially difficult to sell paperbacks to the reading public. Therefore, this segmented market can be reached with the same book by merely binding with a hard cover for the library market and in paper for the consumer. Libraries are willing to pay the extra price to insure that the book will last.   Most consumers are not as concerned with the longevity of their books.

6. What are some of the more important activities expected of a marketing department?

A marketing department's responsibilities generally include the following: The establishment of operating policies and goals, the identification of markets, an evaluation of market share, both for the company and its competitors, sales forecasting, the development of new products, and the establishment of distribution systems.   Also the development of short- and long-range marketing plans, the establishment and management of pricing policies, the development and implementation of sales training, the management of internal sales and order processing, and sales management based on budgets and forecasting.

7. Draw a diagram which illustrates a functionally integrated marketing organization.

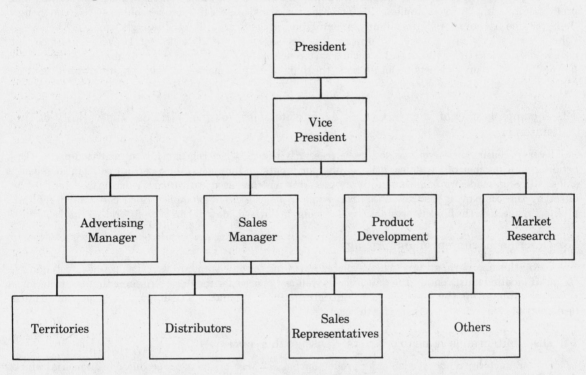

8. What are some of the factors to be considered when planning the size of a sales force?

Once the territory potential has been determined, and the characteristics of the people who would be successful have been discovered, it becomes necessary to decide just how many people will be needed to make the most productive use of each territory.   This depends mainly on the size of the territory and the concentration of prospects.   In some major cities, it is not uncommon for people selling products such as office supplies, to be assigned to only one building.   Consider the number of businesses that are located in metropolitan skyscrapers, such as New York's World Trade Center and you can see that a city territory can be defined vertically as well as horizontally.   Another basis for determining the number of salespeople is the share of the market the company wishes to acquire.   At first, the company may be willing to have more salespeople in a territory, in essence sacrificing profits to secure customers.   When the desired market share is achieved, such a company may thin out the territory to an economically practical level by transferring some of the salespeople to other areas.

9. Describe the product life cycle.

Not unlike people, products pass through cycles which begin with birth and progress to death.   Not all products go through all stages, and the product life cycle may last a few weeks or many years.   The proportionate amount of time in each phase of the cycle also varies.   From a planning point of view, it is important to recognize the steps through which the product will pass and then plan for each accordingly. The four stages of the product life cycle are the introductory, growth, maturity, and decline stages.

10. Describe the introductory stage of the product life cycle.

In the introductory stage, the product is unknown and considerable effort and money are usually expended to familiarize potential customers with it. The promotion may be aimed directly at customers and may be tailored to motivate wholesalers and retailers who would stock and sell the product. It is not uncommon for the product to sustain losses during this period, but if the planning and forecasting were accurate, future profits will more than make up for early losses.

11. Describe the profit maximization approach to pricing.

Using this system, price is increased to the point where a decrease in the number of items sold is noted, and profits begin to drop. For example, a 10% increase in price may reduce the number sold by 4%. Even though there may be few items sold, it still may be profitable for the firm to charge the higher price. The loss in volume is offset by higher profits. To make this system work, the increased total revenue must be just balanced by an increase in total cost. Such a system is easier for a smaller company to manage than for a larger one with many products. But for both, the dynamics of the market make it a system which requires constant attention and fine-tuning.

12. A company should always seek to expand its sales volume. Discuss the validity of this statement.

Ever-increasing sales volume does not necessarily bear a direct relationship to increased profits. Depending on a number of variables, it is possible for profits to diminish after a certain point in increasing sales. Savings made in volume buying of raw materials and increased utilization of existing facilities may be offset by the company's need to subcontract some of its work, for example. Such costs could cut into profits. Therefore, the final determination for pricing should be made in terms of profits, rather than volume.

13. Describe the concept of unit pricing.

Using this approach, all products are priced according to some standard unit, i.e., pounds, feet, quarts, etc. All labeling must contain the unit price as well as the price for the item. Assume that the price for a pound of butter is $1.00, but the package being sold contains two pounds. The unit price of $1 per pound must be displayed along with the $2 price for the package.

14. Distribution adds value to products. Discuss this concept.

Few products are made on a job-order production basis. Most products are produced in quantities which the manufacturers feel they can sell and then are released through the appropriate marketing channel. Because of this system, products can be delivered when and where they are wanted and have had value added by the process of distribution.

15. What is a manufacturer's agent?

The manufacturer's agent is a company or an individual that works for several companies that make related, but noncompeting products. Agents, or manufacturers' representatives as they are also called, receive commissions on the products they sell. Manufacturers' agents usually have limited and well-defined geographical territories, and it is not uncommon for a manufacturer to cover the entire country by using a network of independent agents. The agent is able to keep selling costs down by representing several companies that sell to the same people, making each sales call most productive. For example, an agent might represent a company that makes pipe, another that makes valves and yet another that makes pipe fittings. The individuals in industry who need these products are usually happy to see agents because they can see a number of products in which they are interested in a single sales call.

Chapter 7

Marketing Research

7.1 INTRODUCTION

A successful marketing program depends heavily on information about the market and competitive products and services as well as on an understanding of how prospective customers will respond to each aspect of the marketing mix.   Even when this information is readily available, it must be remembered that every market is in a state of flux at any given time.   The information may be valid at the time it is gathered, but it may not be acted on for months, or even years.   Therefore, any research must include a statement as to the validity of the predictions that can be made when the product or service is actually marketed.

7.2 MARKET RESEARCH DEFINED

The function of market research is to collect, analyze, and interpret, in a systematic manner, data relevant to a particular marketing question.   It is twofold: (1) to develop facts and forecasts that will help marketing personnel do their job, and (2) to interpret the information for other management personnel within the company.

EXAMPLE 1.

Research findings must be communicated to all who will have product responsibility.   A market research study may show the marketing director that a significant market exists for products made by the company. Marketing personnel may plan to go ahead with a product to meet the demand, but if the research people fail to convey their findings to all those in the company who will have responsibility for the product, problems could develop.   For example, if the product must be made of material that is in short supply and the researcher failed to communicate with the materials requirement planning manager, a lot of money and effort can be wasted before a decision is made to abandon the idea.

Market researchers must be able to work with all of the available tools (i.e., mathematics, experimental design, psychology, etc.) and must also be able to translate their terms into meaningful language for nonresearch people.   However, marketing management people should be able to understand, without the interpretation required for other corporate managers, just what research is driving at and what will result from each of several possible courses of action taken.

7.3 MARKET RESEARCH: FOR DEVELOPMENT AND FEEDBACK

Developing strategic answers to marketing problems is not the only use for market research. It should also be used to monitor on-going marketing activities as strategies are implemented. This feedback function allows marketing personnel to "fine tune" a plan as it is tested and used in the marketplace.

7.4 APPLICATION OF THE SCIENTIFIC METHOD

Market research, like other types of formal investigation, makes use of the scientific method. The formal steps of the scientific method provide a systematic approach to the analysis and solution of a specific problem.   The four stages of the scientific method are *observation, hypothesis formation, prediction of outcome,* and *hypothesis testing.*

The hypothesis for marketing applications is generally a statement as to what the anticipated outcome will be.   Sections 7.5–7.10 describe the typical sequence of events in a market research project.

EXAMPLE 2.

A practical application of the techniques of research is contained in this example.   A bicycle manufacturer notices that a competitor has begun to sell more bikes than had been sold in the past.   The competitor had recently added a built-in light generator in the wheel hub of the bikes.   This is an observation.   Next, the manufacturer forms a hypothesis that attributes the competitor's increased sales to the built-in generator. The prediction might be that the manufacturer, too, could increase sales if a similar built-in generator were installed.   To test this hypothesis, the manufacturer would have to make sample models and try them in the market.   If the hypothesis tested correctly, sales would increase.   If the test failed to produce the anticipated increase in sales other hypotheses would have to be formulated and tested until sales increased.   For example, it is possible that the competitor may have simply done a superior job of advertising and that the built-in generator did not contribute at all to the increased sales.   The point is that good research would have disclosed all of the variables that might have contributed to the increase, and each one would have had to be tested independently.

7.5   DEFINING THE PROBLEM

The key to a successful marketing research project is a clear definition of the problem.   Considerable research time is wasted every year simply because people thought they had defined the problem adequately.   Good research done on the wrong problem also represents a cost to the company in terms of lost time in a competitive market.

EXAMPLE 3.

A company must find the reason for a decline in sales before it can attempt to solve the problem.   Consider the position of a company selling in a competitive market which suddenly finds itself losing sales.   Asking the wrong question could only hasten the end of the company in such a situation.   To simply ask "What can we do to build sales" is to neglect the reasons for the sales decline.   A company taking this approach might try any of a number of traditional sales-building approaches (e.g., a sales contest, special bonuses, a beefed-up advertising campaign, etc.).   However, if they had asked *why* sales had dropped off, well-planned research might have turned up the fact that they were being undersold by a competitor who was dropping an equivalent line.   Under such circumstances, the best move probably would have been to stand pat until the competitor's supply was exhausted and the market returned to normal.

7.6   PRELIMINARY ANALYSIS

Once the marketing problem has been clearly defined, it should be subjected to a preliminary, or situation, analysis.   The *situation analysis* is essentially an evaluation of the company, its markets, and its competition based on information gathered from within the company and from published data.   Its purpose is twofold: to test the accuracy of the problem statement and to provide the background for hypothesis formulation.

Information for the situation analysis should be obtained from company executives, managers, and dealers, as well as from company financial and sales records.   The company library is a good source of both historical data and industry-related information.   The key to this step in a market research project is that it is an *internal* process—the researcher works with others within the company to be sure that the project is on course.

EXAMPLE 4.

There are many sources of secondary data.   A situation analysis is concerned with *secondary data;* that is, information that has already been published.   Current information should be sought, but historical data should be used in order to determine if specific trends are occurring.   Considerable secondary data can be gathered from many of the state and federal governmental agencies that deal with business.   For example, the Department of Commerce should be the first place to begin a search. Among the many studies it publishes is the annual Statistical Abstracts of the United States which, along with its detailed footnotes, can provide a wealth of national and international business information. In addition, it is possible to get secondary information from other companies (if they are willing to share it) as well as from trade and professional associations that may have an interest in the markets being served by your company.

The situation analysis may turn up the fact that someone else has already faced the same problem and solved it. This would, obviously, conclude the project. However, since most researchers are not this lucky, the project would proceed as described in the next sections.

7.7   CONDUCTING AN INFORMAL INVESTIGATION

Once the researcher has gathered all the material that is relevant to the problem from secondary sources, the next step is the informal investigation. During the *informal investigation,* the researcher goes *outside* the firm to gather information. While the problem may still not be as sharply defined as it should be, the researcher has the advantage of being able to ask enlightened questions of the right people. Sources of information for the informal investigation vary and might include some or all of the following: wholesalers, retailers, advertising people, and customers—of the company's own and/or the competition's product. Again, it may be possible to solve the problem at this point without undertaking a formal research project. Note that when time is of the essence, management often bases a decision on the information that becomes available from the informal investigation.

7.8   PLANNING THE RESEARCH PROJECT

If all of the work done thus far has failed to yield an answer to the problem, the researcher must plan a *formal* research program, which involves the acquisition of *primary data.* Basically, there are three approaches open to the researcher: *observation, survey,* and *experiment.*

EXAMPLE 5.

Observational research is done without personal contact. Using the *observation* method, there is seldom any direct contact with the individuals who are expected to provide the information being sought. For example, if a researcher is interested in seeing which of two labels attracts more attention, he or she would create two situations which are equal in all respects except for the differently labeled products. By standing in a strategic position, or by simply counting the number of products sold in each situation over a fixed period of time, the researcher can observe consumer preferences with reasonable accuracy.

EXAMPLE 6.

Survey research involves personal contact. Using the *survey* method, the researcher would gather information from a population sample; that is, a group selected from a larger group randomly or because of some specific characteristic. Surveys can be taken by phone, face to face, or through the mail. To be most reliable, careful control of the survey situation as well as a rigid use of statistical mathematics in the sampling and analysis are necessary.

EXAMPLE 7.

Experimental research is based on a simulated marketing situation. When the *experimental* method is used, considerable attention is paid to rigorous definition of the problem as well as the methods by which the data will be gathered and analyzed. But the most important characteristic of this method is that two groups are used—an experimental group and a control group. The control group is not presented the information or products that are to be tested, and thus forms a baseline by which results of a study conducted with the experimental group can be evaluated.

7.9   CARRYING OUT THE RESEARCH PROJECT

It is not possible for a book such as this to go into the details of how to carry out a research project by each of the three traditional methods.   Entire books have been devoted to each.   However, it's important that the research people and the marketing managers work in concert from the conception of the project through the implementation of the marketing program.   The marketing people will have to act on the data gathered by the researchers and they should be able to understand the research processes well enough so that they can short-stop problems in the final stages as well as be able to interpret and use the data.

7.10   RESEARCH INTERPRETATION

Most market research is aimed at guiding marketing policy, whether it is for the general management of the entire marketing function, or for use in marketing a specific product or service.   Therefore, the results of a well-conceived and carefully carried out research project should provide specific recommendations for courses of action, rather than simply state the facts that have been uncovered.   The operating manager should know what research methods were used and should be given some idea of the validity of the results.   This can be done mathematically as well as by having the researcher simply state that decisions can or cannot be made with any specific level of confidence based on the data.

Review Questions

1.   Marketing intelligence, once gathered, is valid and usable with confidence at any point in the future. True or false?

     Ans.   False.   See Section 7.1.

2.   Market research must not only develop facts and forecasts, but must also present it in such a way that it can be used by managers within the company.   True or false?

     Ans.   True.   See Section 7.2.

3.   In addition to developing answers to strategic problems, market research should (*a*) help sell the product, (*b*) monitor ongoing activities and provide appropriate feedback, (*c*) overcome consumer resistance, (*d*) provide immediate sales leads.

     Ans.   (*b*)   See Section 7.3.

4.   The four stages of the scientific method are observation, hypothesis formation, prediction of outcome, and hypothesis testing.   True or false?

     Ans.   True.   See Section 7.4.

5.   The hypothesis for market research tries to anticipate the outcome.   True or false?

     Ans.   True.   See Section 7.4.

6.   Good research should locate all of the variables that could account for different marketing conditions. True or false?

     Ans.   True.   See Example 2.

7.   A market research problem always defines itself because of obvious marketing conditions.   True or false?

     Ans.   False.   See Section 7.5.

8.   Once a problem has been tentatively identified, the next step is to perform (*a*) a situation analysis, (*b*) an hypothesis validation, (*c*) a formal investigation, (*d*) none of these.

     Ans.   (*a*)   See Section 7.6.

9. When performing the situation analysis, it is important to seek information (a) outside of the company, (b) inside the company, (c) by mailing survey questionnaires to customers, (d) by whatever means is practical with anyone who is not connected with the company.

    Ans. (b) See Section 7.6.

10. The situation analysis is undertaken specifically to defend the choice of problem if there is any doubt in the minds of other marketing executives.   True or false?

    Ans. False. See Section 7.6.

11. A situation analysis is concerned with (a) primary data, (b) secondary data, (c) tertiary data, (d) all of these.

    Ans. (b) See Example 4.

12. A situation analysis is never concerned with trends, only with information as it exists as of the moment.   True or false?

    Ans. False. See Example 4.

13. The research problem can never be solved at the point of the situation analysis.   True or false?

    Ans. False. See Example 4.

14. Once a research project has reached the point of the informal investigation, the problem must be sharply in focus.   True or false?

    Ans. False. See Section 7.7.

15. During the informal investigation, the researcher talks with (a) only those within the company sponsoring the research, (b) those outside the firm who are best qualified to supply information, (c) top management within the sponsoring company, (d) all of these.

    Ans. (b) See Section 7.7.

16. It may be possible to reach a valid conclusion during the informal investigation.   True or false?

    Ans. True. See Section 7.7.

17. When using observation to conduct a research study, researchers seldom, if ever, have any personal contact with the people who are best able to supply answers they need.   True or false?

    Ans. True. See Example 5.

18. Surveys can be made (a) by phone, (b) face-to-face, (c) by mail, (d) all of these.

    Ans. (d) See Example 6.

19. An important characteristic of the experimental method is the utilization of a control group to provide a baseline for information gathered with an experimental group.   True or false?

    Ans. True. See Example 7.

20. Well-conceived and carefully developed research should provide specific recommendations for a course of action.   True or false?

    Ans. True. See Section 7.10.

Solved Problems

7.1.   The cost and complexity of consumer research generally exceeds that of industrial market research by a large amount.   What accounts for this?

   In general, the market for consumer goods is much larger and often more complex than the market for most industrial products.   Add to this regional tastes and preferences and it becomes evident that the cost to research a consumer product can be very expensive.

   In contrast, industrial markets are often smaller, and their needs are seldom affected by regional differences, other than those which require costly shipping of raw materials and finished products.   A valve is a valve; it can be used for the same application just about anywhere.   This doesn't mean that all industrial market research can be done inexpensively, but comparatively, consumer research is generally more expensive.

7.2.   Are there any guidelines that can help to determine how much should be spent for a specific market research project?

Ths cost of research is generally proportional to the risk involved and the anticipated return. However, while great sums can be invested in a given project to increase the precision of the study, no research can ever guarantee that the product or service will be a success.   At the same time, research does predict success in terms of probabilities.   When it is felt that the risk of an enterprise can be reduced substantially by a reasonable investment in research, such projects should be undertaken.   However, note that it is up to top management and those in charge of finance to agree with marketing personnel as to how the word *reasonable* should be interpreted.

7.3.   Some firms have gone beyond the traditional market research function and developed corporate marketing information systems.   What is this system and what are its principal benefits?

One of the highest costs of running a business is the cost of information.   With the advent of the marketing information system, there has been a shift from the traditional fact-finding function of market research to an integrated problem-solving function.   Such a system stresses continual interaction and an orderly flow of information through every phase of the operation.

A marketing information system is a formalized set of operational procedures using a variety of resources to generate and disperse relevant market-related data for use in managerial decision-making.   It is generally comprised of people and data processing equipment which may range from the simpler office machines to sophisticated computers.   Large, decentralized companies have made extensive use of advanced computer systems which can be programmed to process, store, and provide information when it is needed, thus leading to better management performance.   Such systems are especially helpful in providing each location with the information it needs, and integrating it with the other corporate locations.

When such a system functions well, it is especially practical in the application of the marketing concept.   Many firms have found that information they collected before going on to an integrated marketing system was not useful in its raw state.   A carefully planned system can integrate the data in a meaningful way for corporate and marketing executives.   Such a system can reduce human bias, such as the desire to avoid information that may have unpleasant consequences.   For example, there comes a time in most product life cycles when the product should be retired.   Unfortunately, there are often people who have been involved with the product for many years who want to believe that it can go on forever.   This hope, and the reality of the marketplace, are often at odds; a good marketing information system will point out the problem and suggest appropriate alternatives.

7.4.   How does marketing research fit in with a marketing information system?

Marketing research tends to be project oriented.   That is, when a company wants to know if a particular product will have market acceptance and be profitable, it conducts a market research study.   A market information system is, in essence, an overall information system which is geared to the market, but which forms the basics from which management as well as marketing decisions are made.   When a marketing information system is in use, the data generated by market research can be put to more productive use because the system will provide the guidelines for interpretation and implementation.

7.5.   Describe the major sources of secondary data that are useful in marketing research.

All research should begin with an investigation of the firm's own records as well as with discussions with employees.   Sales records, territorial productivity, an analysis of the profitability of each product as well as an analysis of each product's performance in different territories are only a few of the areas that often yield helpful information.

Virtually every department of the federal and state government has information that may be valuable to a firm.   There are many private firms that not only undertake specific research projects for a client, but also conduct independent research projects to sell to those who need the specific information.   Known as multi-client reports, these studies are usually general in nature, but often have enough basic information to be useful.   The cost of such reports is considerably less than a single company would have to pay if they commissioned the research firm to do the study only for them.

Trade and professional associations also have a wealth of information, but it is usually available only to its members.   However, some associations will sell information to others.   Magazines and journals published by these trade associations are often available to nonmembers on a paid subscription basis.   These magazines are usually a good source of ongoing information since they comment on matters that are of interest to companies within the fields served by the associations.

Advertising media are excellent sources of information.   To help advertisers and to win over new accounts, magazines, newspapers, TV, and radio stations do considerable research.   Advertisers are usually entitled to this information without charge; the data is often given away to entice companies to use the medium.

Colleges and universities often have their own research centers from which a company can get helpful information.   This is big business for many schools that do research for small businesses with the help of graduate students.   In addition, faculty members frequently serve as consultants to business and are able to utilize the facilities of the university to help them provide this service.

The company library as well as a local community library can be one of the best sources of secondary data.   Now that many libraries have formed into regional networks, the researcher has the capabilities available at many libraries.

7.6.   Survey research is the most popular way to gather primary data, but there are a number of problems associated with the method.   Describe these problems.

Unless the universe is very small, survey data is gathered by means of contacting a small portion, called the sample.   For survey research to be successful, the sample must have the same characteristics as the entire universe.   If the sample is not planned carefully and does not approximate the universe, any interpretations and predictions based on data collected may be subject to error.   There is also the possibility of having errors in the design of the questionnaire, as well as in its editing, tabulation, and analysis.

Another problem involves money.   Greater reliability is generally attributed to surveys in which a large sample is used, however, the larger the sample, the greater the cost.   As previously discussed, marketing is and always will be dependent upon a certain amount of risk.   Therefore, the decision point must be based upon the allowable risk and the amount of time and money that can be spent to get data.

Apart from the research instruments, it is often very difficult to get people to provide the information needed.   There is a vast difference between a behavioral intention and a behavioral act.   That is, people may simply tell you what they think you would like to hear—that they will buy your product when it is on the market.   But, when the chips are down and the product is in the stores, it may be yet another story.   There is also a growing reluctance for respondents to take the time to answer a survey.   Business people are faced with more and more inquiries, and the time it takes to answer direct questions or to write responses on a mail questionnaire represents time away from a business.   Finally, there have been a number of organizations that have hidden behind the respectability of market research in order to gain access to an individual to make a sale.   This results in awkward situations for bona fide researchers.

7.7.   Which of the three types of research interviews (person-to-person, telephone, and mail) is the most flexible?

The personal interview is generally thought of as the most flexible of the three.   It is possible for the interviewer to observe the respondent during the interview and to probe more deeply for information when an appropriate lead presents itself.   However, interviewers must be carefully trained when this probing is to be done to avoid introducing any bias by leading the respondent.   It is also possible to record other conditions which cannot be gathered by any other survey method.

Household or business physical locations and conditions, status, and other observational items can be included, if needed to add information to the report.

7.8.   The personal interview is the most flexible and productive of the methods, but it has its limitations.   Describe them.

The most limiting factor of the personal interview is cost.   Good interviewers are expensive, and a national survey could be prohibitive.   Also, personal interviews are time consuming, both in the planning and the actual survey stage.   A well-planned personal interview study is usually begun with a pilot study in which the researchers try to eliminate the problems that could endanger the validity of the final study.   When a national personal interview study is planned, the advantage of personal probing must be eliminated.   In a large study, this helpful technique could turn into a problem by introducing bias from virtually every interviewer.   Therefore, interviewers must be instructed to follow the questionnaire rigidly.   Even when well-trained interviewers are used, the compounding of all the collective bias that could creep into the study could raise serious questions about the results.

7.9.   Telephone surveys are less flexible than personal interviews but more flexible than research conducted by mail.   What are some of the advantages of using the telephone to conduct market research?

The telephone study can be conducted more rapidly and at less cost than the personal study, for the same number of respondents.   It is possible to sample wide geographic areas without locating and using local interviewers or sending professionals to the area just for the project.   Because the time required to make the calls is less for the telephone interview than for the personal interview, it is possible to gather data more quickly than it would be by using personal interviews.   This is, perhaps, one of the most important advantages of the telephone interview.   When a timely subject must be researched, it can be done almost immediately by phone.   The research done on television viewing habits makes use of the adaptability of the phone survey by calling at the time of the show.   Political research is conducted by phone for the same reasons.

7.10.   Discuss the major limitations of the telephone survey.

In general, people do not like to grant long interviews by phone.   It is difficult and often impossible to gather some of the peripheral data that can be obtained in a personal interview.   Observational information, such as socioeconomic factors, can only be inferred by phone.   In a face-to-face meeting, the interviewer can see just what the conditions are.   Because most survey research is done by contacting people who are randomly selected, the telephone adds a significant bias to the results.   Not everyone has a phone, and of those who do, not everyone has a listed number.   And, of course, not everyone is at home when the call is made.   It is possible to call back until the call is completed, but if the research is timely, such as checking TV viewing habits during prime time, a call after show hours will invalidate the conditions of the study.

7.11.   Mail surveys are used by manufacturers of both consumer and industrial goods.   Discuss the more important advantages of using the mail to gather marketing information.

Because there is no personal contact, the problem of interviewer bias is eliminated in a mail survey.   Mail surveys are less costly than personal interviews and lend themselves to wide-ranging applications.   When respondents are guaranteed anonymity in a mail survey, the chances are that they will be more inclined to give truthful answers.   Respondents to mail surveys feel less inclined to try to impress than they do when the survey is done face-to-face or by phone.   Also, because of the vast organization of mail list houses and businesses that compile their own lists, it is easy to identify and reach very specific audiences.   This, of course, helps to insure that the answers given will be more reliable than if a segment of a less well-defined audience were to be used.   However, seldom do all those who are surveyed respond to the questionnaire.   The characteristics of the nonrespondents may be just as important as those of respondents.   If such a problem exists, it may be necessary to weight the responses with a factor that will correct for the nonrespondents. It is also possible to do further research with the nonrespondents to correct the problem.

7.12. What are some of the major difficulties encountered in mail survey research?

As mentioned in Problem 7.11, the use of mail research is enhanced by the availability of many lists of people and companies with specific characteristics in common. But, in some esoteric areas and in areas where the categories are very broad, the selection of an appropriate sample can become a problem. Sample reliability must be considered, especially when the desired population sample has characteristics which differentiate it from nonrespondents. Also, it is difficult to conduct a mail survey if timeliness is especially critical. Apart from mail delays, respondents themselves seldom answer questionnaires immediately. Generally speaking approximately 80% of the responses are returned within ten days of receipt of the survey.

Because there is no person to guide the interview, the questions must be short and easily understood. This becomes difficult when the marketing problem is complex and requires more than a simple answer. Other difficulties associated with mail surveys include the absence of an opportunity to observe the respondents and the small number of questionnaires that are actually completed and returned. Mail researchers often include something to insure a higher return, such as a shiny new quarter. The respondent is told that the quarter can never possibly repay the person for the time taken to answer the questionnaire, but it is a symbol of appreciation that might be appreciated by a child. While this tactic is often seen as unduly influencing the response, any bias created can be compensated for if the design and analysis of the study are carefully planned.

7.13. Observational research can be conducted on a face-to-face basis or through film or video-taping equipment. It is considered to be one of the most accurate ways of gathering data. Describe its major benefits.

When the observational method is used, there is little chance for the people being watched to bias the information according to any personal characteristics. Because they are unaware that their behavior is being monitored, their responses are completely natural. Much of the possibility of researcher bias is removed at the same time, because there is no contact between the person conducting the study and those being studied. Note, however, that it is still possible for the researcher to add personal bias in the interpretation of the data. For example, consider the situation where a research organization attached recording devices to the televisions and radios of a sample of people in the market being studied. The devices recorded the stations to which the sets were tuned, the time of use, and the total time the sets were in use. A review of the records simply showed what had happened in the market, and there can be no disputing the impartiality of such research. However, no matter how carefully the data collection is controlled, there is always a possibility of bias entering when conclusions are drawn from the facts by the researcher.

7.14. Discuss some of the drawbacks associated with observational research.

As already mentioned, observer bias can cloud results. Also, the technique has limited application. The problem under study must be adaptable to observational research, and not too many marketing problems can be studied this way. In addition, because all this system provides is a picture of what has happened in a particular situation, it is difficult to tell why it happened. If, however, this method is combined with an experimental approach in which subjects react to a stimulus situation, more direct inferences can be drawn. It should also be noted that observational research is generally expensive relative to the number of situations observed, compared with the number of interviews that could be conducted by phone, for example.

7.15. A marketing experiment attempts to create a scale model of what will be encountered in the real world when the product is actually marketed. From the results, researchers can make corrections and then scale up for the actual marketing of the product or service. Discuss the major benefits of the use of marketing experimentation.

Of the methods used to gather primary data, only the experimental approach creates and measures marketing situations. In survey research, for example, people are asked what they would do *if* something were to occur. In an experiment, an event occurs, and people do what they might do in a real market situation. Different types of ads can be tested and results can be compared. Such pragmatic evidence is much more reliable than the data collected from a survey in which people tell which ad they would be more affected by. In addition, the techniques used in experimentation lend themselves to critical qualitative analysis and extrapolation. Thus, some feel that it is possible to make decisions with less data than would be needed if a decision were to be made on the basis of a survey.

7.16. Discuss the problems which tend to limit the value of experimental research.

Perhaps the most difficult problem in an experimental research project is selecting markets that will match the market at large. Over the years, various research organizations have set up test markets in towns, counties, and cities that they have felt mirrored a total market. But after a while, the very fact that the people in the area have been the subjects of a number of tests tends to reduce the reliability of the experimental market. If competitors learn that a marketing experiment is being conducted in a specific area, they can, and often do, try to sabotage it. For example, a competitor might increase its advertising, or could artificially inflate results by having ringers buy the test product in large quantities.

Experimental research is expensive and time consuming; thus, it requires very careful planning. There is a story told of a company that manufactured shaving lotion. When it conducted a test marketing experiment, the first batch delivered to the stores sold exceedingly well, but there were very few repeat sales. The company concluded that the product was a dud and withdrew it from the market. However, six months later, after the product had already been scrapped, the demand flared up. It turned out that the bottle the company used was much too large, and it took six months for those who bought it to use it up and return to the stores for more.

7.17. What are some of the problems that can reduce or destroy the value of a survey questionnaire?

No matter what type of survey is to be done, a questionnaire must be developed. A telephone questionnaire must be short, but a mail questionnaire can be somewhat longer. Personal interview questionnaires can be longer still and can allow for some flexibility. For example, the personal interview can provide for the use of in-depth probing if the interviewers are trained in the use of psychological methods. However, errors can creep in if the design is faulty.

Often, personal questions can backfire. This is especially noticeable in personal and phone interviews. It can be less of a problem in a mail survey when the responses are anonymous. Questions about age, finances, sex, and health are subject to considerable error unless extreme care is used.

When a question is too general and does not have a good baseline, results can be misleading. For example, when a respondent is asked if he or she likes big cars, the answers could be confusing because one person's definition of a big car is not the same as another's.

When questions require answers in unfamiliar terms, the value of the answers may be questionable. For example, few people could say how many gallons of beer they drink in a year. But most could tell you how many six-packs each week. A simple calculation will provide the gallonage, if it is needed.

People don't like to be embarassed when they don't know an answer and often will make up one. To a question such as, "What kind of shoes does your wife wear?" a respondent may feel expected to have the answer and might fabricate one as an ego defense. When questions are positioned in the wrong order, problems can occur. For example, if it is important to get answers to personal questions, it is often wise to put them last, and start instead with a number of innocuous questions to establish some kind of rapport with the subject.

7.18. A questionnaire is seldom used without a pretest. Discuss the concept of pretesting and the points that should be considered when the pretest is done.

Not unlike new products which must be tested in the prototype stage before production runs are considered, the marketing research questionnaire should be given a similar shakedown cruise with an appropriate sample of individuals drawn from those who will be given the final questionnaire. It is important for the researcher to determine whether the questions are clear and in the proper order. An unclear question can lead to interpretation problems and distorted results. It is just as important to test the instructions to the interviewer as it is to test the questionnaire. An interviewer-introduced error has the same effect as an unclear question. Lastly, it is important to determine whether there will be any problems in the editing and tabulation of the completed questionnaires.

7.19.   What is the fundamental idea behind the selection of a sample for survey research? What is a random sample? An area sample? A quota sample?

Implicit in all sampling is the notion that if a small number of people are chosen from a larger number, the sample will tend to have the same characteristics in approximately the same proportion as the total population or the *universe*.

When a *random sample* is drawn, every unit in the universe must have a known and equal chance of being selected. An *area sample* is used when it is not possible, for economic or practical reasons, to get the full universe. In a consumer study, for example, blocks would be chosen and everyone or a specific sample of individuals on the chosen blocks would be interviewed. The blocks would be selected randomly.

A *quota sample* has none of the qualities of a random probability sample. Respondents are selected specifically because they have certain characteristics that enable them to supply answers.

Note that sampling done on a strict probability basis permits the reliability of the results to be expressed with a measure of mathematical precision.

7.20.   Describe the final steps in a market research study.

The research data must be analyzed, the findings interpreted, and a report written. The final step is the presentation of the researcher's conclusions in written or oral form, or both. Remember that all research has as its goal the possibility of being able to recommend specific courses of action for accomplishing the marketing task.

Chapter 8

Market Planning and Forecasting

8.1 INTRODUCTION

Because clearcut choices are so rare in business activity, marketing planning, which takes into account all of the factors influencing a product's market performance, has assumed a major role in firms of all sizes. In essence, planning can be viewed as one way of insuring that all elements of the marketing mix combine in the most productive way. A marketing plan is an integrating system which is as relevant to the head of every department as it is to the director of marketing. Successful firms encourage the interaction of all departments and personnel as they "fine tune" their activities to be sure that the marketing mix is correct.

8.2 FOCUSING THE MARKETING MIX

One of the goals of the marketing concept is to insure that the energies of all departments are focused on target markets. To develop and implement a successful marketing plan, it is essential that the needs and idiosyncracies of the target market be understood by everyone involved. However, even in companies with extensive research capabilities it is virtually impossible to know everything about a market's needs and characteristics.

EXAMPLE 1.

The effects of competition are an important consideration because competitors are constantly forcing each other to face new marketing situations. Thus, while the marketing plan must give firm direction, it must also be flexible enough to allow for strategy modification with no loss of momentum. The elements of the marketing mix—product planning, distribution strategy, promotion and price—can all be adjusted in a marketing plan to counter competitive activities. For example, price competition is common in food marketing, and a company which has planned its pricing structure to accommodate revisions in the face of competitive action may maneuver successfully in such a situation.

8.3 BARRIERS TO SUCCESSFUL MARKETING PLANNING

Despite the documented benefits of sound marketing planning, few companies do extensive *formal* planning. The fault often lies with top management, when it fails to communicate corporate goals to those responsible for implementing them. Other barriers to good marketing planning are the inability to judge accurately the strengths and strategies of competitors, the lack of interdepartmental communication, and an overdependence on rigid planning and stereotyped management. And, of course, if a company's marketing goals are unrealistic and out of proportion with its capabilities, its planning can hardly be expected to succeed.

Many firms lack a clearcut definition of who their customers really are. In this age of specialization, it's difficult and economically dangerous to try to be all things to all people.

8.4 ANTICIPATING RESPONSE TO MARKET VARIATIONS

A well-conceived marketing plan attempts to show how target customers will react as marketing variables change. In general, an attempt is made to show how sales or profits will shift as a result of increasing or reducing the amount of money spent on each of the elements of the marketing mix. The task is not easy; since every market is always in a state of flux, any analysis is truly valid only at the moment it is made.   And, finally, because each different market exhibits unique characteristics, marketing plans are generally not interchangeable.

EXAMPLE 2.

Spending money on expanding *product variety* might increase sales, but at some point the increased costs would reach a point where profits would decline, regardless of the increased number of units sold.   This is a common problem for companies manufacturing clothing in which fashion and style varieties are significant, and one which should be considered during planning.

Example 2 illustrates an important economic concept—the *law of diminishing returns*.   In economic terms, an increase in input (money spent to expand product variety in this case) causes total output to increase.   However, after a point, the income from the extra output (product variety) becomes less and less.   When the money spent to expand the line exceeds income, the point of diminishing returns has been reached.

EXAMPLE 3.

An increase of expenditures on *distribution* could increase sales and profits up to a point.   However, when the saturation point is reached, the sales increase slows down, profits drop and it becomes uneconomical to continue with the expansion.   An accurate analysis of this situation should give management an idea of where the saturation point is long before any expansion of distribution is undertaken.   This, too, is a diminishing returns condition.   When money spent to expand distribution exceeds income, it is no longer practical to continue the expansion.

EXAMPLE 4.

The saturation problem also occurs when an *advertising appropriation* is increased.   Up to a point, the increase should produce greater sales and profits, but at some point (which is dictated by the specific situation), the added amount spent on advertising will result in diminishing returns.   Again, an attempt to predict the point where this would occur should be part of a sound marketing plan.

EXAMPLE 5.

Because it is not possible to expand sales indefinitely, a marketing plan should try to predict when there will be a sales rate decline.   A market can absorb just so many units of a product for a given period of time, and this factor, coupled with an analysis of the rate at which a market will accept the products, should be included in the plan.

Example 5 illustrates the concept of *marginal utility*.   As units of a product or service are consumed, the value of the product or service declines to the consumer.   Economists use the word utility to describe the benefit derived from a product, and can show how utility decreases as the consumption of the product increases.   Thus, it is important for marketing people to be able to determine the point at which the market will no longer be able to absorb products and still produce a profit.

8.5   PLANNING BASED ON A COMPOSITE OF MARKETING MIXES

Only when all the elements of several different marketing mixes are studied as a composite will it be possible to determine the best plan.   A marketing plan can be considered well-conceived when sales or profits are predicted as a function of budgeted expenses for all the elements of the marketing mix.   However, such an analysis must consider both short- and long-range objectives (see Section 8.6).   One plan may maximize profits in the short run, but lose money in the long run.   The goals established for the product by management must also be taken into account in any planning.

8.6   LONG- AND SHORT-RANGE MARKETING PLANNING

In general, *long-range planning* has a greater effect on corporate growth than the work accomplished in short-range planning and is generally the responsibility of top management. Long-range planning usually includes major considerations such as market and product line expansion, plant expansion, and acquisitions, as well as decisions to eliminate major product lines.

In contrast, short-range planning is frequently a middle management function. It seldom covers periods longer than one year and is often concerned with immediate problems such as price adjustments in the face of competition.

8.7   MARKETING AND TOTAL CORPORATE PLANNING

Total corporate planning involves the development of long-term goals and strategies relating to the full spectrum of a company's ongoing activities (i.e., finance, production, staffing, research and development, etc., as well as marketing). *Marketing planning* is an ongoing activity that projects long-term marketing efforts for the various elements of the marketing mix (see Section 1.3). Since profits and sales emanate directly from proper management of the marketing mix, it is inevitable that these two planning approaches will overlap when a company adopts the marketing concept.

EXAMPLE 6.

While approaches to marketing planning vary, they all include the following steps:

(1) *Review the company's position.* Before projecting future plans, executives must determine just where the company is in terms of competition as well as in the absolute sense of growth and profitability rates. This analysis should also provide a clear idea of where the company is headed.

(2) *Determine long-range goals.* Because goals give direction to a company's activities, they should be specific statements of objectives that can realistically be achieved. Goals that are beyond the company's capabilities only create problems.

(3) *Select appropriate strategies.* Once goals have been established, the plan for their achievement is developed. The interdependency of the various elements of the marketing mix makes this a delicate process requiring careful consideration.

(4) *Evaluate the plan.* Because planning is an ongoing process, the marketing effort must be constantly monitored so that results can be measured against established goals. This keeps the plan on course and enables management to adjust strategies as needed.

8.8   THE ANNUAL MARKETING PLAN

The *annual marketing plan* takes the long-term goals and strategies of the marketing plan and makes them operative. It is performance oriented, and deals with short-term needs—i.e., specific problems requiring immediate solution—as well as parts of larger projects slated for completion in the current year. Because it deals in specifics, the annual marketing plan is also easily subjected to evaluation and necessary adjustment.

8.9   MARKET DEMAND FORECASTING

There is perhaps no element more crucial to successful marketing planning than an accurate forecast of market demand. This information is essential to the planning in every department within the company. For example, manufacturing departments plan work requirements and material needs on the basis of market demand predictions. Sales and budgeting projections can be made only after such information is in hand.

Generally market demand is forecasted using either a *breakdown analysis* or a *build-up approach*.

EXAMPLE 7.

Using breakdown analysis, the firm first evaluates general economic conditions to determine the industry-wide market potential for the product or service. Next, the firm's current share of the market is determined. With this information, the firm can project potential market shares at various expenditure levels. This is the sales forecast. Realistic figures obtained in this manner provide the basis for departmental budgeting as well as other operational planning.

EXAMPLE 8.

When the build-up approach is used, forecasting is based on the total of estimates of future demand provided by organizational units within the company. Such information is usually obtained from salespeople, distributors, retailers, and any other people within the organization that management believes can contribute worthwhile data. The forecast is then derived from a careful analysis of accumulated information.

8.10 MARKET POTENTIAL AND MARKET SHARE

The term *market potential* is defined as the total sales volume of all sellers of a specific product in a specific market over a specified period of time, usually a year. Note that if one product is sold in several markets, a separate potential exists for each individual market.

A company's *market share* is the ratio of its sales to total industry sales. This figure can be stated in terms of either actual or potential sales.

EXAMPLE 9.

Market potential is often classified in terms of geography. That is, the potential success of a particular style of clothing may be greater on the west coast than on the east coast. Regional preferences often make it necessary for such planning, but when all regional market potential figures are available, they are combined and used as the basis for total planning. This planning includes the product variations that will be needed in different markets as well as budgetary allocations for all activities needed to bring the product to market.

EXAMPLE 10.

Trade associations often can provide information needed to determine a company's market share. For a small company, the task of gathering national market potential information may be too difficult and expensive. Yet to compete, this information may be crucial. In some cases, trade and professional associations to which these companies belong will provide the basic data, allowing the individual members to estimate their market shares and develop their marketing plans.

EXAMPLE 11.

National economic trends are used in forecasting. For some products, the job of determining market potential is greatly simplified. The potential for housing sales, for example, fluctuates in direct proportion to the supply of money, interest rates, and the birth rate. When money is short and interest high, few houses will be sold. Those who market consumer as well as industrial products find that gross national product figures and other economic factors often correlate with their marketing success. Predicting future sales thus becomes a simple matter of historical analysis—correlating economic conditions with past sales performance.

Review Questions

1. Marketing planning is seldom as important for small firms as it is for larger firms. True or false?

   Ans. False. See Section 8.1.

2. Marketing planning enhances the possibility of success of a product or service by insuring that the elements of the marketing mix combine in the most productive way. True or false?

   Ans. True. See Section 8.1.

3. A marketing plan must be completely rigid.   Any flexibility will result in loose management and reduce the possibility of achieving the marketing goals.   True or false?

Ans.   False.   See Example 1.

4. Most companies fail to plan adequately because (*a*) there are seldom people on staff with the requisite experience, (*b*) top management fails to communicate corporate goals to those who do the planning, (*c*) planning is considered something for the classroom and not for the real world, (*d*) none of these.

Ans.   (*b*)   See Section 8.3.

5. Other reasons for the failure to plan adequately are (*a*) an inability to judge the strengths and strategies of the competitors, (*b*) a lack of interdepartmental communications, (*c*) stereotyped management style, (*d*) all of these.

Ans.   (*d*)   See Section 8.3.

6. A well-conceived marketing plan attempts to show how target customers will react as marketing variables shift.   True or false?

Ans.   True.   See Section 8.4.

7. A marketing plan attempts to predict how sales or profits will vary as a result of increasing or decreasing expenditures on various elements of the marketing mix.   This is greatly complicated by (*a*) lack of support from suppliers, (*b*) sales department indifference, (*c*) the fact that markets are always in a state of flux, (*d*) lack of management cooperation.

Ans.   (*c*)   See Section 8.4.

8. Increased spending on product distribution will always result in continued growth.   True or false?

Ans.   False.   See Example 3.

9. To be effective, a marketing plan should predict when market saturation will occur as well as determine the growth factors.   True or false?

Ans.   True.   See Example 5.

10. Sales and profits are never planned as a function of expenses for all elements of the marketing mix. True or false?

Ans.   False.   See Section 8.5.

11. Long-range planning has a greater effect on overall corporate growth than does short-range market planning.   True or false?

Ans.   True.   See Section 8.6.

12. Long-range planning includes (*a*) product line expansion, (*b*) plant expansion, (*c*) acquisitions, (*d*) all of these.

Ans.   (*d*)   See Section 8.6.

13. Short-range planning, often delegated to middle management, seldom covers periods in excess of (*a*) three months, (*b*) six months, (*c*) nine months, (*d*) one year.

Ans.   (*d*)   See Section 8.6.

14. In firms which have adopted the marketing concept, corporate and marketing planning tend to blend. True or false?

Ans.   True.   See Section 8.7.

15. Marketing planning is an ongoing activity, but the annual marketing plan is concerned with immediate goals and problems.   True or false?

Ans.   True.   See Section 8.8.

16. Among other things, a marketing plan should include (*a*) a review of the present position of the company, (*b*) a determination of its goals, (*c*) the selection of appropriate strategies, (*d*) all of these.

Ans.   (*d*)   See Example 6.

17. Once the plan is put into action, all planning should be stopped in order to cope with the day-to-day problems.   True or false?

Ans.   False.   See Example 6.

18. Only the marketing department is dependent on an accurate forecast of demand for a product or service.   True or false?

Ans.   False.   See Section 8.9.

19. A breakdown analysis of demand includes (*a*) a general evaluation of economic conditions for all producers in the industry, (*b*) an analysis of the share of market held by the company, (*c*) a determination of how much market share could be acquired at various levels of marketing expenditures, (*d*) all of these.

Ans.   (*d*)   See Example 7.

20. A market share is the total sales volume of all sellers of a specific product or service over a period of time.   True or false?

Ans.   False.   See Section 8.10.

Solved Problems

8.1. A sales forecast is an estimate of sales in dollars or physical units for a specified future period under a proposed marketing plan and under an assumed set of economic and other outside conditions.   Which comes first, the sales forecast or the marketing plan? Why?

Marketing goals and strategies must be determined first, because this is the point at which data relating to market potential is accumulated and analyzed.   The accuracy and reliability of any sales forecast depends on the appropriate use of such information.   For example, it would be impossible to forecast sales before the decision is made to add a particular product to the line.   Only when factors like this are specified is it possible to accomplish any forecasting.   Note again that once the marketing plan has been accepted, it becomes the central element in all operational planning within the company.

8.2 Is a sales forecast the same as the sales potential? Explain.

No.   A sales forecast is based on a marketing plan, which is usually not based on perfect conditions.   It simply may not be possible to capture the entire market.   While there are times for some companies when a sales forecast and a sales potential might be the same, in most cases the sales forecast will be less than the sales potential.   The sales forecast is based on limiting factors, such as budget, personnel, and plant capacity factors.   But sales potential is based on ideal conditions in which the company could spend to whatever limit is required to capture the total market.

8.3. Why does a forecast generally cover a one-year period? When are longer and shorter forecasting periods used?

Annual planning correlates with most economic systems, such as taxation, budgeting, and economic forecasting.   Firms seldom allow their annual plans to go unmonitored; they are reviewed on a regular basis so that any necessary corrections can be implemented.

Short-run forecasting is generally done when product and competitive conditions tend to fluctuate widely.   Companies whose products are seasonal or subject to the influence of fads must plan for shorter periods to insure flexibility.   Planning beyond the traditional year is usually undertaken when the company intends to expand its facilities or the product line in a significant way.

8.4. Describe the procedure most commonly used to forecast market demand by a company with many products and many markets.

To begin with, individual estimates for each item in each product line are prepared. This is done in such detail that economic as well as unit sale forecasts for each territory or marketing unit are available. These individual forecasts can be used by each department within the company for planning; collectively, they can be integrated with the elements of corporate planning for financial and other general management purposes.

8.5. What is a market factor? How is this concept used to predict product demand?

A market factor is a condition or element of a market which can be subjected to quantitative measurement and which is directly related to the demand for a product or service. For example, the number of cameras sold in a given period is a factor which can be measured and used to predict the demand for photographic film and film processing. When the factors used bear close relationship like cameras and film, prediction can be made with a high degree of certainty. Therefore, the choice of appropriate factors is of prime importance. Note that the number of factors used should be kept to a minimum. As the number of factors used increases, it becomes more difficult to determine the extent to which each individual factor influences demand.

8.6. Using the camera illustration in Problem 8.5, explain how information can be derived directly from camera sales in order to predict the sale of accessory equipment.

If it can be shown that of all people who buy cameras in a given period, a certain percentage will expand their interest in photography within a year to include the purchase and use of accessories such as additional lenses, a predictive model can be constructed. For example, if twenty percent of camera owners are interested in extending their photographic interests, a manufacturer can derive the total market demand for accessories simply by applying the percentage to the industry sales figure. Then, by analyzing such factors as product quality and price, position in the industry, distribution system capabilities, and competition and past performance, the manufacturer can project a potential share of the market for its products. The system is simple, direct, and relatively effective when reliable market factor information is available.

8.7. How is a correlation statistic used to predict market demand? Why is the technique difficult to use?

A correlation of any sort shows that when one item, or variable, in a situation changes, other items or variables change in a predictable way. In very simple terms, if swimsuit sales go up, and picnic basket sales increase at the same time, it could be said that the two are interacting, and that one is affecting the sale of the other. Note, however, that such methods are subject to error unless trends can be watched over a relatively long period. While certain circumstances may appear to be interrelated, the assumption of causality must be supported by considerable statistical history of sales in order to prove the relationship. At the same time, when such information does exist, correlation analysis can be a very reliable predictive tool.

8.8. Market demand can be predicted by simply surveying a sample of buyers and asking if they intend to buy. Discuss the benefits and limitations of this approach.

A survey of buying intentions often can be made quickly and easily for consumer as well as industrial products and services. The study can be made face-to-face, by mail, or over the telephone. However, because of certain limitations the results must be interpreted carefully. It may be difficult to get a large enough sample if the product is to be sold to a general consumer audience. Where industrial products are involved it may be difficult to identify and contact the potential users. The major limitation of this technique, however, is psychological. Survey respondents tend to tell research people what they think they want to hear, as long as there is no commitment on their part. If, for example, a researcher asked questions about future purchases of a product, the respondent might feel that a less than enthusiastic answer would be taken personally, and inflate his or her estimate of buying intentions. Then, when the product hits the market, these less than honest responses result in sales that seldom meet the forecast. Because problems such as this are widely recognized by researchers, raw survey data is generally weighted so that results allow for any limitations.   Note that in general the data gathered in any research project is interpreted in terms of specific experience and historical data that is directly relevant to the problem being considered.

8.9.   Describe how test marketing is used to predict market demand and how it overcomes the problem inherent in a survey of buying intentions.

When a test market is used, the company markets its product for a short time in a limited geographic area, using all the strategies that it would normally use in a full-scale marketing program.   From the results of a test market, the company can predict what conditions will be if and when the product is marketed to the entire market.   In addition to providing excellent economic information, a test market can be used to determine the relative merits of different product features.   That is, a single product can be marketed emphasizing different features in each of several markets simultaneously.   When all variables but one are held constant, the most desirable feature can be determined.

Perhaps the most important feature of a test market is that the results show exactly what will be bought, rather than a behavioral intention.   The data is real and directly measurable in terms of the product and the marketing effort behind it.   Subjectivity is reduced considerably when this method is used, but, at the same time, note that such research can be very costly.

Test marketing is a powerful technique and is one that is used effectively by companies who have made a major investment in a new product.   However, it can be distorted by competitors who discover when a test marketing campaign is being conducted.   Research sabotage in the form of special sales of competitive products can invalidate test market results; this possibility introduces a degree of risk in any decision to invest in a test market project.

8.10.   How can some of the problems inherent in test marketing be overcome?

In the past, test marketing was traditionally done in medium-sized cities, and test periods often covered several months.   Now, to combat potential sabotage, it is often done using much larger areas and much shorter test periods.   The intention is not necessarily to reduce the cost, but to make it difficult for a competitor to mobilize an effort that could distort the results.

8.11.   Companies serving relatively stable markets often base their forecasts on the previous year's sales.   This is safe and effective under some circumstances, but when used unwisely, the results can be misleading.   How is such forecasting done? What problems can occur?

When a company does business in a steady market with a long reliable history, it often applies a flat percentage increase to a previous year's sales as a forecast.   Note, however, that most markets are not stable, and not all products of the company can be treated in the same way.   Different products have different demand characteristics that must be taken into consideration.   Also, changes in a marketing program will change results, destroying the ability to depend strongly on historical data.   However, when this information is used with other data, it can be very helpful.

8.12.   Sales forecasting can be based on data collected by people representing the company in sales positions.   They may be salaried salespeople, independent manufacturers' representatives, or others who either as employees or independent agents are in contact with the market directly.   How is this method implemented?

All salespeople are asked to prepare an evaluation of what their territories will produce for an upcoming year.   When all of the data has been gathered, it is totaled to provide an overall projection of sales for the year.   The data is useful in the composite for general planning as well as a means of setting individual sales goals.   This is a buildup method that can be used most effectively by companies that have a few large customers rather than many small ones.   The degree of success also depends on the research abilities of the salespeople.

8.13. Although it is possible to gather meaningful and useful information by using the company sales force, there are serious disadvantages. What are they?

When salespeople are used to gather marketing intelligence, they are taken away from their prime work—selling. Many companies have reported sales slumps for the periods when their sales force was gathering marketing intelligence. In addition, salespeople are not necessarily the best researchers. They may not have the skills or patience to extract necessary data from their customers and prospects. Finally, because most salespeople are optimistic, personal enthusiasm can cloud the results.

8.14. Why is it important to consider the product life cycle in all marketing planning?

The product life cycle is a significant factor in marketing planning because it is directly related to profits. For example, suppose a product with an estimated three-year life cycle cannot be expected to reach its breakeven point (i.e., the point at which all investment costs have been recovered and the product is making a profit) until the third year. If a substantial profit can be anticipated in the third year, the plan may be viable despite the required carrying cost. On the other hand, the projection of a modest profit might require an alternative marketing plan or even the cancellation of a planned new product.

8.15. There are times when even significant profit potential may not warrant implementation of a plan. The ROI is one indicator of such a situation. Discuss.

The anticipation of profits in itself is not always enough to justify project implementation. The expenses involved in generating profits must also be considered. By calculating the rate of return on investment (ROI) for a plan, a company can determine whether its financial assets are being put to their best use. The ROI is particularly useful when alternative plans are being considered. Suppose the implementation of one plan requires considerable investment in machinery and people, while another requires a lesser investment in goods purchased for resale. If the same profit goals, short- and long-term, can be achieved with either plan, the one with the higher ROI is probably the better choice. At the same time it is important to note that the nature of the investment must be carefully considered. For example, a large up-front investment in machinery which results in an initially low ROI may actually be a viable long-term investment as long as the product life cycle can support the operation, or if the equipment has uses that transcend the plan being considered.

8.16. What is the most common method used to establish a budget for marketing?

In a company with a stable history, it is usually possible to establish a marketing budget by computing a percentage of past or predicted sales. Industry guidelines, which are often available from trade associations, frequently serve as the basis for such budgeting. This method, however, is somewhat limiting in that it tends to narrow creative planning. It just may be possible to increase sales considerably by spending slightly more than the comfortable percentage that has worked in the past. Executives who use the percentage method are robbed of the ability to see the possibilities. It has certain apparent safety features in that it can often be shown by correlation that the percentage spent in the past has been successful. However, correlation statistics are not very robust; even though the percentage spent appears to have been responsible for growth, it may have no relationship to sales.

8.17. Describe the greatest weakness of budgeting for marketing using the percentage of sales method.

When this method is used, budgets expand when sales are good, and contract when sales are off. Rigid adherence to such a system makes it impossible for company executives to see that an increased marketing expenditure during a downturn might be called for. Often the aggressive marketer does better by spending more heavily during lean periods than when sales are up.

8.18. Some executives set marketing budgets by estimating what their competitors are spending. What is wrong with this method?

> To assume that a company is successful just because it runs four-color advertisements in a dozen magazines is a big mistake. The competitor may be pursuing a disastrous marketing program; to copy its style is to invite the disaster that will surely catch up with the company being emulated.

8.19. The task method of establishing a marketing budget is practical and useable by nearly any firm. Describe the method and its goals.

> When a company states its goals clearly, it can plan a marketing program that will help achieve them. Budgeting for goals then becomes a matter of determining exactly what costs are required to maximize each of the elements of the marketing mix. If the costs are too high, the company can either borrow to meet them or scale down its goals. The system is appealing because it is practical and employs real-world figures. It is, of course, possible to state the figure estimated for the total marketing budget derived this way as a percentage of sales, but the number has more use in task-related terms. The plan should have built-in checkpoints in order to keep in touch with expenditures and sales as it is being implemented. Minor fine-tuning of the plan and goal modifications based on on-going experience usually result in greater sales than a rigid attention to the plan.

8.20. The use of computers in sales forecasting is increasing rapidly. What are some of the important areas in which computers are being used?

> The computer has made it possible to assemble, store, and process huge amounts of data, gathered from inside as well as outside the company. It permits rapid statistical evaluations of such conditions as seasonal variations. It can correlate large amounts of information. Many use the computer to generate models of their markets which can then be subjected to various plans. Such pretest modeling not only helps to perfect the plans, but also provides levels of confidence with which the plans can be used in the real world. In addition, it greatly simplifies the task of revising a sales forecast as data is gathered during the year.

Chapter 9

Consumer Behavior

9.1 INTRODUCTION

Anyone interested in satisfying consumer needs should understand what motivates people to buy one product and reject another. While some reasons are purely functional and economic, others involve elements of human behavior that, once understood, not only help make a sale, but help a company produce products that satisfy psychological as well as practical needs.

In recent years, behavioral scientists have teamed up with marketing people and an entire new discipline has emerged—the study of consumer behavior. One of the organizations within the American Psychological Association is the Division of Consumer Behavior, and the American Marketing Association has active committees engaged in theoretical as well as practical research in the field.

The field of psychology includes numerous theoretical approaches to the study of human behavior. While it is difficult to say with any certainty whether one school of psychology has more to offer the marketing person than another, it is possible to select the practical contributions made by each to the marketing concept.

9.2 LEARNING THEORIES OF BEHAVIOR

Theoretical and applied psychology diverge on numerous points, but the main difference is between those who hold behavioral theories as the key to understanding human behavior (see Sections 9.3–9.5) and those who adhere to the psychoanalytical theories developed by Sigmund Freud (see Section 9.6). The behavioral theorists tend to be more practical and eclectic in their approach. Neither approach had provided a unified theory, but each has produced psychological working tools that have practical marketing applications.

9.3 STIMULUS-RESPONSE THEORIES

Stimulus-response (S-R) theories state that learning takes place when a person responds to a stimulus and is either rewarded for a correct response, or penalized for an incorrect response. The earliest S-R theories can be traced to Pavlov, a Russian scientist who showed that it was possible to make a dog salivate when a conditioned stimulus, such as meat powder, and an unconditioned stimulus (i.e., one that did not normally evoke the response) were paired in the proper sequence. The theories have been refined and modified by a number of later, contemporary psychologists.

EXAMPLE 1.

In an advertising campaign, an ad is often used repeatedly. This is due to the work of Dr. John Watson, a psychologist who was the first consumer behavior specialist. He noted a phenomenon that has remained important in marketing. Through experimentation, he proved that the repetition of a stimulus tends to strengthen the response that is made. The practical marketing applications of this observation can be seen in the repetitive advertising designed to reinforce buying habits. Although Watson's work was productive and some of his applied work survives, his major theories have since been modified by other behaviorists.

9.4 COGNITIVE LEARNING THEORIES

Cognitive theorists believe that such things as personal attitudes, beliefs, and past experiences are combined mentally to produce insight into a situation. For the cognitivists, the brain, or the central nervous system, is dominant. In most cases, cognitive theories of learning reject the theories of the strict stimulus-response behaviorists as too mechanistic. Behaviorists, on the other hand, reject the "mentalism" of cognitive theories. Insisting that behavior is visible and measurable, they consider theirs to be the practical approach to the study of psychology.

EXAMPLE 2.

It is easy to see that consumer attitudes influence buying behavior, and this is where cognitive theory comes into play. While a behaviorist would look for stimulus-response connections in the buying situation, a cognitivist would attribute the buying behavior to the use of past experience and a set of specific attitudes. Strongly held attitudes tend to prevent people from paying attention to conflicting stimuli. In a marketing situation, these stimuli are the advertising and selling efforts of competitors.

Ordinarily it requires very persuasive advertising and selling to change a person's attitude about a product or service that has been providing satisfaction. Food brand preference, for example, is extremely difficult to change. There can be no brand switching until prospects have sampled other products, and food marketers have worked hard to induce prospects simply to try another product. The cents-off and discount coupon techniques have been effective, but once the prospect buys a competitive product it must be better than the one he or she has been using, or there will be no lasting change in buying behavior.

9.5 THE GESTALT THEORY OF LEARNING

Roughly translated from the German, the word *gestalt* means pattern or configuration. The Gestalt theory of behavior is based on perception, experience, and a definite goal orientation. Gestalt psychologists believe that a person perceives a whole situation, rather than the individual elements if it. Thus, the whole is more than merely a sum of the elements because people tend to organize the elements of a situation, and then add elements of past experience, thus making the experience greater than the sum of the individual perceptions.

EXAMPLE 3.

By providing certain meaningful cues it is possible, according to Gestalt theory, to imply more than is given in a situation. For example, if an advertiser of tooth brushes wants to imply that dentists approve of the product, the use of a person dressed as a dentist is sufficient to transmit this message. Even without saying that the person is a dentist or providing a dental office setting, the implication is made.

9.6 PSYCHOANALYTICAL THEORIES OF LEARNING

Based on original work done by Sigmund Freud, psychoanalytical theories assume that people are born with instinctive biological urges which are seldom found to be socially acceptable. As a person matures and learns that these desires cannot be satisfied directly, other means of satisfaction are sought. Thus, Freud talked of sublimation, substitution, and other constructs to account for the way people behave. As tensions are repressed, feelings of guilt or fear often appear, but basic urges are always present. The result is complicated behavior that is understandable to the psychologist and useful to the marketing person.

EXAMPLE 4.

Understanding consumer motivation is crucial to successful marketing, and one of the more important benefits derived from psychoanalytical theory is the work done in motivational research. Using analytical theory as well as some of the practical methods for uncovering motivations, researchers are able to enhance a product or service's chance of success before a major investment is made. Motivational research is used not only to test products and promotional strategies, but also to aid in product development. While many practical benefits have been derived from analytical theory, its use as a popular theory is minimal today. The most productive theories seem to be those of the behaviorists, because they are more observable and useable.

Note that motivation research ranges from simple observation to determine why people buy certain products to the use of sophisticated psychological tests. An example of the latter is the depth interview.

Such research is nothing more than nonstandardized questioning to probe a person's needs. Projective tests try to get answers by indirect means. Instead of asking why "you" buy product X, a projective question would ask "why do you think your neighbor buys product X?" This leads the respondent to feel that his or her biases will not be revealed.

9.7 MOTIVATION

As confusing as the various theories may seem, they do provide practical elements which can be used effectively in product development and marketing. The concept of motivation is hotly debated from many theoretical points of view. However, by viewing it as a stimulated need, it becomes an accessible and useful concept for marketing people. Arousing a need creates a condition of motivation with accompanying tensions that must be resolved. Needs do not become motivators until the individual is aware of the condition. For example, until a person becomes hungry, there is no motivation to eat.

EXAMPLE 5.

Early psychologists attempted to describe behavior by creating long lists of motives and needs, but this provided little in terms of explanation. Today most psychologists, whether theoreticians or applied scientists working in marketing, assume that two classes of motives exist. *Biogenic motives* are those related to bodily needs such as food, drink, sex, and comfort. *Psychogenic motives* are those which arise from a state of psychological tension. For the most part, marketing psychologists are concerned with psychogenic needs. A hungry person will eat just about anything if he or she is hungry enough. But, in the absence of biogenic need, the appeal to psychologically derived motives determines which brands are chosen, which products are used, etc. These are learned, or *culturally induced*, motives. Appeals to psychological motives are most obvious in consumer advertising: "Don't offend with bad breath" or "Have the biggest car on the block." These may not be the headlines, but they are the messages of advertising designed to appeal to psychogenic needs.

9.8 PERCEPTION

Perception should not be confused with sensation. *Sensation* is the raw data received by an individual through the senses. Perception is the interpretation of sensation (stimulus) on the basis of its physical attributes, its relationship to its surroundings, and the conditions present within the individual at a specific point in time. Thus, perception is directly related to the individual's frame of reference, and a single stimulus will be perceived differently by the same individual at different times, depending on changing conditions. The elements that contribute most to the process of perception are the characteristics of the stimulus, and the individual's past experiences, attitudes, and personality characteristics.

EXAMPLE 6.

To select the appropriate stimulus, a marketer must know as much as possible about the target market. Perception is selective. Every individual has characteristics which determine the level and amount of this selectivity. On a broad scale, a new sports car may mean fun, enjoyment, and/or status to its new owner, but it also means a commission to the salesperson who sold it. Therefore, it is important for marketing people to know how each market will respond. An interpretive error at this point could completely doom a marketing campaign.

Review Questions

1. In addition to producing products that meet practical consumer needs, it is important to understand psychological needs as well. True or false?

   Ans. True. See Section 9.1.

2. Theories of human behavior have resulted in schisms within psychology, but the practical applications of conflicting schools of thought have immense value to marketing people.   True or false?

    Ans.   True.   See Sections 9.1 and 9.2.

3. The more practical work of the behaviorists tends to be less in vogue today.   True or false?

    Ans.   False.   See Section 9.2.

4. Stimulus-response theories state that learning takes place when (*a*) a bell is rung, (*b*) a person is rewarded for making a correct response to a stimulus, (*c*) a cognitive connection is made, (*d*) the ego is satisfied.

    Ans.   (*b*)   See Section 9.3.

5. Dr. John Watson stated that repetition of a stimulus tends to (*a*) weaken a response, (*b*) strengthen a response, (*c*) generalize a response, (*d*) cause cognitive overloading.

    Ans.   (*b*)   See Example 1.

6. Cognitive theorists believe that insight is developed from (*a*) attitudes, (*b*) beliefs, (*c*) past experiences, (*d*) all of these.

    Ans.   (*d*)   See Section 9.4.

7. Much practical marketing research is based on theories which are essentially cognitive in origin.   True or false?

    Ans.   True.   See Example 2.

8. Those who work within a Gestalt framework tend to feel that behavior is determined mainly by (*a*) perception, (*b*) experience, (*c*) goal orientation, (*d*) all of these.

    Ans.   (*d*)   See Section 9.5.

9. To the Gestalt psychologist, the whole of experience is more than simply the sum of the parts.   Therefore, much can be conveyed in marketing by inference.   True or false?

    Ans.   True.   See Section 9.5 and Example 3.

10. Theories based on Freudian concepts deal with instinctive biological urges which are seldom considered to be socially acceptable.   True or false?

    Ans.   True.   See Section 9.6.

11. According to psychoanalytical theories, the tensions created by instinctive biological urges are repressed.   They are, however, influenced by advertising which suggests reducing the tension by using a product or service.   True or false?

    Ans.   True.   See Section 9.6.

12. Motivational research is based mainly on psychoanalytical theories.   True or false?

    Ans.   True.   See Example 4.

13. From a marketing point of view, when a need is aroused, a condition of motivation exists.   True or false?

    Ans.   True.   See Section 9.7.

14. Motivation produces tension within an individual and he or she will strive to reduce this tension.   Marketing people use the individual's need to reduce the tension produced by motivation to build demand for a product or service.   True or false?

    Ans.   True.   See Section 9.7.

15. Biogenic motives are related to basic bodily needs such as food, drink, sex, and comfort.   True or false?

    Ans.   True.   See Example 5.

16. Psychogenic motives are culturally learned.   True or false?

    Ans.   True.   See Example 5.

17. Psychogenic motives are those which are most responsive to advertising claims.   True or false?

    Ans.   True.   See Example 5.

18. Perception and sensation are the same.   True or false?

   Ans.   False.   See Section 9.8.

19. Perception is defined as the interpretation of sensation based on (*a*) physical attributes of the stimulus, (*b*) the relationship of the stimulus to its surroundings, (*c*) the conditions present within the individual, (*d*) all of these.

   Ans.   (*d*)   See Section 9.8.

20. Every individual perceives a stimulus in the same way.   True or false?

   Ans.   False.   See Example 6.

Solved Problems

9.1. Attitudes are considered to be lasting favorable or unfavorable evaluations, emotional feelings, or behavioral tendencies toward a thing or an idea.   It has been shown that buying intentions as well as actual purchasing behavior are, in part, determined by an individual's attitudes.   How are attitudes formed?

Attitudes are formed as a result of information accumulated by an individual through past experiences, from relationships with other individuals and groups, and by individual personality traits.   Once formed, attitudes are largely responsible for repeated purchases of products which are difficult to distinguish from others in absolute terms.   For example, most cigarettes taste the same, despite the protestations of smokers.   But few smokers will accept a substitute when a store is out of the brand they smoke regularly.

9.2. In order to enhance the potential success of a marketing program, attitudes toward the product or other aspects of the program are measured.   What techniques are used to do this? Which is most often used?

At best, attitudes are difficult to measure.   It may seem reasonable simply to ask a person how he or she feels about something, but many uncontrollable factors can cloud the results of this seemingly direct approach (see Problem 7.6).   For example, many people try to give the researcher the answer they think is being sought, rather than their true feelings.

Much motivation research tries to approach attitudes in indirect ways by using what psychologists call *projective tests*.   Rather than asking direct questions, these tests require a subject to talk about specific, albeit ambiguous, stimuli, such as pictures or statements.   The intention is to cloud the real meaning of the test so that respondents are unable to perceive it.   This reduces the tendency of respondents to provide answers that they think will please the researcher.   From the responses obtained in this manner, researchers are able to infer what the attitudes are.

Perhaps the most widely used and most practical method of determining attitudes is found in some of the *scaling* technques.   When subjects are asked to rank things, an order of preference emerges.   This technique is often refined by showing subjects pairs of items, leaving a series of individual choices which then can be placed in rank order.   There are many ways of constructing attitude scales, and each has advantages and disadvantages.   In general, however, scaling techniques are considered more representative of true attitudes than many of the projective tests.   At the same time, when it is difficult to present several concrete concepts in a scaling situation, projective tests can be effective.

9.3. How can a marketer deal with unfavorable consumer attitudes toward a product?

Research has shown that consumer attitudes strongly affect buying decisions.   If consumer attitudes do not favor a product, the marketer can either try to change the attitudes or modify the product.   Generally, an attempt to change attitudes is effective only in situations where a new or unusual product is being introduced to a market already served by several look-alike competitors. Product modification is considerably simpler.   If market research can provide a clear picture of attitudes that will be consonant with a modified product, this is the most reasonable and economical strategy.

9.4.   Under what conditions will a marketer most likely be able to modify a consumer attitude? What conditions make it most difficult to change an attitude?

A shift in attitude is most likely to occur in individuals who are open-minded and/or have relatively weak existing attitudes.   When there is little solid information to support an existing attitude, it will be easier to change than if the attitude were backed up by strong evidence.   Also, if there is little ego, or personal involvement with the attitude, it will be easier to change.   Brand loyalty is a strong attitude, and is therefore difficult to change.

In general, the probability of change varies inversely with the strength of the attitude.   Attitudes intimately related to self-concept, values, and personal motives are especially difficult to change.   Thus, attitudes related to family ties, prestige products, and one's peers are especially resistant to change.   Also, when attitudes are interrelated they are difficult to change.   A change in one attitude that would require changes in others is quite difficult to effect.

9.5.   Describe three ways a marketer might be able to change consumer attitudes.

Strongly held attitudes can be changed only with highly persuasive communications.   The communication may be face-to-face selling or it may be advertising.   In order to be effective, the communication should try to modify one or more of the attitude dimensions.   A marketer who wants to work on the cognitive aspects of an attitude might provide strong information relating to product benefits, or the deficiencies of competitive products.   Another technique is to appeal to the emotional aspects of an attitude by providing a strong emotional argument, such as a testimonial.   However, most attitude shifts take place when the marketer convinces the prospect to act contrary to his or her conventional behavior.   Special promotions such as the cents-off coupon attempt to break an established attitudinal and behavioral pattern.

9.6.   Attitudes toward products and services can be changed by using negative as well as positive promotional appeals.   Describe how some major advertisers use negative appeals.   Will a strong negative appeal be more effective than a weaker one?

Perhaps the most obvious use of negative appeals can be seen in the promotion and sale of insurance.   Advertising emphasizes what can happen to a person with little or no insurance.   Life and fire insurance ads demonstrate this approach most graphically.   Some grooming aid manufacturers also occasionally use negative appeals.   For example an ad might show a person who failed to use the advertiser's mouthwash being ostracized because of bad breath.

Oddly enough, the stronger the fear appeal, the less effective the ad.   A low-key negative appeal will be much more effective than one which pulls out all the stops.   Consumers are more likely to identify with and react positively to ads portraying small problems than to those based on major crises.

9.7.   Although anti-smoking campaigns have been in use for a number of years, there has been little change in the number of people who smoke.   While most of the campaigns have been low-key, none have been especially effective.   Explain this lack of success.

Research has shown that fear, or negative appeal promotions, are much more effective with people who have less of a commitment to something than those who are heavily committed.   Thus, heavy smokers are much less likely to stop smoking as a result of any particular campaign than those who are only moderate tobacco users.   Evaluations of anti-smoking campaigns indicate that the heavy smokers react defensively by avoiding all information that points out the dangers of smoking.   Exactly the same effect has been noticed in brand preference studies.   It's much more difficult to switch a person from one brand to another when the person is a committed user.

9.8.   What are the psychological dynamics of brand loyalty? How do these dynamics operate to the benefit of the manufacturer who has won brand loyalty from customers?

Even though consumers are deluged with advertising of all kinds for virtually every type of product, very little gets through their perceptual defenses. In other words, once a product is perceived as being satisfying, consumers tend to filter out messages that are in opposition to the attitudes they hold. This selective perception tends to account for brand loyalty. It has been shown that people will often seek information on products they use just to reinforce their choice.

9.9.   Claims have been made that buying decisions can be influenced without consumer awareness through subliminal advertising. However, follow-up tests have shown that consumer fears are unwarranted and that the effects of such advertising have been grossly overstated. What are the problems involved in subliminal perception that make its effective use impossible?

Subliminal advertising attempts to change attitudes without awareness. In the experiments that were conducted, messages that were beyond the recognition and awareness of many of the viewers were flashed on a movie screen. The researchers claimed that popcorn and soft drink sales increased every time the message was flashed. However, other researchers who attempted to replicate the results of the experiment were unable to do so.

Subliminal advertising is ineffective for several reasons. First, the subliminal stimulus is much too weak to gain any attention. Within the time period of such an exposure, only an extremely short message can be transmitted. This period simply does not permit enough of a suggestion to take hold. Second, every individual's threshold for stimulus recognition is different. For a given stimulus, one person might perceive it, while another would miss it completely. Therefore, subliminal stimulation is neither the ultimate tool of the marketer, nor the weapon of the devious politician as many fear.

9.10.   In addition to the psychological dimensions of consumer behavior, social influences also affect buying decisions. Define the terms *status* and *role* and differentiate between them.

Whether the groups with which an individual identifies are formal, such as the PTA, or informal, such as the middle class, social affiliation occurs. *Status* is the relative position a person has within a specific group. Status can be acquired by specific effort, or conferred simply on the basis of social interaction. While one person might strive to be president of a club, another achieves status by studiously avoiding such activity. In other words, status defines a point on a social continuum rather than a state of high achievement. *Role* refers to the rights and obligations that are expected of an individual by other individuals in specific positions within the group.

Status and role considerations influence the way people perceive themselves as well as their buying decisions. For example, as status within a neighborhood increases, many people feel obliged to display their upward mobility. They may do this by redecorating, adding a garage they don't need, or hiring a gardener. Astute marketers are aware of such motivation, and plan marketing campaigns to capitalize on this situation.

9.11.   Purchases are often influenced by reference groups. What is a reference group? What is its effect on purchasing behavior?

Reference groups are those with which a person identifies, but does not necessarily belong to. People tend to dress in clothing that positions them with groups with which they identify. Children wear shirts of the baseball teams they admire. Adults often choose clothes that imply a certain class status. They may, in fact, belong to the class, but as mentioned before, membership is not a prerequisite for creating the impression.

Generally, products which are purchased under the influence of reference group identification must be visible and somewhat conspicuous. Expensive clothing with identifiable logos, such as Calvin Klein, are bought because of reference group pressures. The same clothes, but without the Klein logo, would have much lower sales. The buyers want to be identified with a group that can afford to spend a lot of money for something as basic as a pair of jeans—the logo gets this message across.

9.12.   Social class plays a role in determining the types of products an individual will buy.   How might a marketer use sociological information which describes prospects for a product?

Considerable research has been done both by academic social scientists and commercial firms to determine what types of products are bought by different types of people and why.   When a marketer understands the social factors that influence a purchasing decision, the product as well as the marketing effort can be tailored to suit the conditions.   For example, upper middle class people tend to buy fewer pieces of furniture, but look for quality in the pieces they buy.   Lower middle class families prefer to have more furniture; quality is less important because they will spend less for it than would the upper middle class individual.   Under these circumstances, entire lines of furniture can be created and priced to meet these conditions that are socially induced.

9.13.   In every social structure, whether it is a small local club, or an international organization with millions of members, opinion leaders tend to set the pace.   For the marketer, product endorsement by opinion leaders often means immense success.   Describe several situations where this social situation can be used to aid in marketing a product.

The marketing of fashion clothing is one of the best examples of the use of opinion leaders.   An astute fashion firm that can get a famous personality, such as a TV star, to wear and endorse a new style will probably have little trouble moving merchandise.   Auto companies try to have automobile experts and racing drivers use and endorse their cars for the same reason.   However, it should be noted that Federal law prohibits opinion leaders from making such endorsements unless they really use the product.   Apart from the use of such obvious opinion leaders, it is possible and practical to entice leaders in any group to be the first to use a new product.   It is hoped that others in the group will follow the lead of these people.

9.14.   Describe how shifting family relationships can create marketing possibilities.

Every individual goes through a number of family relationships during a lifetime.   The family to which one is born represents the first family exposure and one set of marketing opportunities. Once a person leaves the family to start another, other marketing opportunities become available.   The new family needs furniture and appliances, and baby items when the family expands.   When the children have grown and left home, a smaller home may be needed.   As old age arrives, family needs shift to more health-oriented products.   Products aimed at various stages of family development can be marketed to a specific target audience.   For example, a number of health tonics are marketed in this country for an older family audience.   Can you think of others that attempt to reach the family in a specific stage of development?

9.15.   There are distinct cultural differences between people of different countries.   Discuss the possibility of successfully marketing a deodorant in countries with attitudes that differ from ours.

In America, consistent advertising has made most of the population very conscious of the way they smell.   Even those who work in air-conditioned offices and seldom do enough exercise to cause an odor regularly use a deodorant.   However, in other countries, body odor is not considered a particular problem.   Before marketing such a product, it would be prudent to determine what local attitudes prevail toward the "problem" seen by Americans.   If enough of a market exists, a program might be planned.

However, it is important to note that cultural differences often make it impossible to sell the same product in different countries.   While it might be possible to create a market for the product in the foreign country by using the same techniques that created the market here, such a decision would probably involve a considerable financial commitment as well as a high degree of risk.

9.16.   Social scientists, working with marketing people, have identified a series of steps through which most people learn of and ultimately buy products.   Describe each.

1.   *Awareness.*   A person must be aware of the product for the decision-making process to begin.

2. *Interest.* Once the person is aware of the product's existence, and becomes interested in it, relevant information can be gathered.   If no interest is aroused, the process will stop here.

3. *Evaluation.* At this point, information has been gathered and assimilated.   The person now begins to make mental evaluations of the product, trying to see if it will solve a particular problem or meet a specific need.

4. *Trial.* A trial is next in the sequence.   If the product is inexpensive, it will be purchased and assessed.   If it is an expensive purchase, such as a car, some kind of demonstration will be sought, such as a test drive.   When trials are difficult to accomplish, many products are eliminated.   This is why most publishers who sell books through the mail offer a free inspection period before requesting payment.   Books sold in bookstores can be examined immediately prior to making the decision and are not sold with a money-back guarantee.

5. *Decision.* After the trial, a decision is made.   The product is either rejected or purchased.

6. *Confirmation.* Seldom is a person totally convinced that the purchase was right.   However, at this point a conflict, called *cognitive dissonance,* is resolved by selectively avoiding advertising for competitive products and reading only information that will confirm the correctness of the decision.

9.17.   Discuss the element of risk in buying an unknown product.   What steps can a marketer take to overcome the problem?

Risk, in a marketing sense, is directly proportionate to the price of the product.   A person is much more likely to spend a dollar to test a new brand of food than to risk a few hundred dollars on an untried brand of appliance.   The higher the price, the more important it becomes to eliminate the possibility of risk for the prospect.   Apart from the devices used to convince, such as celebrity testimonials, money-back guarantees are the best means of eliminating the problem of risk from the purchasing decision.

9.18.   What factors, other than psychological and social conditions, influence buying decisions?

A purchase decision is seldom made on the basis of one factor alone.   Even though practical factors must be considered, decisions are rarely made on the basis of need alone.   Purchase decisions involve a blend of emotional and factual points.   For example, dependability may seem to be a purely rational factor, but it can be affected by other considerations.   Reliability, durability, economy, and other factors are often part of the decision process.   From a marketing point of view, it is important to isolate the factors that seem to be uppermost in the minds of prospective customers when they consider the purchase of a product.   Psychological and practical buying motives are often difficult to separate.   Price is a definite consideration, but under many circumstances people are willing to spend more for psychological reasons.   For example, a clothing manufacturer may market one line with a status logo on it for a higher price than the same line without the prestige logo sold at a lesser price.   If pure reason prevailed, the purchasing decision would be made on the basis of price and quality.   But when the logo tells others that more money was spent, psychological considerations must be taken into account.   For the marketer, it is important to know the extent to which psychological and practical considerations are considered in the buying decision.

9.19.   Very few people are totally oblivious to the ego enhancement that accompanies the use of status symbols.   The automobile is one of the most obvious of such symbols.   Describe a few others that are less obvious, but strong enough to warrant the attention of marketing people.

A few years ago, the brand of scotch a person drank was considered a strong symbol, but it has been replaced to some degree by certain wines and even non-alcoholic drinks such as carbonated water.   A man's haircut can also be a status symbol.   When men first wore their hair longer, they were identified with a certain group.   The hair was, for many, styled by specialists, not cut by barbers.   Having a stylist was a symbol that was responsible for many barber shops changing formats and charging many times the price of a conventional haircut.   Now that most people have more leisure time, the symbols of success have become travel, vacation home, and membership in social organizations such as boat and tennis clubs. The marketer who can anticipate or create effective symbols will be ahead of the competitors.

9.20. Why is it important to differentiate between where a product is bought and where the decision to buy is made?

For some products, the decision to buy and the act of purchasing take place at the same time and in the same place. Impulse purchases, such as those made at a supermarket which are not on the shopper's original list, must be promoted differently than those products which require a longer and more complex evaluation. Heavy in-store displays can make the most of products that are bought on impulse. But when a person buys an automobile, the decision takes longer and the effort to make it is much more complex. Most of the decisions to buy expensive items are made away from the point of sale, after many stores have been visited and many competitive products seen. Therefore, any advertising that is done for these products should reach the people where the buying decision will be made. This could be newspaper advertising which reaches homes in the trading area, or it could be direct mail sent out to those who have visited stores to evaluate the items being considered.

Chapter 10

Advertising and Sales Promotion

10.1 INTRODUCTION

A general model of communications shows that a message starts with a sender, is then encoded (words, type, etc.), then transmitted (spoken, printed, etc.), and decoded (received) by the person for whom the message is intended. This model is basic to any communications process; its understanding and application are essential to the success of advertising and sales promotion.

Applying the process, a promotional message can start with a company that has a product to sell. The encoding phase might be magazine ads, television commercials, or publicity. The transfer of the encoded message is handled by salespeople, informative packaging, and other selling media. At the consumer end, the prospect for the product receives the message, decodes and interprets it on the basis of subjective external and internal factors, and either buys or rejects the product. Note that there is "noise," or interference, at every step of the communications process; that is, advertisements compete with each other, and even the content of a TV show can interefere with the commercial..

This straight-line model doesn't end with a sale or a rejection. Instead, it becomes a feedback loop when the company seeks information from the point of sale, the last step in the chain. Feedback can help turn a loser into a winner and a marginal success into a big winner.

This model is more than a descriptive system. It provides a strategy in which each step can be tested, evaluated, and fine-tuned to optimize the promotional effort and budget. (See *Theory and Problems of Advertising,* Schaum's Outline Series.)

EXAMPLE 1.

The flowchart in Fig. 10–1 illustrates the communication process and its application to advertising and sales promotion.

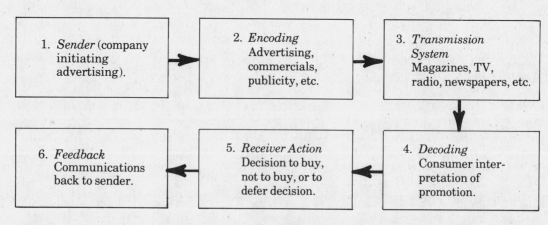

Fig. 10-1

10.2 THE PROMOTION MIX

Effective promotion relies on a careful blend of all of the promotion mix elements: advertising, sales promotion, personal selling, and public relations. No one element is more important than another in absolute terms. However, in order to derive maximum benefit from its promotional plan, a company should place greatest emphasis on the elements that are most appropriate to its particular marketing programs and products.

EXAMPLE 2.

Advertising is, in general, a nonpersonal sales presentation. In some cases, advertising is strictly product-oriented and expected to result in direct sales. In others, advertising is used to attract people to stores where the sales will be made. And in others, advertising may be *institutional;* that is, used simply to create a good image of the company, rather than to generate sales.

EXAMPLE 3.

Sales promotion is any activity other than advertising, personal selling, and publicity. For example, in-store displays, brochures which describe industrial products, discount coupons, and give-aways used to build store traffic are all considered sales promotion activity.

EXAMPLE 4.

Personal selling is done in a face-to-face situation. The activities of the store salesperson, the independent representative of several companies, and the door-to-door salesperson are just a few examples of personal selling. In recent years, there has been a marked increase in the use of the telephone to sell products directly. Even though the seller and prospect never meet face-to-face, this is still personal selling.

EXAMPLE 5.

Public relations is any kind of communication to customers, dealers, and others involved in the marketing mix for the purpose of enhancing the image of a product or service. Most definitions limit this activity to unpaid promotion. Although this is a big part of a public relations campaign, it is by no means the only facet of the activity. Newspaper and magazine articles in which a product is mentioned as well as attempts by the manufacturer to have its products appear in places where they will be seen by prospects are public relations activities. Consumer products seen in movies and TV shows are often public relations plants. Manufacturers try to have their brand names appear in such non-advertising contexts whenever they can.

10.3   ESTABLISHING AN OPTIMUM PROMOTIONAL MIX

The actual blend of promotional mix elements depends on the products being sold, the nature of the market, and the channels of distribution. Planning for the optimal mix is best begun by working backwards from the market. The marketing manager should begin by analyzing the techniques used for successful competitive products. This does not imply a lack of room for innovation, but rather that if enough producers have found one way to be successful, the others probably are unproductive. For example, if the individuals or companies in the market are accustomed to being called on directly, this approach should be tried, unless it can be shown that all of the competitors are operating inefficiently. Once the major thrust of the mix has been determined, the amount of emphasis to be placed on each of the other elements can be determined.

EXAMPLE 6.

The promotional mix for a product should be determined by the manufacturer. A manufacturer of heavy machinery would probably emphasize personal selling and make only minimal use of advertising. This would make sense because the sale of such equipment often requires specialized selling and servicing by people outside the marketing department. Advertising would be used primarily to locate prospects for the sales force. Thus, for this manufacturer, direct selling expenses would be high, while advertising costs would be low. Many salespeople gain access to prospects by showing a copy of their most recent national advertisement.

In contrast, a company producing popular records would stress the mass-marketing elements of the promotional mix. It might try to build store traffic with local tie-in newspaper ads. It might spend a considerable amount on TV to create direct mail order sales. This promotional mix is the antitheses of the one the industrial company would choose.

10.4   THE GOALS OF PROMOTIONAL ACTIVITY

Creating clever ads may be fun, but unless they are designed to achieve specific goals, money can be wasted. Therefore, whether the planning is for advertising, publicity, selling, or promotion, very specific marketing-oriented goals should be established. That is, they should be established to accomplish a specific task within the marketing mix for the product or service.

Although goals will vary with the situation there are some objectives that most marketing situations have in common. To wit,

(1) providing information,

(2) increasing demand,

(3) differentiating the product,

(4) establishing the value of a product, and,

(5) maintaining a certain sales level.

EXAMPLE 7.

Industrial advertising seeks to inform and locate prospects. Much industrial advertising is designed to supply information. Rather than try the "hard sell" in such advertising, industrial companies often give magazine readers as much information as they can about the product. Since such products are seldom bought on impulse, this approach is very effective when an in-depth knowledge of the product is required for a sound buying decision. Note, however, that such advertising generally supplies just enough information to interest the prospect. When the ad offers more information and readers are urged to send for a brochure, a face-to-face sales program can begin.

EXAMPLE 8.

The main objective of most promotional activity is to increase demand. With a greater promotional effort, demand for the product should rise. However, it should be noted that there is a point for all products and markets where an increase in promotional expense will no longer produce a profitable level of sales. The cost of the sale becomes too expensive, and a lower, but optimum level is then used. See Section 8.4.

EXAMPLE 9.

Differentiation is very important in markets where the product or service is difficult to distinguish from others. Soft drinks, liquors, food, and even some automobiles have this problem. It is often wise to try to position the product, service or company in an effort to gain an increased market share. Avis, number two in the car rental business according to its advertising, is using such an approach.

EXAMPLE 10.

Testimonials convey a strong sales message. When promotion in any form extols the benefits that will accrue to the user, the value of the product can be greatly enhanced. It is seldom enough to say simply that the product is the best—proof must be given. Testimonials and comparisons with other products (when the comparison is legitimate and not an invitation to the competitor to engage in a war of meaningless words) are techniques often used to convey such a message.

EXAMPLE 11.

Advertising is used to stabilize sales. A company may want to stabilize sales for a number of reasons. For example, an uneven cash flow caused by the effects of a seasonal business can be a serious problem. Companies in trendy fields, such as clothing, often look to other products to stabilize their cash flow by advertising them regularly. The steady sale of work clothes can often make up for the ups and downs that occur in seasonally advertised merchandise, such as beachwear.

10.5   ESTABLISHING A PROMOTIONAL BUDGET

The amount of money spent on promotion varies widely from industry to industry. It also varies among competitive manufacturers of the same or similar products. Essentially, every company tailors its promotional budget to its individual characteristics and the way it operates. It should be noted that, in general, as more money is spent on effective promotion, greater sales are achieved. However, this is not a limitless equation, and few companies are in a position to test this notion. There does come a point in every company where an extra expenditure on promotion no longer produces additional profitable sales. For this reason, most promotional budgets are planned on a more pragmatic basis.

EXAMPLE 12.

Many companies, especially those with a pragmatic orientation, try to establish promotional budgets as a percentage of sales. The budget may be based on sales of the previous year, or on an estimate of anticipated sales for the year to come. Despite its popularity, the method is not especially practical because it limits the flexibility of those responsible for sales and marketing. If, for example, an unanticipated marketing opportunity occurred during a year in which the promotional budget were fixed and tied to sales, it might be difficult to get management to allocate additional funds.

EXAMPLE 13.

A variation of the percentage of sales method of budget allocation allows a fixed amount of promotional money for each unit produced. This method has the same defects as the method described in Example 12, except that more money becomes available as more units are produced. However, it is still a limiting system.

EXAMPLE 14.

Some companies rely on what they think their competitors spend on advertising as an indicator of what they should spend. There is some merit for this approach when the figures are averages based on a number of competitors in the industry. However, there is also a lot of room for error. The company which is considered successful may be wasting money without knowing it. The copycat may be doomed to commit the same mistake.

EXAMPLE 15.

The most practical way to plan a promotional budget is to base the dollars to be spent on specific goals. Traditionally referred to as the task method, this approach not only provides more flexibility than other budgetary methods, but also allows management to determine the productivity of the program when it is over.

When the task method is used, company management first states a specific goal, such as a percentage increase in sales, or a larger segment of the market. Whatever measure is used, this is a quantitative goal. Once all concerned agree on the goals, the next step is to estimate how much money will be required for promotion to accomplish the task. The determination of dollar amounts must be made in conjunction with the development of the program implementation. It is necessary to develop specific budget figures for all of the promotion that will be involved. For example, if the goal of a mail order company is to increase its share of a TV viewing audience by a certain amount, it will be necessary to determine how much more advertising will be needed and when it should be run. When this has been determined, the cost of the programming must be computed. Some goals, of course, are more ambitious than the resources of the company. If necessary, funds can be borrowed, or the program can be scaled down to be more realistic in terms of funds available.

10.6   EVALUATING PROMOTIONAL EFFECTIVENESS

For some, the measure of promotional effectiveness is immediate and obvious. If, for example, a retailer runs an ad in a local newspaper and enough people respond to make it profitable, the retailer has a direct measure of promotional effectiveness.

However, for others it may be more difficult. Consider the situation faced by a manufacturer of automobiles who uses, among other promotional elements, national TV advertising. The ads may sell hard, but unless they are keyed to local dealers, their effect will be difficult to measure. Those who see the commercial may be impressed, but unless it stimulates them to go to a local dealer, there is no way to determine the ad's impact. For this reason, most automobile manufacturers time their promotions with local dealer advertising so that the effect is not only immediate, but measurable.

Those who sell products by mail have the advantage of being able to determine promotional effectiveness almost immediately. If their mailing piece doesn't produce sufficient orders to cover costs and make a profit, it hasn't been effective. But mail-order marketers are in a better position than most. They are able to test their mailing pieces with only small portions of their mailing lists before they spend large sums on a big mailing.   If they encounter problems in the test, they can determine the causes and correct them before a mailing is made to the total list.

EXAMPLE 16.

It is often possible to pretest advertising without the bother, expense, and risk of using it first in the marketplace.   When this is done, several ads are prepared, each with specific variations on the basic concept.   There may be different approaches to the headline, text, or illustrations.   Each version is tested with a group of people considered to be representative of those in the market.   Usually, such testing is done by placing the different versions of the ad in segmented editions of a publication covering the same demographic area.   A coded coupon is often used to determine just which ad pulled best.   There are other ways to accomplish the same purpose, but each is based on this approach.

The same technique is often used to test TV commercials, except that a jury is made up of individuals who respond to a request to preview a "new show" at a TV studio.   Actually it is the commercial that is being tested, and the "show" is used to normalize the testing situation.   The true intent of the project is masked to make the testing situation seem as close to at-home viewing as possible.   Questions are asked after the presentation, but only the answers to the questions about the commercial are considered.

Review Questions

1. The basic communications model includes a sender which encodes and transmits a message to a receiver who decodes the message.   True or false?

   Ans.   True.   See Section 10.1.

2. To be most effective, the communications model described should be a circular, rather than a straight-line process.   The last step is provision for (*a*) market research, (*b*) product diversification, (*c*) consumer feedback, (*d*) product positioning.

   Ans.   (*c*)   See Section 10.1.

3. Which of these is *not* part of the promotional mix? (*a*) Advertising, (*b*) product design, (*c*) personal selling, (*d*) public relations.

   Ans.   (*b*)   See Section 10.2.

4. Regardless of the company, the product, and the market, all elements of the promotional mix should be blended in the same proportion to be most effective.   True or false?

   Ans.   False.   See Section 10.2.

5. Advertising is never used to produce direct sales.   True or false?

   Ans.   False.   See Example 2.

6. Personal selling is always done in a face-to-face situation.   True or false?

   Ans.   False.   See Example 4.

7. Specific efforts to enhance the image of the product or service fall within the activity of (*a*) sales promotion, (*b*) direct selling, (*c*) public relations, (*d*) advertising.

   Ans.   (*c*)   See Example 5.

8. The blend of the promotional mix elements depends on (*a*) the products being sold, (*b*) the nature of the market, (*c*) the channels of distribution, (*d*) all of these.

   Ans.   (*d*)   See Section 10.3.

9. Innovation should be discouraged if it is found that others selling the same product or service are all promoting in the same way.   True or false?

   Ans.   False.   See Section 10.3.

10. A manufacturer of heavy machinery would probably spend more on advertising than on direct selling. True or false?

   Ans.   False.   See Example 6.

11. Much industrial advertising is designed to (a) sell directly, (b) provide information, (c) create a favorable image of the company, (d) all of these.

    Ans. (b) See Example 7.

12. The main objective of most promotion is to (a) increase demand, (b) provide feedback, (c) harass competitors, (d) none of these.

    Ans. (a) See Example 8.

13. When a product is similar to others on the market, the promotional effort should (a) create a strong image of the company, (b) knock the competitors, (c) differentiate the advertiser's products from all others, (d) all of these.

    Ans. (c) See Example 9.

14. Advertising is not always used to increase sales. It can be used to stabilize sales in a fluctuating market. True or false?

    Ans. True. See Example 11.

15. When an advertising budget is prepared as a percentage of sales, sales can be expressed in terms of (a) a future period, (b) an earlier period, (c) neither of these, (d) both of these.

    Ans. (d) See Example 12.

16. A variation of the percentage-of-sales method of budget allocation allows a fixed amount of promotional money for each unit produced. True or false?

    Ans. True. See Example 13.

17. The most practical approach to advertising budgeting is (a) as a percent of sales, (b) as a fixed amount of the number of units produced, (c) based on the task to be accomplished, (d) based on an estimate of what is spent by competitors.

    Ans. (c) See Example 15.

18. When the task method is used to plan a promotional budget, the first step is to (a) review last year's budget, (b) seek information on competitors' budgets, (c) plan the creative strategy to see if it will be affordable, (d) set specific marketing goals.

    Ans. (d) See Example 15.

19. The major drawback of the task method of budget development is that it does not provide information which can be used to evaluate the effort of the program. True or false?

    Ans. False. See Example 15.

20. Because it is difficult to evaluate the effects of advertising in all but directly measurable situations such as mail order, advertisers have turned to pretesting elements of a program, such as ad headline, copy, and illustration. True or false?

    Ans. True. See Example 16.

Solved Problems

10.1. Advertising and sales promotion are the essential elements of a sales approach called a pulling strategy. Discuss.

> When a pulling strategy is employed, a very strong promotional effort is directed at the final consumers, temporarily bypassing any of the intermediaries who might handle the product. The intention is to create consumer demand so that the channels of distribution will respond to the potential of pre-established demand and stock the product for resale.
>
> The intermediaries involved may include jobbers and wholesalers as well as the final link in the chain, the retailer.

The technique is especially effective when there are already many products competing for the desired outlets, and when the outlets are unwilling to take on a new product.   This technique is used frequently with such products as soap and foods.

10.2.   A pushing strategy depends less on advertising and more on personal selling.   Describe the dynamics of this approach.

When a manufacturer uses this strategy, heavy emphasis is placed on direct selling to the channels of distribution.   These may include the same channels that are involved in a pulling strategy, but in this case the thrust of the effort is directly to intermediaries who will buy and sell the product.   In this situation, the manufacturer depends on aggressive intermediaries selling to get the product to the retail outlets.   Normally, the manufacturer will help the retailer with cooperative advertising allowances, trade discounts, any other dealer aids.   Pushing and pulling strategies were presented here as alternatives, but they are most often used in combination.   The emphasis depends on the job to be done.

10.3.   Describe the advertising approaches that would be most appropriate at each stage of the product life cycle.

During the *introductory stage* of a new product, the promotion must sell the idea of the product. If it's an entirely new idea, the concept must be sold; if it's a new product based on an accepted idea, the promotion must stress the product as something new from the company.   It's important to stimulate primary demand with promotional efforts.

During the *growth stage,* competitors begin to enter the market.   At this point, there should be a shift in promotional emphasis to a stimulation of selective demand.   That is, the promotion should tell why the product is better than those with which it competes.

Once a product has reached the *stage of maturity,* advertising generally shifts to a maintenance program designed to retain that share of market which has been captured.   At this point, price reductions are often advertised.   Of course, as market conditions change, it is possible for a firm to find itself back in a competitive growth situation again.   When this occurs, the company may elect to launch a new competitive promotional effort, or it may simply phase out the product.

A decision to eliminate the product marks the beginning of a *sales decline phase.*   The promotion in this stage is designed primarily to build enough sales at a sufficient profit to allow the firm to phase the product out over a period of time.

10.4.   Market conditions are seldom stable for long periods of time.   How must advertising react to changing conditions?

It seldom occurs that all competitors are satisfied with their share of the market.   Expansion is the nature of business, and it usually requires that more product or service must be sold.   If one company in a market noted for unaggressive advertising suddenly takes the initiative with forceful advertising, its competitors must either follow suit or develop other means of promotion.   This must often be done just to retain current business, not to mention gaining a larger share of the market. Under such circumstances, it is unwise for those responsible for promotion to assume that a given promotional program will be effective at any time in the future.

10.5.   In general, promotion used to sell consumer market products follows certain well-established patterns.   Describe these patterns.

Because the consumer market is large and geographically widespread, mass promotion is most often used.   Even though a product may be sold in many small, local retail stores, mass promotion combined with tied-in local promotion is usually most effective.   National campaigns for consumer products may be placed on TV, radio, and appear in national circulation magazines.   But, such products are also advertised in local newspapers and on local stations in greater detail (i.e., telling the prospects where they can buy the products).

10.6. The promotion of industrial products depends less on advertising than it does on personal selling. Describe how advertising is used as part of the promotional mix to sell products to industry.

There are many more magazines serving industry and the professions than those published for general consumers. Those who want to reach special markets select the magazines which reach their audience and place ads in them. The ads, for the most part, try to provide information about the product and to stimulate the reader to seek additional information. Many of these magazines have reader service cards which the reader can use postage-free in order to request more information. The manufacturer not only sends the information requested, but sends its sales people to discuss the product and to try to fit it to the needs of those who responded to the ads. Because many industrial products carry high prices, the actual sale often takes considerably more time and money than is expended on the sale of most consumer products. Therefore, more time and money is usually allocated to direct selling than to advertising for many industrial products.

10.7. Promotion to wholesalers requires an entirely different approach than that needed for other markets. What should be considered when planning a program to reach and influence them?

Wholesalers, when they are used, are the firm's customers. Even though the wholesaler may sell to the retailer who then sells to the consumer, the customer is the wholesaler. Therefore, the promotional message will be entirely different from any used to stimulate consumers at the retail level. The wholesaler wants to know how much promotion the firm will do to stimulate retail sales so it can plan its stocking levels and profit margins. It wants to know how the firm will meet its competitors in terms of price, service, and product quality. And, it wants to know many of the financial details of the transactions such as shipping and promotional allowances. Therefore, the promotional effort aimed at the wholesaler will try to answer these kinds of questions.

10.8. Differentiate between product and institutional advertising.

When a firm uses product advertising, it intends to build sales directly. Ads for special sales in stores are seeking direct action, store traffic, and high sales. Product advertising can be indirect; that is, it may not strive for immediate orders. Instead, it may be designed to stimulate enough interest in a product or service so that when the need arises, the firm's message will be remembered. Much of the advertising in national consumer magazines can be considered indirect product advertising. The products are all sold in local retail stores, but the intention of the ads is not necessarily to build store traffic. Instead, it is to build interest so that when the product is needed, the firm's brand will be selected.

On the other hand, institutional advertising strives to create a favorable attitude toward the firm and to build good will rather than to sell products directly. Retailers who change their selling hours to accommodate evening shoppers may advertise this fact without saying anything specific about individual products they sell. They are selling the institution as a convenient place to shop. Considerable advertising is placed by major industrial companies in consumer magazines to explain their efforts on behalf of public interest programs. Especially popular today are ads which describe a company's efforts to curb pollution. They are not selling their products directly, but are telling the readers that they are good firms to deal with because of their public-spirited interest.

10.9. Differentiate between national and local advertising.

The language of advertising can be imprecise, and this is one example in which words don't mean what they seem. National advertising is that sponsored and placed by a manufacturer, while local advertising is placed by retail establishments to bring in business from their area. On the surface it would seem that a national advertiser is one who advertises and sells nationally, or across the entire country. This may be the case, but to be classified as a national advertiser all that is necessary is that the ad be for a manufacturer rather than a retailer. For example, there are regional meat processing companies all over the country. When they advertise in their trading area for themselves, it is considered national advertising. But, if a retailer who sells the meat products places the ad, it would be considered local advertising. Note that there are different rates for national and local advertisers in newspapers. The local rate is generally lower then the national rate, but the national rate is commissionable to advertising agencies.

10.10. The aim of any advertising, whether it is institutional or hard sell, is ultimately to sell a product, service, or an idea. Discuss some of the more effective ways advertising can be used to accomplish this goal.

Advertising, especially that done by industrial companies, is used to develop leads for salespeople. The advertising helps to pre-sell by acquainting prospects with the product; it can go further by telling the reader to contact the company for additional information. This becomes a lead for a sales follow-up. It also helps make the salespeople more effective. When they have valid leads they can be more productive than if they had to hunt unknown prospects. It also helps by reaching people whom salespeople find difficult to reach personally. Top managers and many professionals guard their time and seldom grant interviews to salespeople unless they initiated the call. Ads, in whatever medium, can often get to these people when sales people cannot. Advertising can be used to expand a dealer or distributor network. There is hardly a business or professional field that isn't served by a few magazines or journals. When it becomes important to expand the intermediary network, advertising can often play a key role. Advertising can be used to pioneer a new market, and to introduce new products. In addition, it can be used to expand a share of the market.

Advertising is also used to build good will. The effectiveness of institutional advertising is hard to measure, but when used with a campaign that stresses sales, it can be an effective adjunct to a well-planned campaign. Institutional advertising by itself is seldom effective. But when the company has a good reputation, it often pays to trade on it with some institutional advertising.

10.11. One of the most common problems associated with an advertising campaign is the selection of appropriate media. No matter how good an ad is, it will never work if it is placed in the wrong publication. What are the basic considerations of media selection?

The first determination is which of the basic media types (radio, TV, newspapers, magazines, direct mail, out-of-home, etc,) will be most effective. This decision must be based on a sound knowledge of the market and the ways potential customers get their product information. The next step is to narrow the selection to smaller categories. If magazines are to be used, will the best media buy be a news magazine or one aimed at family living? Once this decision has been made, specific magazines must be selected. This step involves a very careful analysis of readership, circulation areas, and data reflecting the experience of similar advertisers in the publications. Such media analysis can be very involved and deal with extremely sophisticated research. It may be necessary to get a psychological composite as well as an economic profile of the average reader. And it may be necessary to test the ads in regional editions of selected publications before a full campaign is undertaken.

10.12. Explain how advertising goals affect media selection.

Consider the case of a manufacturer of consumer products that are sold nationally through chain stores. Should its advertising be national, local, or a combination of the two? If its advertising goals are to generate immediate sales for the retail outlets, it might forego a national program and place all its ads locally to stimulate traffic. Such ads are generally run on a cooperative basis with the retailers who sell the products. That is, the manufacturer either provides a direct allowance on ads placed by the retailer, or offers merchandise discounts proportional to the amount of advertising done.

If, on the other hand, the manufacturer is more interested in building a steady business at the retail level, it might elect to use steady national advertising with a smaller program at the local level.

One of the industrial manufacturer's key advertising goals is invariably to encourage direct inquiries which can be used as sales leads. To reach potential customers, such manufacturers generally place the bulk of their advertising in specialized publications designed for the markets their products serve.

10.13. Discuss the circulation factors to be considered when selecting magazines for advertising.

To begin with, there are three types of circulation which must be evaluated. *Net paid* circulation refers to the number of copies bought or subscribed for per issue. It's important to relate this figure to the estimated total market for the product being advertised and to compare it with similar circulation figures for competitive magazines. Next, the advertiser should look at *primary circulation,* or the other members of the purchaser's household who also read the magazine. These people may also be prospects for the products being advertised. *Pass-on* readers are those who read, but do not buy, the issues. Copies are passed along to them after they have been read by those who bought the issue. If the advertising is to be of a timely nature, pass-on circulation may have little value.

It is also important to know whether a magazine penetrates its audience vertically or horizontally. A horizontal publication reaches readers who have similar interests or qualifications, regardless of other classifications. For example, a purchasing magazine would reach every purchasing agent, regardless of the industry or type of company which employed him or her. A vertical magazine is one with its editorial content directed at a specific industry or profession, regardless of individual job categories. For example, a magazine aimed at ham radio operators has a vertical interest orientation, but slices through the horizontal characteristic of income by including children with no income at all and wealthy adults at the other end. There are also magazines that are sent without charge to individuals with specific characteristics wanted by advertisers. These are controlled circulation publications, and those receiving them are presumed to be potential prospects for the products of the advertisers. Most controlled circulation magazines are found in trade, industrial, and professional fields.

It is also important for the buyer of magazine space to have knowledge of the demographic characteristics of the circulation. Income, age, and educational level are some of the factors that may be considered. Buying power is also important. Advertisers will want to know if readers are in a position to buy the products, regardless of their income levels. Advertising Jaguar automobiles in *Boy's Life* would, obviously, be a mistake.

10.14. What effect does the product itself have on the selection of advertising media?

Many products are sold more effectively in some media than in others. For example, products with a high visual impact would be better advertised on TV and in print than on the radio. Clothing, furniture, and other products which have esthetic appeal fall into this category. However, when advertising involves a special sales campaign where the main thrust is price, nonvisual radio can often do the job.

Products which are to be sold quickly should be advertised in publications which will reach the target audience on time. Daily newspapers have this flexibility; monthly magazines do not. Radio and television are especially effective when timing is important.

10.15. What are the major advantages of newspaper advertising?

Most newspapers provide intense local coverage of a market. Good paid circulation papers are generally read by most of the people advertisers would want to reach. However, controlled circulation papers which are distributed free to everyone in a defined geographic area can also be very effective. Another advantage of newspaper advertising is that it offers great flexibility. Ads can be scheduled or cancelled on short notice, often within 24 hours. They can also be placed on a standing order basis, to appear at regular intervals, or when certain conditions exist. For example, a manufacturer of automobile antifreeze might give a paper an order to run its ad every time the temperature in the area drops below freezing. Such flexibility is not possible with publications such as monthly magazines.

National advertisers enjoy another kind of flexibility by being able to adapt their ads to suit specific local conditions when they advertise in newspapers serving different geographic areas. A variety of sensibilities can be appealed to, e.g., the slant can be ethnic, economic, social, etc. Finally, most newspapers can provide excellent market information to help advertisers make a media choice, as well as create ads that will appeal to the specific readership.

10.16. What are some of the major reasons for advertising in national magazines?

Unlike most newspapers, magazines generally offer high quality reproduction of process color photography. Color can be used in newspapers, but it is subject to the limitations of the paper and press equipment normally used. A magazine can be used to reach a national market at a relatively low cost. Many can also be used to reach specific audiences. That is, some magazines offer separate editions that either serve specific geographic or demographic audiences. This approach can eliminate considerable waste and expense when only a portion of the publication's circulation is of interest to the advertiser.

In addition, magazines are read leisurely. The life of a magazine can be weeks, compared with one day for a daily newspaper. This long life bodes well for a cumulative exposure of advertising.

10.17. Why would an advertiser consider using television advertising? What are some of the disadvantages?

Television is, perhaps, the most flexible advertising medium available. It reaches its audience in both sight and sound, and allows for visual demonstrations of the product. Television air time can be purchased for local as well as national viewing, and offers the advantage of extreme timeliness. It is often possible to buy time on a TV show a day before air time. However, national TV air time is considerably more difficult to arrange.

Perhaps the greatest single drawback is the high cost. And because the message, once transmitted, is lost forever, the effective life of a television ad is extremely short when compared to that of print ads. Finally, since copy must be short to be effective, there is no time to go into the detail that is possible when print is used. Note, however, that many products are best sold with short, oft-repeated televised messages. For example, patent medicines, such as headache remedies, appear frequently; each exposure is seldom more than 10 or 20 seconds.

10.18. Out-of-home advertising has both special benefits and serious limitations. Discuss.

Out-of-home advertising, such as outdoor signs, transit displays, and point-of-purchase devices, can be very effective. When properly used, this technique affords the advertiser the advantages of high impact advertising with potentially widespread coverage at relatively low cost per exposure. It should be noted, however, that the success of such advertising is largely dependent on its being placed in the right spot. Unlike most other advertising, which is *delivered* to a more-or-less captive audience, out-of-home advertising is presented to an audience-at-large.

The high impact nature of such advertising requires short, to the point messages. Since most products that can be advertised effectively by out-of-home media are those already enjoying widespread consumer use, the high impact ad functions primarily as a reinforcement of other promotional efforts. This factor limits its use. The cost involved in a national outdoor campaign may also be prohibitive. However, when used locally, this technique can be a relatively inexpensive way to get extensive exposure.

10.19. Discuss the benefits and drawbacks of direct mail advertising.

The strength of direct mail lies in its ability to be very personal and direct. Most direct mail is prepared for a very specific audience, and when the characteristics of the audience are known and understood, the copy can be tailored to suit its needs, wants, and personal traits. Because direct mail offers the utmost in selectivity, it is possible to write copy that doesn't waste words or the reader's time. Apart from general mailings that most people classify as junk mail, direct mail allows an advertiser to reach only those people who appear to be the most likely prospects for the product or service. Mailing lists of every description are available through mailing list brokers as well as directly from those who have compiled them. Such lists may be made up of customers for similar products. Manufacturers often rent their customer lists to those making noncompetitive products. The mailing list broker arranges for these rentals and takes a percentage of the rental as a fee.

Although direct mail tends to be quite costly in terms of the number of people reached, this factor is offset by the fact that it offers the selectivity that other media lack. There can be enormous circulation waste in radio, TV, newspapers, and magazines if only a small segment of the audience can be considered prospects. Another drawback is that it can be difficult to build, buy, and maintain good direct mail lists. Some specialists claim that 2% of most lists become obsolete each month. This, of course, means that 24% of a list can be wasted each year unless it is updated regularly. List maintenance can be as expensive as list development. But when the product, the promotion and the list are good, direct mail can be one of the best ways to sell.

Unlike most other media, it is possible for a direct mail advertiser to get a good feel for the entire campaign before large amounts of money are committed to a program. The sales letters and the offer can be tested on small portions of the list so that necessary changes can be made before the campaign is launched.

10.20. Describe the process involved in creating an advertisement that will appear in a print medium.

Before any creative work is done, the advertising goal must be established: Will it be expected to bring in store traffic? Develop leads for salespeople? Remind people that the product is on dealer shelves? Whatever the purpose, the goal must be clearly established and used to test every element of the ad as it is being created. An ad must attract attention, hold interest, and stimulate the reader to take the desired action. Therefore, careful attention must be paid to the headline, layout, and illustrations—these are the elements which attract attention. The copy is the sales message. It should be short enough to hold attention yet long enough to tell the story. Some industrial copy can run hundreds of words in length, but most retail copy seldom exceeds 50 words. An ad, like a direct sales presentation, should end with a request for some action to be taken. If a catalog is offered, the copy should emphasize this and suggest that the reader send for it. If the ad is for a sale in a store, it should urge readers to visit the store and specify sale dates. Even low-key institutional ads usually end with some suggestion for action, even though such advertising is considered soft sell. Soft sell is defined as not suggesting or requiring immediate action.

10.21. Describe some of the marketing situations which benefit most from advertising, personal selling, and dealer promotion.

Advertising

The condition of primary demand, in which consumer interest exists for a product without regard for a specific brand, is an excellent climate for the use of advertising. In recent times, wood stoves have become popular as an alternate heating source. Those who advertise their brands have been able to capitalize on primary demand by building interest in their products.

When products are easily differentiated, advertising can be used to create selective demand. For example, luxury automobiles are easily differentiated from each other as well as from economy cars. Look at automotive advertising and you will see the lengths to which the manufacturers of automobiles go to differentiate their products from others. When a product has hidden qualities that cannot be judged at the time of purchase, advertising can be used to help move the prospect closer to the sale. For example, advertising for vacation tours must convince the tourist that the trip will be worth the expense. There is just no way of knowing what the trip will be like at the point of sale. When a product is bought for emotional reasons, advertising can often be used effectively. Insurance, for example, is sold by playing on emotions. Picture a family in a magazine ad watching its home burn and you have a strong emotional scene that is conveyed effectively by advertising.

Personal selling

Advertising can be used to motivate a prospect to inquire about a product or service, but if a high price is involved, personal selling is usually required to close the sale. Real estate agencies are usually heavy advertisers, but very few houses are sold without considerable personal selling. Products that are purchased infrequently also often require personal selling. Expensive services, such as house painting, are bought infrequently and require personal selling by the contractor.

When a demonstration is important, there is usually little that can be done without personal selling. Much farm machinery is sold as a result of demonstrations, as are technical products and industrial equipment. When the product is too big to bring to the prospect for a demonstration, the prospects are often taken to see it at the plant. Industrial trade shows fulfill this function by having manufacturers' equipment on display where many people can see it in operation.

If a trade-in is involved, personal selling is most important. Such situations usually require some negotiation over the value of the product being traded, and it is difficult to do this without face-to-face selling. Everything from used cars to printing equipment and commercial aircraft can be sold this way.

Dealer promotion

A product that is not easily differentiated from its competitors usually requires some dealer promotion. When the dealer can be convinced to give the product more attention than might be given to a competitive product, the effort usually pays off in greater exposure and sales.

If the product must be judged at the point of sale, dealer promotion to emphasize the product is usually needed to attract consumer attention. For example, in department stores which carry different brands of clothing, quality is one of the characteristics judged by consumers. If the store can be persuaded by dealer promotion to display a product prominently, its virtues can be determined easily. Because there may be little qualitative difference between brands carried in a single store, the more prominently displayed product is often preferred by the shoppers. Of course, there are stores in which the merchandise is graded. But, even within the good, better, and best classifications usually used in these stores, there are subtle differences. Again, the more prominently displayed product is usually preferred. Impulse items are very sensitive to relative position within a store. Effective promotion to the dealers handling these products can help get them placed where they will be easily seen and picked up.

Chapter 11

The Legal Environment of Marketing

11.1 INTRODUCTION

American economic philosophy has long favored a free-enterprise system which encourages competition among business firms. Such competition tends to regulate prices to the benefit of consumers, and stimulates product innovation. This relative freedom can, however, also work against consumers. For example, when a number of small producers band together to control prices rather than allowing them to respond to natural market conditions, the consumers' best interests are not served. Situations like this have prompted the enactment of considerable federal and state legislation over the years. Many government regulations are designed to protect the consumer, while others promote the competitive marketplace.

Today, more than ever, the government is active in economic legislation. Some of it is badly needed, and some has had negative effects on the free-enterprise system. However, all of the legislation now being enacted can be traced to one or more of the policies and laws described in this chapter.

11.2 A SUMMARY OF MAJOR ACTS AFFECTING MARKETING

American public policy has long favored and tended to regulate a competitive marketing system. The laws that have been passed fall into two major categories: those that maintain a competitive environment and those that regulate a specific marketing climate.

Laws that maintain a competitive environment:

Sherman Antitrust Act (1890). This law, passed in an effort to prohibit monopolies in interstate commerce, outlaws any agreements which are in restraint of trade. See Section 11.3.

Clayton Act (1914). An attempt to supplement the Sherman Act by outlawing price discrimination, this law prohibits exclusive and tying contracts, interlocking directorates, and intercorporate stockholdings. See Section 11.4.

Federal Trade Commission Act (1914). This act set forth specific prohibitions against unfair methods of competition in commerce, and established the Federal Trade Commission to regulate the legal aspects of business activity.

Cellar-Kefauver Act (1950). A modification of the Clayton Act, this law makes the acquisition of assets that tend to lessen competition or create a monopoly illegal.

Webb-Pomerene Act (1918). This law made organizations engaged in export trade exempt from federal antitrust laws.

Laws that regulate specific marketing activities:

Robinson-Patman Act (1936). Created to strengthen the Clayton Act, this law specifically prohibits certain discriminatory pricing practices. Among the problems treated are fictitious brokerages, disproportional supplementary services and allowances, indefensible quantity discounts, and the knowing inducement of discriminatory prices.

Pure Food and Drug Act (1906). The Food and Drug Administration was created by this act to enforce laws relating to misbranding and adulterated food and drugs.

Miller-Tydings Act (1937). This amendment of the Sherman Act attempted to protect competitors when price fixing was allowed by individual state laws.

113

McGuire-Keogh Act (1952).   This act permitted a manufacturer or a wholesaler to sign price-fixing agreements with retailers in states which permitted such contracts.

Wheeler-Lea Act (1938).   This act makes unfair or deceptive acts or practices used in interstate commerce illegal.   It is an amendment of the Federal Trade Commission Act.

Wool Products Labeling Act (1939).   This act states that products which contain wool must be labeled accurately as to the content of wool and other materials.

Fur Products Labeling Act (1951).   This act required the identification of the type of fur used in garments, as well as the origin of the fur.

Textile Fiber Products Identification Act (1958).   This law required that the natural and synthetic components of many textile items be accurately identified by label.

Hazardous Substances Labeling Act (1960).   This act gave the Food and Drug Administration the power to judge household products hazardous under certain circumstances and to require that appropriate warnings be given to the consumer.

Food, Drug and Cosmetic Act (1938).   This act modified previous related legislation and strengthened the regulations relating to adulteration and misbranding of cosmetics and therapeutic devices.

Truth in Lending Act (1968).   This act requires the disclosure of the annual interest rates on loans and credit purchases to make it easier for consumers to compare sources of credit.   This act also gives the consumer a 72-hour period during which he or she can back out of a contract in which a home is used as security.

Fair Packing and Labeling Act (1966).   This act requires that manufacturers provide the identification of component producers, the quantity of the product packed, as well as certain other factors that are important to the consumer.

11.3   THE SHERMAN ANTITRUST ACT

This pioneering act has had far-reaching effects on the marketing efforts of most American companies.   Its major significance is that it makes illegal: (1) any contract, combination in the form of trust or otherwise, or conspiracy in restraint of trade; and (2) monopolization, the attempt to monopolize, or a conspiracy or combination to monopolize.   Equally important is the fact that individuals who are injured by the actions described in the act have the right to sue for damages.

Even though the act and its subsequent modifications are fairly specific, the law has been interpreted less than literally.   The rule of reason has prevailed and some activities which are construed by the court to be not unduly restrictive or improperly exercised have been held to be legal.

EXAMPLE 1.

The courts have ruled that activity which impedes, obstructs, or interferes with competition is in restraint of trade.   However, note that the Sherman Act protects the *concept* of competition, not individual competitors.   Businesses acting in legitimate ways may cause others to suffer loss, but this is not considered restraint of trade in the legal sense.   To invoke the provisions of the act, it must be shown that the main purpose of a business activity was to restrain trade.

In a free-enterprise system, price competition is considered one of the factors that will result in the best price to the consumer.   Therefore, perhaps the strongest admonitions handed down by the courts have involved price-fixing cases.   Price fixing is prohibited by the Sherman Antitrust Act.   So strong is the act on this point that proof of harm to the general public is not needed for a judgement.   The act of price fixing itself is sufficient.   It does not matter whether a group of companies agreed to raise, lower, or simply stabilize prices.

EXAMPLE 2.

In addition to unfair competition, the Sherman Act states that monopolies are also illegal. While defining a monopoly can be difficult, in general, the courts have held that a monopoly exists when a firm is in a position to fix prices or to exclude competitors from the market. Size alone is not sufficient to constitute a monopoly. But, the larger the firm becomes, the greater the possibility that it can engage in monopolistic practices. For this reason, the U.S. government has always kept close watch on its corporate giants.

EXAMPLE 3.

In some instances price-fixing information has been filtered through industry trade associations under the guise of general information. While the Sherman Act does not prohibit the dissemination of pricing information to members of an association, it can be invoked when it can be shown that the dissemination was for the specific purpose of producing collusive price fixing to the detriment of others.

EXAMPLE 4.

Certain provisions of the Sherman Antitrust Act prohibit boycotts when the intention is to restrain trade. The provisions of the Act can be applied to those who conspire with others to withhold or prevent sales.

11.4   THE CLAYTON AND ROBINSON-PATMAN ACTS

Even though these two acts were passed twenty-three years apart, they are best considered as one. Indeed, the Robinson-Patman Act was passed to eliminate some of the defects in the earlier Clayton Act.

The Clayton Act was conceived to alleviate the problems of price discrimination that harmed local sellers in different geographic areas. It restricted price discrimination, exclusive dealing, tying contracts, and interlocking boards of directors when the intention was to create a monopoly. It also contained one loose clause stating that if price differences resulted from negotiations made in good faith to meet competition, no illegal act had occurred. This clause was interpreted to apply only to competition between sellers.

The Robinson-Patman Act expanded the coverage of this last point to include situations where large buyers were receiving price differentials that were much greater than those offered to smaller customers.

Among its various sections, the Robinson-Patman Act also does the following:

(1) Prohibits the practice of making product sales or leases contingent upon an agreement not to use competitors' products produced by a competitor.

(2) Limits the amount of stock one company may acquire in another if that acquisition might lessen competition or tend to create a monopoly.

(3) Prohibits interlocking corporate directorates, when a trend to monopoly or the reduction of competition can be cited.

(4) Outlaws direct and indirect price competition on commodities in interstate commerce.

(5) Prohibits brokerage, discount, and other allowance payments except for services rendered.

(6) Requires that promotional services and allowances be made available to all customers purchasing goods for resale on a proportionally equal basis.

Review Questions

1. Competition tends to regulate prices in favor of manufacturers, wholesalers and retailers. True or false?

   Ans. False. See Section 11.1.

2. The Robinson-Patman Act was created mainly to strengthen the (*a*) Clayton Act, (*b*) Miller-Tydings Act, (*c*) McGuire-Keogh Act, (*d*) none of these.

   Ans. (*a*) See Section 11.2.

3. Businesses created solely for the purpose of engaging in export trade were exempted from Federal antitrust laws by the (a) Miller-Tydings Act, (b) McGuire-Keogh Act, (c) the Webb-Pomerene Act, (d) the Wheeler-Lea Act.

   Ans. (c) See Section 11.2.

4. According to the Sherman Antitrust Act, contracts, trusts, and conspiracies which enhance trade are legal. True or false?

   Ans. False. See Section 11.3.

5. Under the Sherman Act, monopolies are considered beneficial, and are to be encouraged. True or false?

   Ans. False. See Section 11.3.

6. The Sherman Act is an attempt to protect (a) competitors, (b) competition, (c) small businesses only, (d) only those businesses dealing in foreign trade.

   Ans. (b) See Example 1.

7. Under the Sherman Antitrust Act, it is necessary to show that the general public has been harmed by price fixing before action can be taken. True or false?

   Ans. False. See Example 1.

8. In a free-enterprise system, price competition (a) is illegal, (b) must be tightly controlled, (c) results in the best price to a customer, (d) raises prices and profits for sellers.

   Ans. (c) See Example 1.

9. Generally speaking, a monopoly exists when a firm is in a position to (a) fix prices, (b) exclude competitors, (c) neither of these, (d) both of these.

   Ans. (d) See Example 2.

10. The Sherman Act prohibits the dissemination of all information on the subject of prices and costs to trade association members. True or false?

    Ans. False. See Example 3.

11. According to the Clayton Act, valid reasons for price differences were (a) selling cost variations, (b) products of different quality, (c) quantity of the product sold, (d) all of these.

    Ans. (d) See Section 11.4.

12. Even if price differences are granted to a number of customers in good faith to meet competition, a violation of the Clayton Act still exists. True or false?

    Ans. False. See Section 11.4.

13. Under the original Robinson-Patman Act, it is illegal to negotiate sales or leases when they are contingent upon an agreement by the buyer not to use a competitive product. True or false?

    Ans. True. See Section 11.4.

14. Under the Clayton Act, interlocking directorates are permitted as long as they do not create a monopoly or tend to reduce competition. True or false?

    Ans. True. See Section 11.4.

15. Direct and indirect price competition is forbidden under all circumstances by both the Clayton and the Robinson-Patman acts. True or false?

    Ans. False. See Problem 11.19.

16. No violation of the Clayton and Robinson-Patman acts occurs when price differences are the result of (a) differences in cost of manufacture, (b) varying sales costs, (c) varying quantities, (d) all of these.

    Ans. (d) See Problem 11.19.

17. Even when price differences are necessary to meet competition, there is no legal justification for price discrimination. True or false?

    Ans. False. See Problem 11.19.

18. It is possible to circumvent the provisions of the Clayton Act by adding brokerage charges to a price, even if such brokerage operations were not actually performed.   True or false?

Ans.   False.   See Problem 11.20.

19. The use of promotional services and allowances as a subterfuge to create advantages for favored customers is strictly prohibited by the Sherman Antitrust Act.   True or false?

Ans.   False.   See Problem 11.21.

20. When promotional allowances are provided by a manufacturer, the same offer must be made to all of its retailer customers, and each should have the opportunity to participate in the program on a proportional basis.   True or false?

Ans.   True.   See Problem 11.21.

Solved Problems

11.1. A trademark can be one of the most important assets in marketing a product or service. Discuss the concept.

A trademark is a legally registered device giving immediate and exclusive identification to the goods or services of a particular company or individual.   It may be a word or a symbol.   Many trademarks can be made-up words, such as Kodak, or ordinary words used in a meaningful sense, such as Mustang automobile.   Suggestive words are often effective trademarks.   For example, Sine-off suggests that its use will alleviate sinus problems; First Prize Sausages implies quality. Letters used as acronyms are also effective; for example, CBS, NBC, RCA, etc.

Distinctive designs, whether or not accompanied by descriptive words, are another kind of effective trademark.   The MGM lion has been around and recognized for years.

11.2. According to copyright law, family surnames, geographical places, and descriptive words which simply identify the product cannot be legally protected.   Why, then, have such names as Ford, Oxford, and Tasty Crust been granted copyrights?

These names were in use for many years before being granted copyright status.   The courts ruled that extended use of a name or word had created a distinctiveness that should be protected.

11.3. Under what circumstances would a trademark lose the full protection of the copyright law?

Over the years, many words originally coined to identify specific products have become generic.   That is, the trade name has come to describe the product itself.   When this occurs, the courts may rule that a trade name can no longer be protected under copyright law.   For example, such words as cellophane, linoleum, thermos, and aspirin were once brand names.

11.4. From a legal point of view, what is the most desirable grammatical form for a trademark?

The trademark should be a modifier that can be used with the product name.   A suggestive rather than descriptive modifier has the best chance of never becoming a generic name, and thereby losing copyright protection.   The states of Florida and California are both used as trademarks for different types of oranges.   In contrast, if a noun is selected as a trademark, its owner may experience the problems described in Problem 11.3.

11.5. What copyright problem is faced when a company invents and markets a product which never existed before?

The introduction of an innovative new product requires the creation of two names. One, the generic name, will be open for use by any other manufacturer. The other, the trade name, can be used only by the company holding the copyright. Today, there are many companies marketing aspirin, each with their own trademark identifying the product. How many different brands of thermos bottles have you seen?

11.6. What is the first and most important step to take when adopting a trademark?

It is most important to determine whether the new trademark is already in use by someone else, or whether there is a mark which is similar enough to cause confusion. If the proposed mark is already being used by a similar product, the use of the new mark would be an infringement on the rights of the original trademark holder. If the proposed trademark is similar, but not identical, to one already being used, there may still be sufficient resemblance so that the use of the proposed trademark would cause confusion in the eyes of consumers and possible loss to the holder of the original mark. Because trademark similarities and differences can be subtle, but have far-reaching consequences, it is essential to consult with an attorney who has specific experience in this field when a new trademark is being formulated.

11.7. Explain why trademark protection is guaranteed, even if the trademark has not been officially registered with the U.S. Patent Office. What additional protection does registration provide?

The courts will uphold the prior use of a trademark to protect goodwill created by its usage, even if it has not been officially registered. The key here is *usage*. In order to receive this protection, a trademark must have been used actively in interstate commerce.

The simple act of filing an application makes the trademark a matter of public record that will be obvious to others who might contemplate using the same mark. When the trademark is registered, the certificate of registration provided by the Patent Office serves as legal notice of the owner's rights. This means that even an unintentional infringement can be stopped. The life of the registration is twenty years. However, to cut down the clutter in the Patent Office, all registrations may be cancelled by the Commissioner unless the trademark owner makes a sworn statement between the fifth and sixth year of use that the trademark is still in active use. Trademarks may be renewed for twenty year periods indefinitely, as long as they are actively used.

11.8. Unlike patents and copyrights, trademarks live on forever if used correctly. How should a trademark be used to avoid being considered abandoned and in the public domain?

Perhaps the most important consideration is that the mark chosen will be something that will always be recognized as a trademark, and not one that could become a generic word in common usage. This applies to trademarks used for company advertising, communications, and product labeling. The following points will further insure the rights of the trademark owner:

(1) The trademark should always be displayed in a distinctive style that will set it apart from non-trademark copy. The distinctive lettering of the Ford name stands out from the type used in text material.

(2) Use of words such as "trademark," "brand," or other official language prescribed by the Patent Office with the mark is suggested. When the mark has been registered, use R, Reg. U.S. Patent Office, or Registered in U.S. Patent Office. Every time the name Coca Cola is used, it is followed by ®. The company guards its rights zealously with this usage.

(3) The trademark should be used only in its correct grammatical form. That is, it should be used only as an adjective; never as a noun, a verb, or a root to form a word.

(4) The generic word which identifies the product should always follow the use of the trade-

mark. Even though the name Bayer is synonymous with aspirin, both words are always used together.

(5) The trademark should be used without modification. Do not change the spelling, add hyphens, or modify it in any way.

11.9. Is an American trademark protected in the rest of the world?

No, each foreign country has its own copyright laws. In order to insure total protection, more than 200 registrations outside the United States would be required. However, it has been estimated that protection in the most commercially advanced countries would require about 75 foreign trademark registrations. Before such registration is undertaken, the trademark should be checked with each country to make sure that the word or style doesn't have a negative local meaning. There can be problems with colors as well as words. For example, the color for mourning in Japan is white. The use of this color with certain products might be distasteful and could result in commercial problems.

11.10. Marketing people enter into contracts with many different people and companies. Give a working definition of a contract. Describe the major elements of a contract.

A contract is a promise or a set of promises which when breached can be remedied by law. Implicit in any definition of a contract are the notions of *legal obligation* and *legal right*. Parties to a contract must not only assent to its terms, but must also assume responsibility for the right and obligation which will be upheld by law. Whether the contract is written or spoken, there must be mutual assent between the contracting parties. In legal terms, this is an offer and an acceptance. To be binding, some form of consideration must be given. Note that each party to a contract must have the legal ability to enter into an agreement. For example, agreements with minors have no legal force. The subject matter of the contract must also be legal. That is, a contract can be held null and void if its purposes are illegal.

11.11. Under law, what constitutes an offer and an acceptance of a contract?

The parties to a contract must agree with each other to the same terms at the same time in order for an offer and acceptance to be valid. To be certain that both parties have exactly the same thing in mind, it is important that the person making the offer state its terms in language that the offeree understands. If the offeree accepts, a contract has been made. The acceptance must be absolute and unequivocal and it must meet the conditions of the offer. Note that advertisements, catalogs, and other marketing communications are not considered offers in the legal sense. They are simply invitations to buy. The purpose of such materials is to inform and interest people in the products and services; there is no contractual intent.

11.12. In order for a contract to be legal and binding, consideration must be given. Must this consideration always be in the form of money?

No, but money is one of the strongest forms of contract consideration. Parties to a contract may agree to give up certain legal rights or duties that they would normally perform. In this case, consideration becomes the price paid for a promise. It should be noted that whatever consideration is given, it must be "legally sufficient."

11.13. Contracts cannot be made with everyone. Who can make contracts, and what are the implications of the limitation?

The decision as to who can enter into contractual agreements is based on competency. In the main, the concern is with minors, the insane, and corporations. Most contracts made by marketing people are with corporations.

A corporation is considered by law to be an artificially created being, and its ability to contract is limited by its charter or the powers implied by the charter.   If a corporation enters into a contractual agreement that is not within the power granted by its charter, the agreement will be unenforceable by either party.   Clearly, before any agreement is made with a corporation, corporate powers to contract should be ascertained.

11.14.   A contract may not violate a specific law, but may still be held null and void.   Under what circumstances can this occur?

Any contract which violates a law is unenforceable.   In addition, the law will not respect contracts which may be damaging to the health, morals and general welfare of society.   Such contracts are considered to be contrary to public interest and therefore are not enforceable.

11.15.   Some business is still concluded with a handshake.   Is such an action considered a contract?

Yes, a handshake as well as an oral agreement are still enforceable as legal contracts.   However, the problems associated with such agreements are seldom worth the money saved by not using an attorney to prepare a written contract.   In general, it's difficult for parties to an oral contract to agree on its points at a later time.   Each party usually remembers only the things that were most important to her or him.   Also, over the years, memory of an agreement can fade or become muddled.   Finally, such contracts can cause all sorts of problems for the survivors of individuals who entered into them.   A written contract is much more functional, because it is a document which, when read by the contracting parties can be affirmed, modified, or dropped.

11.16.   Once a contract has been agreed upon and signed, is it possible to change it?

Yes.   Any contract can be modified at any time, as long as the contracting parties agree to the changes.

11.17.   In the United States there has been considerable activity to systemize commercial transactions.   The first bits of concerted work resulted in the Uniform Sales Act.   However, weaknesses in this Act have lead to the adoption of the Uniform Commercial Code. Eventually, the Code will replace Uniform Sales Act.   What is the most important point of the Code as it relates to marketing activities?

According to the Code, property ownership passes once the goods contracted for are in a deliverable state.   Therefore, when goods have been set aside for the customer with whom the manufacturer has entered into a contract, title to the goods has passed.   This is a very much abbreviated summary of the law.   It would be wise for any businessperson to have a copy of the complete Code and to understand it before entering into any sales agreements.

11.18.   The points made in previous problems relating to contractual law relate to many things, including sales.   However, to be specific, certain business terms must be defined precisely.   What are the definitions, according to the Code, of the words "goods," and "contract?"

The Code states that goods must exist and have been legally identified before any interest in them can pass.   Existing goods are presently owned or possessed.   This distinction is made to differentiate existing goods from future goods which have not yet been identified.   According to the Code, a *contract* is an agreement which is generally limited to the present or future sale of goods. Thus, a contract may be made at the time goods are transferred and consideration is received.   A contract may also be made to sell at a future date; it is considered executed when goods and consideration change hands.

11.19. With respect to the interstate commerce price competition clause of the Robinson-Patman Act, (a) under what conditions can it be invoked?   (b) How can prosecution be avoided?

(a) Before the Robinson-Patman interstate commerce clause can be invoked, it must be shown that the price discrimination tends to create a monopoly or might have adverse affects on competitors.

(b) The circumstances under which a person accused of these violations may avoid prosecution are as follows:

(1) If it can be proven that the price differences are the result of differences in cost of manufacture, sale, or delivery; or of different quantities sold.

(2) If it can be shown that the price differences were necessary to meet competition and that the price reductions were made in good faith.

11.20. What purpose is served by the brokerage payment clause of the Robinson-Patman Act?

By making brokerage and other allowance payments illegal except where a legitimate service was performed, this law tries to prevent hidden price concessions.   The clause does not prohibit legitimate brokerage activity and charges.   It deals only with those who would grant unjustified price concessions, since doing so might tend to create a monopoly or exert undue pressure on other companies in a less advantageous position.

11.21. Discuss the promotional services section of the Robinson-Patman Act.

According to the Robinson-Patman Act, a company that offers promotional services to its resale customers must make them available to all such customers on proportionally equal terms.   For example, many food manufacturers provide extensive advertising allowances as well as direct promotional help to the individual stores and chains that buy and sell their products.   Under the law, all must be treated in an equal fashion; different terms for different customers would have the same effect as price discrimination.

The intent of this section of the law is good, but it is difficult to interpret.   Among the major areas of difficulty are:

(1) The problem of adequately defining promotional allowances, services, and facilities.

(2) The ease with which price discrimination attempts can be disguised (e.g., by providing hard-to-document promotional services).

(3) The problem of defining competing customers.   Two food chains might be considered competitors, but would promotional allowances to one when competition is minimal be justified? There are other areas in which this section of the act become ambiguous, but these are beyond the scope of this book.   However, it is important to note that there has been considerable litigation over the years on this portion of the act.

Chapter 12

Marketing Management and Control

12.1 INTRODUCTION

The need for information is ever-present in the marketing environment. A successful marketing program should begin with good research. A steady input of marketing data is needed to keep an active program on course. The completion of a program signals the need for evaluation; a program's successes and failures can help determine the direction and probable success of future programs.

The information generated by a well-conceived and carefully managed marketing program can be used throughout the company. Periodic progress reports alert those in positions of responsibility (e.g., finance, manufacturing, purchasing, etc.) to potential problems as well as good results that can be further enhanced.

Planning for large companies usually involves the use of elaborate systems which are integrated with electronic data processing. The smaller company plans in a less complicated way, but the need for planning and information is just as important to them as it is for the giants.

12.2 MARKET PLANNING, MANAGEMENT, AND CONTROL

Marketing planning and a control system should be developed concurrently to insure optimal effectiveness. Essentially, most of what has been stated in previous chapters relates to planning. Pricing strategy, distribution systems, research, and legal considerations, as well as product planning and promotion all provide guidance as well as benchmarks for the measurement and control of the marketing program once it gets under way.

EXAMPLE 1.

Plans and controls should be made for both short- and long-range conditions. When the product life cycle can be determined, such planning builds in various checkpoints for reviewing marketing activity. This is one of the most important aspects of a control system, because periodic reviews of a particular program enable management to detect and deal with potential problems before they reach crisis proportions.

For example, a company planning marketing strategy for a new camera may anticipate user demand for additional accessories and plan to introduce these products at a strategic time. Feedback from the distribution system should give the manufacturer a good idea of the plan's results. Sales that exceed the estimate are an indication of the need to increase production. Less encouraging results require explanations that will enable the manufacturer to make appropriate course corrections.

12.3 THE BASICS OF MARKETING CONTROL

The following elements are essential to the establishment of an efficient system of marketing control:

(1) A clear description of the characteristics and sizes of the markets involved.

(2) A review of the results of previous marketing programs.

(3) A clear and concise definition of the goals of the marketing program. See Section 12.5.

(4) A detailed description of the sales, marketing, and promotional efforts that will be undertaken to reach the goals.

(5) A review of the financial history of the company correlated to marketing efforts.

12.4   SOURCES OF MARKETING CONTROL INFORMATION

The most effective marketing control system draws on information from a variety of sources. While the particular emphasis depends on the company, the product, and the market, some combination of the following sources is generally used: field sales force, distributors, retailers, customers, and potential customers. The information may be derived from internal company reports and records and/or firsthand from field visits, trade shows, etc. In addition to these sources, helpful data can often be gathered from trade magazines and associations as well as government bureaus and consultants.

EXAMPLE 2.

Most trade journals publish reports on various aspects of the industries they serve. In addition to summaries of information that can be relevant to those managing and controlling a marketing program, the editors of these publications will often have panels of experts discuss the trends they anticipate.

12.5   USING THE SALES FORECAST AS A MEASUREMENT TOOL

Once the sales forecast has been developed (see Chapter 8), quotas assigned, and budgets approved, the marketing manager has a basis on which to build a system of marketing control. The figures agreed upon in the marketing plan become the goals against which progress can be measured. The intermediate goals specified in most plans become the benchmarks for periodic measurement and evaluation.

12.6   PLANNING A MARKETING CONTROL REPORT SYSTEM

The development of a marketing control report system begins with a definition of the goals and needs of the organization. Corporate goals as well as the marketing strategy influence the type of system that will be useful, and because each firm is different, each system must be tailored to specific needs.

To be most effective, marketing control reporting should be done formally, regardless of the size of the company. Most large companies use data-based systems which compute and print out data regularly, often on a daily basis. In small firms, reports may be issued weekly or even monthly. Inherent in this process is the ability to respond appropriately when goals do not coincide with actual results. Obviously, the more frequently marketing information is made available, the more quickly a company can respond to problems and successes.

EXAMPLE 3.

The nature of a company determines the sort of marketing control report system it develops. A company dealing with high volume, low margin products in a fairly narrow line, such as a manufacturer of nuts and bolts, will have limited use for complex reports. In contrast, a firm with a broad line of high-margin products, such as a clothing manufacturer of many sizes and styles, would require highly sophisticated data on a regular basis to keep business going.

EXAMPLE 4.

Any reporting system must consider the needs of the individuals who will receive and act on the reports. For example, a company manufacturing sophisticated engineered products requires a system in which engineering and materials requirement people are among those kept informed of progress. The engineers may be able to make minor product changes that will spur lagging sales or add features that will make good sales even stronger. Materials requirement people must plan for raw material needs well in advance. Poor sales may dictate a cutback in material stockpiling while good sales may require greater volume purchasing.

EXAMPLE 5.

Line and staff acceptance of the plan must be secured if it is to be effective. Even though top corporate management may not be interested in every detail, they must be included in the reporting system, and they, like everyone else who is included, should acknowledge receipt of each report.

EXAMPLE 6.

The complexity of the marketing organization must be considered when planning a reporting system. Where the channels of distribution are fairly direct and the layers of management sparse, there is usually less need for complex reporting than there would be for a firm with many geographical sales offices and a heavily layered marketing and management team.

12.7 INFORMATION TO BE INCLUDED IN MARKETING REPORTS

Every company's need for marketing data is different, but in general, the categories given below represent the range of information that will be valuable.

(1) *Sales figures.* Figures which indicate total sales as well as sales by territory, market, distribution channel, customer size, end use, and product line. The dollar value and the number of units sold should be included in the report.

(2) *Market data.* A projection of the firm's comparative share of the market as well as such information as brand awareness, outlet stocking figures, price comparisons, and terms and discounts.

(3) *Promotion and sales activity.* A periodic review of projected sales and advertising activities with actual sales results is useful to keep the marketing plan on course. If, for example, the program is on target in terms of sales expenses, but low in actual sales, there will be an opportunity to evaluate the situation and make changes.

(4) *Inventory data.* By showing trends for sales, marketing report data enables the manufacturing arm of the company to plan inventories that minimize required investment. Inventory data includes backlog information, reasons for merchandise returns, etc.

(5) *Financial data.* All marketing items relating to the company's profit and loss picture, including gross and net sales, discounts, credits, freight charges, and promotion expenses. The usefulness of the information will be determined by the needs of the firm. One firm may be satisfied with a simple comparison of current sales with figures for several recent years. Others may need much more information and require it to be correlated with numerous variables. For example, sales data correlated with advertising expenditures can provide insight into the relative effectiveness of the advertising. The same sales figures related to internal expenses, such as manufacturing, might indicate imbalances or areas for improvement.

12.8 DETERMINING THE VALUE OF A REPORTING SYSTEM

Because a marketing report system can involve considerable expense, before one is instituted, the emphasis it should receive must be determined. In other words, the company must consider the amount of information desired in terms of the cost of acquiring this information. There comes a point in the development of a marketing control program where an additional bit of information is no longer worth the expense and effort. The marginal value of that added bit of information can determine the extent of the system and the money spent to run it. In small companies, this decision is usually based on the amount of employee time required that might otherwise be spent on more productive work.

EXAMPLE 7.

A firm in a rapidly growing, dynamic market would probably need information more quickly and in greater quantities than would a firm in a slower, more stable market. The cost of information needed to compete in a fast-growing field is generally greater than that required to maintain a position in a steady market. But in either case, the cost each company incurs must be in line with all of its other costs of doing business. The price of information, while it may be relatively high in terms of dollars, may be relatively low in terms of the benefits it provides to the company.

Review Questions

1. The information developed during the administration of a marketing program is of very little value to anyone in the company except those charged with responsibility for marketing.   True or false?

   Ans.   False.   See Section 12.1.

2. Marketing planning and a system of control should be developed (*a*) independently, (*b*) concurrently, (*c*) after budgets are approved, (*d*) all of these.

   Ans.   (*b*)   See Section 12.2.

3. The benchmarks for an effective control system are determined by the goals of the marketing plan. True or false?

   Ans.   True.   See Section 12.2.

4. It is seldom necessary to institute a system of control for short-run marketing situations.   True or false?

   Ans.   False.   See Example 1.

5. One of the most important aspects of a marketing control system is its ability to spot problems and opportunity situations early enough so that appropriate action can be taken.   True or false?

   Ans.   True.   See Example 1.

6. The checkpoints in a marketing control system can be best determined from knowledge of (*a*) the product life cycle, (*b*) marketing research, (*c*) competitive sales data, (*d*) inventory figures.

   Ans.   (*a*)   See Example 1.

7. Among other things, a marketing control system should be based on (*a*) characteristics and sizes of markets involved, (*b*) goals of the marketing plan, (*c*) sales figures, (*d*) all of these.

   Ans.   (*d*)   See Section 12.3.

8. An analysis of costs as well as profits is seldom included in a marketing control program.   True or false?

   Ans.   False.   See Section 12.3.

9. In addition to the field sales force, distributors, retailers, and customers, marketing control information can be gathered from (*a*) trade magazines, (*b*) trade associations, (*c*) government bureaus, (*d*) all of these.

   Ans.   (*d*)   See Section 12.4.

10. The figures agreed upon in the marketing plan become the goals against which progress can be measured. True or false?

    Ans.   True.   See Section 12.5.

11. A control reporting system is seldom necessary in a small company.   True or false?

    Ans.   False.   See Section 12.6.

12. A company dealing with high volume, low magin products in a fairly narrow line will have little need for the complex reports needed by a company dealing with a broad line of high margin products.   True or false?

    Ans.   True.   See Example 3.

13. A marketing control reporting system must be geared to the needs of each individual concerned.   True or false?

    Ans.   True.   See Example 4.

14. Seldom is top corporate management interested in every detail of a marketing control report, but they should always be included in the routing.   True or false?

    Ans.   True.   See Example 5.

15. Before any control system is undertaken, the cost of such information and the effect it will have on performance and profits should be determined.   True or false?

    Ans.   True.   See Section 12.8.

16. A firm in a rapidly growing market has less need for information than a firm in a stable field.   True or false?

Ans.   False.   See Example 7.

17. When distribution channels are fairly direct, complex reporting is less necessary than for a firm with many offices and management levels.   True or false?

Ans.   True.   See Example 6.

18. A marketing control report includes all of the following except (*a*) sales figures, (*b*) promotion and sales activity, (*c*) inventory data, (*d*) new product proposals.

Ans.   (*d*)   See Section 12.7.

19. Market information in a control report generally includes (*a*) market share compared with that of the competitors, (*b*) price comparisons, (*c*) brand awareness information, (*d*) all of these.

Ans.   (*d*)   See Section 12.7.

20. Sales promotion activity is seldom relevant or needed in a marketing control report.   True or false?

Ans.   False.   See Section 12.7.

Solved Problems

12.1.   To be most helpful, an analysis of the performance of a marketing program should be made by comparing current results with known standards.   Such an analysis is done to locate variations from anticipated goals.   What aspects of a marketing program can be subjected to a performance analysis?

Virtually all of the activities in a marketing program can be subjected to performance analysis.   Comparisons can be made of salespeople, territories, advertising campaigns, and so on.   The goals of such research are twofold: (1) to correct problems or (2) to improve successful trends. Generally, the results of a performance analysis identify areas which should be studied in detail before any action is taken.

12.2.   Table 1 is one section of an ongoing marketing plan analysis.   It represents summary data for one year.   What general conclusions can be drawn from this information?

Table 1

Salesperson	Number of Sales Calls	Number of Orders (in units)	Sales-to-call Ratio (%)	Volume by Sales-person ($)	Average Sale (in $ per unit)	Number of Customers
North	650	212	32.6	256,000	1207	62
East	520	196	37.7	212,000	1081	49
South	244	104	42.6	123,000	1182	21
West	151	72	47.7	86,000	1194	11

Even though North made the greatest number of sales calls, had the largest dollar volume, and the largest number of orders, his sales-to-call ratio was lowest.   This might indicate that North was in a territory with the largest number of prospects, but that his selling ability was not necessarily the best.   When compared with West, whose sales-to-call ratio was fifteen percent higher than North's and who appeared to have the territory with the least potential, North's selling abilities do not appear to be strong.   It seems that the selling abilities of the two men should be evaluated carefully. West's skills might be beneficial to others (i.e., perhaps he should do sales training) and North's additional training need should be considered.   There appears to be little variance in the average sale, although the number of customers in each territory varies greatly.   The cause of this variation should be determined.   While there is no reason to assume that all territories are equal, if the variations observed can be accounted for by some external factor, such as centralization of customers in certain territories, then the performance of West is indeed outstanding and that of North is mediocre.

12.3.   In terms of Problem 12.2, evaluate the data on the comparative cost of the four salespeople in Table 2.   What action do you think should be taken?

Table 2

Salesperson	Annual Compensation ($)	Expenses ($)	Total Sales Costs ($)	Sales Volume ($)	Cost-to-sales Ratio (%)
North	22,000	5600	27,600	256,000	10.7
East	23,500	5800	29,300	212,000	13.8
South	21,000	5100	26,100	123,000	21.2
West	21,000	3700	24,700	86,000	32.2

Despite the fact that salesperson North appeared to be relatively inefficient in terms of his sale-to-call ratio (see Problem 12.2), his cost-to-sales ratio (found by dividing sales volume into total sales costs) is lowest of all.   North and East are in line, but South and West are out of line.   Since it appeared from Table 1 that West was a superior salesperson, the nature of his territory should be investigated.   Perhaps there is not sufficient business to keep the territory open.   If this is the case, it would be important to find West a territory where his abilities could be used profitably.   Note that these cost-to-sales ratios are used simply for illustration purposes and do not represent any general standards.   In some industries they are considerably higher; in others, much lower.

12.4.   A conventional performance analysis does not always provide all of the answers.   As shown in Problems 12.2 and 12.3, what appears to be poor performance may be due to conditions beyond the control of the individuals.   Explain how index numbers can be used to analyze performance.

When marketing plan goals are set on a realistic basis, which takes into account all of the variables within territories, it is possible to have reliable benchmarks against which a valid review can be made.   The simplest and most popular method uses an index number, which is found using the following formula:

$$\frac{\text{Actual sales (\$)}}{\text{Anticipated goal (\$)}} \times 100 = \text{Index number}$$

This calculation produces a percentage which is multiplied by 100 to eliminate the decimal. Thus 100 would be a perfect sales performance; the salesperson sold the exact volume that was assigned to the territory.   The index numbers make it possible for the marketing manager to see at a glance just how well salespeople are performing, relative to their goals and to each other.

12.5. From the data in Table 3, evaluate each salesperson's performance in terms of an index number.

Table 3

Salesperson	A	B	C
Sales Goal	$200,000	$175,000	$228,000
Actual Sales	$196,000	$162,000	$246,000

$$\text{Salesperson A:} \quad \frac{196,000}{200,000} \times 100 = 98$$

$$\text{Salesperson B:} \quad \frac{162,000}{175,000} \times 100 = 92$$

$$\text{Salesperson C:} \quad \frac{246,000}{228,000} \times 100 = 108$$

From this information, it can be seen that all three salespeople have performed well. Two were very close to their goals, and one exceeded it.

12.6. A manufacturer of machine tools divides its market into four geographical territories. According to the best available information, there are no qualitative differences in the characteristics of each territory other than the qualitative potential for sales. What conclusions might be drawn from the performance analysis of the sales for one year given in Table 4?

Table 4

Territory	Percent of Total Market	Anticipated Sales ($)	Actual Sales ($)	Performance Index
A	30	600,000	650,000	108
B	20	400,000	290,000	73
C	15	300,000	375,000	125
D	35	700,000	480,000	69
	100	2,000,000	1,795,000	

Territories A and C exceeded their sales quotas, while B and D were under budget. It appears that the assumption of no qualitative difference should be challenged. The abilities of the salespeople in B and D might also be evaluated. In addition, it would be instructive to determine why territory C was twenty-five percent ahead of its goals. Is such performance an inherent characteristic of the territory or were the salespeople that much more productive this year? The same analysis would be helpful in understanding Territory A's performance.

12.7. An audit is defined as an examination and verification; the word is generally used to describe an accounting procedure. However, there is also a marketing audit. How did such an audit come into being? How is it defined today?

Marketing audits were originally undertaken by firms that were having marketing difficulties. Those doing the audit were looking for problem causes with the hope of solving them. The intention was to solve an immediate problem; there was seldom any thought of the future.

However, the marketing audit today is a tool for both the troubled company and the successful one. No matter how successful a marketing effort may be, it is sometimes possible to make it even more successful by analyzing the elements of success.   In addition, there are times when the manner in which the elements of the marketing mix are interacting to produce a success is not clear.   The marketing audit helps explain the process so that it can be used even more effectively.

A marketing audit can encompass the entire marketing effort of a company, or it can focus on a specific marketing activity within the program.   Basically, the audit tries to *determine* what is being done, *evaluate* what is being done, and then *recommend* what should be done.

12.8.   What are the general characteristics of a good audit?

The audit should be done on a regular basis, rather than only when trouble arises.   It should evaluate the structure of the marketing activity as well as the performance of the various programs and people involved.   The audit should include all elements of a marketing program, not just those that may be in trouble.

12.9.   The need for a marketing audit is usually caused by one of two things.   What are they?

Success can result in complacency.   When this happens, the marketing people's guard may be down, allowing competitors to steal the show.   A marketing audit can pick up a lackadaisical attitude like this, and help keep a program on course.

Markets are dynamic.   By the time a marketing plan has been approved and put into action, conditions may have changed.   Unless an audit points out this problem, the plan may fail.   Therefore, a marketing audit should not only be concerned with present adjustments, it should anticipate changes in market conditions that may require further adjustments in the future.

12.10.   There are two types of marketing audits.   What are they and how do they differ from each other?

There are horizontal and vertical marketing audits.   The horizontal audit deals with the entire marketing effort of a company.   It is concerned with reviewing the interrelationships of the various elements of the marketing mix, but does not deal with the details of each.   However, during a horizontal audit, discrepancies and problems with the individual components may appear; it is the job of the vertical audit to examine these specific problems.   Unless a specific problem is obvious and a vertical audit can be begun immediately, most audits begin with a horizontal study.

12.11.   What three steps are usually taken in a marketing audit?

The first step is a determination of how the marketing functions are being handled.   Once this information has been gathered, an appraisal of the information is undertaken.   Finally, recommendations are made on the basis of the first two steps.

12.12.   The initial task of a marketing audit is to get a clear picture of the company's marketing objectives.   Discuss some of the steps involved and the problems that may be encountered.

Few companies do any extensive market planning, and their definition of a marketing objective may be as vague as just stating that they want to build a high sales volume.   To complicate matters further, individual executives within the same company may have different ideas of what the marketing objectives are.   A well-planned audit attempts to straighten out this problem.   Obviously, a marketing objective must be very specific and based on goals that can be realistically attained.   If, for example, a company feels that it can, with its present resources, capture ten percent more of a $100,000,000 market, the goal should be to increase the present level of sales by $10,000,000.   Stated in these terms, the goal is specific and can be used for planning and management purposes.

It is quite possible for objectives to become obsolete during the execution of a marketing program.   In periods of inflation, dollar volume goals for a program may not be sufficient by the time the program nears its end.   Therefore, periodic reevaluation is often required.

A marketing audit can have some noneconomic problems to solve as well.   For example, a company whose sole goal is to produce the best cotton sails for sailboat racing has missed the boat in a marketing sense. No one races with cotton sails, no matter how good they may be. If the market wants Dacron, the goal should be to produce the best Dacron sails. This approach begins with a consumer need, rather than with a goal that is internally generated. It may be necessary to reorient a company's objectives in terms of market needs. This often happens in high technology companies where products are the output of fertile technical minds. Those involved in product development are often less concerned with the needs of the market than with the uniqueness of the product.

Finally, a marketing audit helps to focus the company's attention on its most productive markets. A company often has a success in one field, but finds it difficult to expand sales. An audit may turn up a saturation situation and recommend the exploration of new markets.

12.13. After the first stage of a marketing audit has been conducted, the next step is to review the program for achieving the objectives. Describe this process.

At this point, the audit is concerned with the structure of the program. The program areas of greatest value to the audit are those related to decisions and policies involving the allocation of marketing mix elements. The audit will try to determine what level of the company's resources are being directed to the marketing effort, and whether this level is sufficient when related to the company's marketing goals.

It is also important to discover how the total marketing budget is allocated. The aim is to identify specific elements of the market where an increased effort might pay off, as well as the elements on which too much is being spent. After each element has been analyzed, the best level of appropriation and activity for each is determined. The best blend when the plan was first formulated may not be right at the time of the audit. If the audit results show what can be done to improve the mix, then it will have been effective.

12.14. In the next phase of a marketing audit, the procedures for the implementation of the marketing plan are reviewed. Describe the process.

It is entirely possible that the audit may have turned up very few problems in the previous steps, and yet the marketing program may be foundering. The causes are often found at the tactical and operational level. Some of the operational areas that should be investigated include the methods used to choose, train, and supervise salespeople. Creative advertising strategy may be wrong or it might be on target but placed in the wrong media. Distribution methods might be out of sync. There may be problems in order handling. If, for example, the marketing program is producing orders at the anticipated rate, but manufacturing and shipping are lagging, there will be discrepancies between goals and achievements. Trade discounts might be too high. Even with sales on target, this could cause profits to be off. Every element of the implementation of the marketing plan should be scrutinized. When a problem is big enough to be obvious, it is usually taken care of. However, a marketing audit usually turns up a lot of small problems, each of which, in isolation, is not sufficient to cause a firm major difficulties. When combined, their effect can be serious.

12.15. Because the marketing audit is essentially a review of work being done by company individuals, it may be difficult to get unbiased information. How can an audit be undertaken so that bias is reduced or eliminated?

When there are several functioning marketing departments within a company, the bias problem may be solved by having marketing people from other divisions conduct the audit. This does not completely eliminate the possibility of bias, but if the managers of each department recognize the need to be impartial it can be a practical approach.

The audit may be conducted by a senior executive such as a marketing vice-president if the marketing department is large and includes line and staff responsibilities. Usually a person with this title is responsible for overall department activity, while the marketing manager who reports to him has operational marketing responsibilities. Although the possibility of bias remains, enlightened managers are usually able to control most of it.

Large companies often establish separate auditing departments. Conducting a marketing audit might be only one function of such a department. Management audits and evaluations of other functions such as personnel administration are among their additional activities. Sometimes it is advisable to appoint a task force made up of executives from different departments within the company to conduct the audit. This approach can be quite effective because of the knowledge each has of the total operation.

By far the most effective audits are conducted by outside specialists. Not only is the problem of bias eliminated, but also the company benefits from the experience the consultant has had with similar companies. In addition, because the outside consultant is doing only the audit, he or she can devote full time to it. When individuals within the company work on an audit, their regular work may suffer. This problem is eliminated when a consultant is used.

12.16. The net sales portion of an accounting operating statement can be very helpful in controlling the marketing effort. How are these figures generally viewed and what are some of the limitations of their use?

From the operating statement, it is possible to get figures for the total number of unit sales as well as for the dollar volume. The numbers are useful when compared with goals established in a marketing plan, but they become especially helpful when they are analyzed on the basis of different sales territories, product lines, individual markets time frames, and order sizes.

As useful as an analysis of total sales volume can be, it is often difficult to get the information needed to make an accurate and detailed study. However, companies with automatic data processing systems have found that this data can be obtained readily. Even when all the data is current and available, the sales/volume analysis has limited value by itself. When it is used with a review of marketing costs, its value in greatly enhanced. See Problem 12.17.

12.17. The sales/volume analysis can be helpful as a benchmark, but to be most useful, information on the profitability of products, territories, and so on should be analyzed. The term generally applied to this task is distribution analysis. Describe the process and the benefits that accrue to its users.

A marketing or distribution cost analysis is very closely tied to the company's accounting system. When budgetary goals have been established and the raw data for the cost analysis is available in accounting systems, it is then only a matter of identifying variances between budgeted and actual figures. All of the firm's marketing costs, such as those involved in direct sales, advertising, and warehousing, are checked against current figures. When trends can be predicted it is possible for management to react accordingly. If, for example, sales are running ahead of goals, it will be necessary to budget for additional material for the products. Such costs, as well as the anticipated benefits of additional salespersons and increased advertising, can be predicted accurately.

12.18. Marketing cost analyses can be performed in several ways. The simplest and least expensive is an accounting ledger analysis. Describe how the review is done.

When an accounting ledger analysis is prepared, expense totals for all marketing activities are listed and simply compared with similar totals for previous years. These figures may be expressed as percentages of net sales to provide the marketing person with guide numbers on which to base an evaluation. However, note that no business is the same year after year. Competition comes and goes, inflation waxes and wanes, and markets become saturated. When this simple technique is used, the numbers it produces must be viewed against a background of these and other marketing conditions. Trade associations often provide averages with which a firm can compare itself. These comparisons can be misleading, too, and it is important to weigh all the factors to be sure that the comparisons are appropriate.

12.19. When more detail is needed, a functional cost analysis can be performed. Discuss the concept and its use.

Where expense totals are used in a simple ledger analysis, detailed figures for all marketing-related activities are not available. A functional cost analysis focuses on expenses incurred in specific marketing activities.   For example, if it were seen that all expenses were reasonably stable over the past five years, but that advertising costs doubled in one year, further investigation would be indicated.   If this detail can be shown to correlate with a profitable increase in sales, the analysis has provided the feedback needed to increase sales further.

12.20. A company with many territories can go even further with a functional cost analysis.   Describe the process.

A study of the cost and profitability of each market can be made by segmenting the market by territories, products, types of customers, and order sizes.   When management has information on each variable in each territory, it is usually possible to spot problems and successes very quickly.   If, for example, all territories but one had profitable operations, and it is discovered that the weak territory had an abnormal number of small orders and few large ones, it might turn out that the cost of processing these many small orders was eating into profits.

When accounting procedures are standardized for all territories, and all expenses are subtracted from gross margin, the result is net profit.   The net profit figures alone can be a signal to look more deeply into the details of a functional analysis which is done by market segments.

12.21. The best control is possible when volume and cost analysis are used together.   How might decisions to realign sales territories be made with information gathered from volume and cost analysis?

When it is possible to pinpoint the strengths and weaknesses of each territory, the greatest possibility for improvement exists.   Knowing what has been successful in strong territories may be applied to those lagging behind, and it may be possible to make the strong territories even stronger.   Occasionally salespeople can be transferred to places where they will be more effective, and territorial borders can be shifted to accommodate inherent strengths and weaknesses.

If the company has not kept up with changes in the industry it serves, it may find that its customers have moved to areas where sales strengths are lacking.   Major industry shifts have taken place regularly in the United States.   The printing industry moved away from Eastern metropolitan centers, and the South, not New England, is now the center of the furniture making industry.   Of course, any accounting analysis, such as we have been discussing, would not lead to such a conclusion directly.   But when sales in a territory drop, it is important to know why.

Final Examination

The answers you give to the questions in this examination will help you to evaluate how well you have mastered the material in Chapters 7 through 12.

1. Market research must be concerned with management as well as marketing. Discuss this concept.

    The purpose of market research is not only to develop facts and forecasts for marketing personnel, but also to provide information for those in all other departments. For example, the director of production planning must know how much of the product is expected to be sold in order to plan for manufacture without interruption. The personnel department must know whether anticipated sales will require additional people. Financial people must be prepared to plan for the company's capital requirements.

2. What is the difference between primary and secondary data?

    Data collected for the first time from sources other than published information is referred to as primary data. The results of interviews, surveys, and other basic analysis fall into this category.

    Secondary data is found in previously published material. Books, magazines, conference reports, and similar sources provide secondary data.

3. Discuss the build-up approach to marketing forecasting.

    When this technique is used, forecasting is based on estimates of future demand provided by different organizational units within the company. The information is usually requested from salespeople, distributors, retailers, and other people within the organization that management believes can make worthwhile contributions. Forecasts are based on the trends detected in the information collected internally.

4. What is the major disadvantage of using the company sales force to gather marketing information?

    While salespeople may be perfectly capable of gathering information, in doing the research they are kept from doing what they were hired to do—sell. If the research can be undertaken as part of regular selling activity, or if it is designed to take only a small portion of the salespeople's working time, it's often a sound practice. However, the loss in sales that can occur when salespeople are doing research often costs more than the cost to employ professional researchers.

5. What are attitudes and how are they formed?

    Attitudes are lasting favorable or unfavorable evaluations, emotional feelings, or behavioral tendencies toward a thing or an idea. Because buying intentions as well as actual purchasing behavior are, in part, determined by an individual's attitudes, their study and use are important in marketing. Attitudes are formed as a result of information gathered through past experience, in relationships with individuals and groups, and by individual personality traits. From a marketing point of view, attitudes are largely responsible for the repeat purchase of products which are difficult to distinguish from others in absolute terms. Most cigarettes, for example, taste pretty much the same, despite the protestations of smokers. But few smokers will accept a substitute when the store is out of their favorite brand.

6. Discuss three ways attitudes can be changed.

    Attitude change generally requires highly persuasive communications. The communications may be face-to-face, as in a personal selling situation, or in the form of advertising. To be most effective, the communications should try to modify one or more of the dimensions of an attitude. A marketer who wants to work on the cognitive aspects of an attitude might provide strong evidence of the product's benefits, or the deficiencies of a competitor's product. It is also possible to work on the emotional dimension of an attitude by providing a strong argument, such as a testimonial. However, most attitude shifts occur after a person is tempted to act in a way contrary to his or her customary behavior. Thus the cents-off coupon approach tries to break an established attitudinal and behavioral pattern.

7. Describe the elements of the promotional mix.

Effective promotion depends on an appropriate blend of advertising, sales promotion, personal selling, and public relations. Advertising is, in general, a nonpersonal sales presentation. Personal selling involves direct communication between the seller and the prospect. This may be done face to face, or over the telephone. Public relations is communications with the market or audience for a product or service that is placed in print publications or broadcast media at no charge. However, paid advertising is often used to carry a public relations message. Any activity other than advertising, personal selling, and publicity is considered sales promotion. For example, in-store displays, brochures, and give-aways are considered sales promotion.

8. Why does a pushing marketing strategy depend more on personal selling than on advertising?

When this strategy is used, heavy emphasis is usually placed on direct selling to the channels of distribution. This may include the same channels that are involved in a pulling strategy, but in this case the thrust of the effort is directed at the intermediaries who will buy and sell the product to retailers. In this situation, the manufacturer depends on aggressive intermediary selling to get the product to retail outlets. Once the product has reached the retail level, manufacturers often support this selling effort with advertising aimed at the consumer.

9. What is the most practical way to establish a promotional budget? Describe how the method is used.

A budget based on specific goals is generally most effective. This task approach not only provides more flexibility than other budgetary methods, but also gives management a clearer view of ongoing program productivity. When the task method is used, goals must be established first. They may be stated as increases in sales, or the acquisition of a specified larger segment of a market. Whatever measure is used, the budget is based on quantitative goals. Once the goals have been accepted by management, estimates can be made of the cost to reach them. If the costs are out of line, adjustments can be made either in the promotional program or the marketing expectations. Periodic checks of the program's effectiveness permit corrections to be made. If a program is especially effective, more money may be allocated to take advantage of the momentum it generated. Conversely, expenditures may be reduced if a plan doesn't live up to projections.

10. What is a trademark?

A trademark is a symbol that provides immediate identification to the goods or services of a company or individual. Some trademarks are made-up words such as Exxon. Others are words used to convey a specific image, such as the Cougar automobile. Words that suggest a product's uses are effective trademarks. Gum-out says quite a bit about the job that will be done by an automotive additive.

Words that suggest quality can also be used effectively. Blue-Ribbon beer suggests awards and endorsements. Finally, a trademark can be a distinctive graphic design. Consider Arm and Hammer on the box of baking soda.

11. Describe the major point of (1) the Hazardous Substance Labeling Act; (2) the Food, Drug, and Cosmetic Act; and (3) the Fair Packing and Labeling Act.

(1) The Hazardous Substance Labeling Act gives the Food and Drug Administration the power to judge household products as hazardous under certain circumstances and to require that appropriate warnings be given to consumers.

(2) The Food, Drug, and Cosmetic Act modified previous legislation and greatly strengthened regulations relating to adulteration and labeling of cosmetic and therapeutic devices.

(3) The Fair Packing and Labeling Act states that manufacturers must provide the identification of the producer, the quantity of the product packed, and other factors that will be important to the consumer.

12. What five points should be considered first when developing a marketing control program?

   1. A clear description of the characteristics and sizes of the markets involved.
   2. A detailed description of the sales, marketing, and promotional efforts that will be undertaken to reach the goals.
   3. A clear and concise definition of the goals of the marketing program.
   4. A review of the results of previous marketing programs that may bear on the success of the program being planned.
   5. A review of the financial history of the company correlated with the marketing efforts.

13. What are the general characteristics of a soundly conceived marketing audit?

   The audit should be done on a regular basis, and it should provide an evaluation of the structure of the marketing activity as well as the performance of the programs and people involved. All elements of the marketing program should be included, not just those that may seem to be successful, or in trouble. The marketing audit points out ways to improve the performance of successful elements as well as those that may be lagging.

14. What three steps are usually taken in a marketing audit?

   The audit generally begins with a determination of how the marketing functions are being handled. When this information has been gathered, it is evaluated. On the basis of the evaluation, auditors can make specific recommendations for improvement.

15. Cite some of the advantages of using the telephone to conduct market research.

   Telephone surveys are less flexible than personal interviews, but more flexible than studies done by mail. The telephone study can be conducted more rapidly and at less cost than a personal study, for the same number of respondents. It is possible to sample wide geographic areas without the bother of locating and using local interviewers or sending professionals into the area. It is also possible to gather information more quickly by phone than with personal interviews, a point which is important when the questions asked are timely.

Glossary

Adoption process.   The steps in a consumer's decision-making process through which a product passes on its way to acceptance, i.e., awareness, interest, evaluation, trial, and adoption.

Advertising.   A nonpersonal sales presentation, set at a predetermined level, aimed at an audience within a specific period of time, and paid for by an identifiable sponsor.

Agent wholesaling middleman or intermediary.   One who performs wholesaling tasks, but does not take title to the products being handled.

Area sampling.   A market research survey technique which uses geography, such as blocks in a city, as the basis for selecting a random sample test population.

Attitude.   The evaluation a person makes of an idea or an object.

Auction company.   An agent wholesaler who brings buyers and sellers together at one place for the purpose of goods examination and sale through open bidding.

Average cost.   A figure obtained by dividing total cost by the quantity associated with these costs.

Average fixed cost.   A figure which is obtained by dividing total fixed costs by the associated quantity.

Average revenue.   A figure obtained by dividing total revenue by the associated quantity.

Average variable cost.   Total variable costs divided by the relevant quantity.

Basing point.   A system of charging freight costs in which transportation costs from a location nearest the buyer are included in factory billing.

Brand.   Identification in the form of a name, symbol, term, design, or some combination thereof, which differentiates a product from its competition.

Brand insistence.   The final stage of the brand acceptance process, in which consumers refuse to accept substitutes and search for the desired brand.

Brand name.   The portion of product identification that can be verbalized.

Brand preference.   The second stage in the process of brand acceptance, in which consumers select a particular brand based on previous experience with it.

Brand recognition.   The first stage in the brand acceptance process.   At this point the consumer is simply familiar with the existence of a particular product.

Breakeven analysis.   A financial evaluation of the profit potential of alternative prices.

Broker.   An agent wholesaler who specializes in certain products and functions by bringing together buyers and sellers.

Brokerage allowance.   A discount provided for brokerage services.

Buyer's market.   An economic condition in which an abundance of goods exceeds the demand for the goods.

Cash-and-carry wholesaler.   One who sells only for cash; credit and delivery services are not available.

Cash discount.   An amount of money the seller will allow the buyer to deduct from the price of goods or services in return for prompt payment.

Census.   The collection of data for market research purposes.

Chain stores.   A group of stores owned and operated by one company.   Each carries the same merchandise, but operates in different geographical areas.

Class action suit.   A lawsuit instituted by a group of consumers who have a common complaint relating to unfair business practices, against one individual or company.

Closed sales territories. Sales areas in which agents are guaranteed exclusive selling rights by the manufacturer.

Closing. The final step in a selling situation in which the salesperson asks for the order.

Commission merchant. An agent wholesaler who has physical control over the merchandise and earns commissions from the sales of goods handled.

Communication. The transmission of a message from a sender to a receiver.

Comparative advertising. Advertising which makes direct comparisons of the product being promoted with those of competitors.

Competitive bidding. A situation in which several suppliers submit price quotations based on the buyer's specifications for a product or service.

Concentrated marketing. A marketing program in which one market is singled out for intense, exclusive treatment.

Concept testing. The process of evaluating a new product idea prior to its actual physical development.

Consumer behavior. The manner in which an individual reaches decisions related to the selection, purchase, and use of goods and services.

Consumer goods. Products made expressly for use by the final consumer, as opposed to those made for resale or for further use in the manufacture of other goods.

Consumer innovator. One who is among the first to accept and use new products and services.

Consumerism. A movement in which consumers demand that marketers pay more attention to their needs and wants as well as to product quality and service.

Contest. A sales promotion technique in which a company tries to attract attention to its products by offering rewards to winning entrants.

Convenience goods. Items such as cigarettes, beer, and chewing gum which are purchased frequently, immediately, and with little effort.

Cooperative advertising. A system in which advertising costs of particular items are shared by the manufacturers and the retailers.

Corrective advertising. Advertising required by the Federal Trade Commission to correct previous deceptive advertising.

Cost-plus. A pricing system in which the cost of the product or service is used as a base to which a profit factor is added.

Counteradvertising. A Federal Trade Commission plan under which consumer groups can advertise against the sale of a product they consider harmful or uneconomical.

Coupon. A sales promotion device providing a purchase incentive in the form of a price reduction when it is presented with the specified product at the checkout counter.

Creeping inflation. Modest but steady increases in the general price level.

Culture. A system of learned values, ideas, and attitudes.

Decoding. A term used to describe a consumer's interpretation of the message portion of the communications process.

Demand curve. A graphic representation of the quantity of a product or service demanded at various price levels.

Demarketing. A process by which a producer attempts to reduce demand for a product to a point compatible with production capabilities.

Demographics. Statistics which describe prospective buyers in terms of such factors as age, sex, education, and income level.

Department store. A large retail organization in which merchandise is separated into departments for the purpose of service, promotion, and control. There are many departments, each specializing in a different type of merchandise.

Differential marketing. The use of different marketing programs for separate segments of the market.

Diffusion. The process by which new products are accepted by consumers. It begins with innovator use and proceeds through early adapters, early majority, late majority, and laggards.

Discount store. A retail organization offering low prices and minimal customer services.

Discretionary income. That part of a person's income which is left after spending for necessities.

Distribution warehouses. Facilities for product storage and reshipment. Used to facilitate the rapid movement of goods when trading areas are remote from point of manufacture.

Distributor. A wholesaler who takes title to the goods being handled.

Drop shipper. A merchant who sells products which are shipped directly to the buyer by the manufacturer.

Economic order quantity. The optimum quantity of a product as determined by balancing the cost to keep inventory against the cost of making sales.

Engel's Laws. The results of a study done by Ernst Engel which sought to predict economic activity based on an individual's increasing income. They state that as income increases: (1) a smaller percentage will go for food, (2) the percentage spent on housing and household operations and clothing would remain constant, and (3) the percentage spent on other items would increase.

Exclusive dealing contract. A contract which prohibits middlemen (or intermediaries) from handling competitive products, except where such action would have the effect of reducing competition or creating a monopoly.

Exclusive distribution. A situation in which a manufacturer grants exclusive distribution rights to an intermediary in a particular territory.

Family brand. A brand name used to identify the numerous products of a single manufacturer.

Family life cycle. A description of the process of family formation and dissolution. Begins with bachelor stage and proceeds through young married with no children, young married with children, older married with dependent children, older married with no children at home, and solitary survivors. People respond to different sales appeals at different life stages.

Feedback. A term used to describe the process by which information is returned to the sender. For marketing, feedback includes information on sales, customer reactions, etc., that help fine-tune a marketing campaign.

Fixed costs. Costs which do not vary with changes in output; e.g., rent, depreciation, insurance, etc.

F.O.B. origin. A term stating that the price of goods quoted does not include shipping charges, which are the buyer's responsibility.

Form utility. An economic term which states that value increases when raw materials are converted to finished goods.

Franchise. An arrangement by which individuals can sell the products of a manufacturer under terms specified by the manufacturer.

Freight forwarder. An intermediary who consolidates the shipments of several companies to effect cost saving with carload lots.

Full-function wholesaler. An intermediary who provides services such as storage, delivery, credit, return privileges, and marketing intelligence for his or her retail customers.

Functional middleman. See Agent and Broker.

General merchandise stores. Retail stores, such as department and discount stores, which carry a wide range of merchandise in depth.

Generic name.   A commonly used word that describes a particular type of product.

Import quota.   A government-imposed restriction placed on the quantity of certain goods that may enter the country.

Impulse items.   Products that are bought with little thought or effort, and which are usually placed near the store's cash registers.

Industrial distributor.   A wholesaler operating in the industrial goods market.

Industrial goods.   Goods used in the production of other goods for resale.

Inflation.   A rise in price levels which results in reduced consumer purchasing power.

Institutional advertising.   Advertising for the purpose of promoting a concept, or the goodwill of a company or organization.

Jobber.   A wholesaler.

Job-order production.   A production system in which products are made specifically to fill existing customer orders.

Label.   The identifying portion of a package which generally contains the brand name, name of the manufacturer or distributor, product ingredients, and suggested uses.

Life style.   The way in which people live their lives in career, social, and consumer terms.

Limited function wholesaler.   A wholesaler who, by limiting the number of services provided for retail customers, reduces the costs of such servicing.

Limited-line store.   A retail store which offers a complete selection of a narrow line of products.

List price.   The full price that is quoted to a potential customer and is generally recommended by the manufacturer.

Loss leader.   A product that is advertised at a deliberately low price in order to attract customers into a store.

Mail order sales.   A selling system in which products are promoted by mail, space advertising, telephone, radio, television, etc., and orders received are delivered by mail.

Manufacturer's agent.   An intermediary who sells lines of related but noncompetitive products for several manufacturers, usually has a protected territory, and seldom stocks or takes title to the goods sold.

Marginal cost.   The change in total cost resulting from the production of one additional unit.

Marginal revenue.   The change in total revenue resulting from the selling of an additional unit.

Market.   An identifiable group of consumers with purchasing power who have the willingness and ability to pay for a product or service.

Marketing.   The development and implementation of sales and distribution systems for products or services.

Marketing channels.   The paths taken by a product on its way to the consumer.

Marketing communications.   Messages created for the purpose of facilitating the marketing process, e.g., advertising copy, catalogs, etc.

Marketing concept.   The idea that products should be designed and created to fill a consumer need and provide a profit to the producer.

Marketing mix.   The blending of the elements of product planning, distribution strategy, promotion, and price to meet the needs of a specific market.

Marketing research.   The systematic gathering, recording, and analyzing of information relating to the marketing of products and services.

Marketing strategy.   An overall plan for the use of the elements of the marketing mix to carry out a marketing program.

Market segmentation.　The identification of markets which require separate sales approaches.

Market share.　The portion of a market controlled by a particular producer.　Reaching a specified share of market is often stated as a goal of a marketing plan.

Markup.　The amount of money added to cost to determine the selling price.

Merchant wholesaler.　A wholesaler who takes title to the goods handled.

Message.　The information transmitted in a communications system.

Middleman (or intermediary).　An individual or a firm operating between a producer and the consumer or the industrial user.

Missionary sales.　The task of selling from scratch; e.g., introducing a new product, a new company, or a new concept.　Such selling is often used only to introduce the product, and actual sales may be made by other salespeople later on.

Monopolistic competition.　An economic term which describes a condition in which a large number of sellers offer a heterogeneous product.　Product differentiation allows each marketer some control over price.

Monopoly.　An economic term which describes a condition in which one seller dominates the market.

Motive.　The inner state that directs a person toward the satisfaction of a specific goal.

National brands.　Products made and sold by manufacturers.

New product development.　The process of determining market needs and developing products to meet them.

Observational study.　Research conducted by actually watching subjects in test situations.

Odd pricing.　A form of psychological pricing, which uses prices having odd endings, such as $4.95.

Oligopoly.　A market condition characterized by relatively few sellers and which is difficult to penetrate by others.

Open dating.　The marking of perishable or semiperishable goods to show the last possible day they can be sold.

Opinion leader.　An individual whose opinion is respected by and who influences others in a group.

Patent law.　Legislation which guarantees and protects an inventor's rights to a discovery for a specified period of time.

Penetration price.　A low, introductory price designed to encourage purchases of a new product.

Perception.　The attachment of meaning to information received through the five senses.

Personal selling.　Selling done on a one-to-one basis.

Physical distribution.　The process by which goods are moved from the manufacturer, through the various intermediaries on to the customer, including shipping, warehousing inventory control as well as order processing and customer service functions.

Place utility.　Value accruing to a product because it is available where consumers want to buy it.

Planned obsolescence.　The practice of manufacturing products with a predictably limited life, by using materials of lesser quality which allow a lower selling price.

Point-of-purchase advertising.　Displays, signs, and demonstrations which promote a product at a time and place close to the point of sale.

Positioning.　A marketing strategy which concentrates on a specific market segment by attempting to relate a particular product to its competitors.　When Avis said that it was number two, it was an attempt to position itself favorably next to the giant, Hertz.

Premium.　A bonus given without charge when a product is purchased.

Prestige pricing.　The practice of adopting relatively high prices in order to maintain a product's prestige image.

Price leadership. A situation which occurs mostly in an oligopoly in which one firm leads in price changes. One firm usually sets the prices for others implicitly in the steel industry without collusion.

Price limits. A psychological phenomenon which tends to set high and low limits for a product, so that a too-low price implies inferiority and the too-high price limits sales for conventional economic reasons.

Primary data. Original information collected for a specific market research study.

Private brand. A line of merchandise sold by a wholesaler or retailer under its own brand name. See National Brands.

Product advertising. Advertising whose sole purpose is to sell a product.

Product life cycle. The path a product travels from conception to its elimination from the line. The stages include introduction, growth, maturity, and decline.

Product line. All of the products produced by a single firm.

Product manager. An individual within a company who is assigned the responsibility for determining objectives, establishing strategies, and managing a program for a product or a product line.

Promotion. The task of informing, persuading, and influencing individuals to choose a certain product or service.

Promotional allowance. A grant of money made by a manufacturer to those in the distribution channel to help promote a product.

Promotional price. A price created specifically as part of a selling strategy; e.g., "Buy one and get one free."

Prospecting. A step in the selling process in which those selling a product or service attempt to identify its potential customers.

Psychological pricing. Depending on the product and those who make up the market, certain prices have more appeal than others. For example, $99 has more appeal than $100 even though there is only a $1 difference.

Publicity. Public relations activity which is directly related to the promotion of a product or service.

Public relations. The communications and other relationships a firm has with its various audiences (i.e., customers, stock holders, employees, government, and the neighbors of the plant).

Pulling strategy. A plan to build user demand for a product that distribution channels will be forced to meet.

Pushing strategy. A marketing method directed to the channels of distribution, rather than the end user.

Quantity discount. A price reduction offered when large quantities of a product are ordered.

Rack jobber. A wholesaler who handles specialized lines of products for retail stores, and also provides merchandising and stocking services for the retailer.

Receiver. The person in communications model toward whom a message is directed. Marketing communications (advertising) are directed to prospects.

Reciprocity. The practice of giving favorable consideration to suppliers who are also customers for the firm's products.

Reference groups. The groups of people with whom a person identifies.

Research design. An all-encompassing plan used to conduct a market research project.

Retail cooperative. A contractual arrangement made between a group of retailers to form a wholesale warehousing operation for the purpose of stocking their respective stores at lower costs.

Retailer. A person or company in the marketing chain that sells products directly to the final consumer.

Return on investment (ROI). A figure used to measure selling success, which is derived by multiplying the rate of profit (net profit/sales) by turnover (sales/investment).

Sales analysis. The study of sales figures for the purpose of reviewing, improving, or correcting a marketing situation. Sales information is broken down into individual components and examined as it relates to other factors operating within the marketing mix.

Sales branch. A company-owned sales office, remote from headquarters, which may or may not include product warehousing facilities.

Sales forecast. An estimate of anticipated sales in terms of dollars and units. The sales forecast is valid for a specified set of economic conditions and for a limited period of time.

Sales management. The activities of the sales manager and his or her staff directed to recruiting, maintaining, motivating, managing, evaluating, and controlling the efforts of a sales force.

Sales office. A regional office owned and operated by a company for the sole purpose of selling. Stock or inventory is never carried in a sales office.

Sales promotion. Techniques used to supplement advertising, personal selling, etc., such as trade shows, contests, premiums, etc.

Sales quota. An expected performance level established for a salesperson, or for a sales territory, against which actual performance can be measured.

Sampling. The process of selecting a representative number of people from a given universe for the purpose of market research.

Secondary data. Information used in a research project that has been gathered for other purposes and has been published previously. See primary data.

Selective distribution. The use of a small, but carefully selected number of retailers to handle a product line.

Self-concept. A psychological notion that states that the way people envision themselves influences the way they behave as consumers.

Seller's market. A market in which there is a shortage of goods or services.

Selling agent. A wholesaler who markets the products of a manufacturer and has control over pricing decisions and promotional expenditures.

Selling up. A sales technique used to induce a customer to buy a better and more expensive product than was originally being considered.

Sender. In communications terms, the person or organization which originates a message. The manufacturer that places advertising would be a sender. See receiver.

Services. Work performed which does not involve the production of tangible products; e.g., management consulting, tax preparation, personnel selection, etc.

Shopping center. A cluster of retail stores, centrally located to provide easy access for a large number of people.

Shopping goods. Goods purchased only after competitive goods have been evaluated in terms of price, quality, style, and color..

Standard Industrial Classification (SIC) Codes. A coding system which identifies every type of business, and is used in market and research planning, as well as for government industrial census information.

Status. A psychological term which describes an individual's relative position within a specific group.

Stock turnover. The number of times an average inventory is turned over within a given year.

Subculture. A group which can be isolated from a main culture group on the basis of certain specific characteristics.

Subliminal advertising. The attempt to influence people by presenting a stimulus (advertising message) below the threshold of recognition.

Supermarket. A department store for food products which operates as a self-service unit, and often competes with other types of stores by offering lower prices on certain consumer items.

Survey. A market research study which is conducted by asking respondents specific questions in order to obtain information on attitudes, motives, and opinions. Such studies can be conducted face-to-face, by telephone, or through the mail.

Target return objectives. The long- and short-term profit goals sought by a firm, usually stated as a percentage of sales or investment.

Tariffs. Publications giving rates for shipping various commodities. Also refers to taxes levied on imported goods.

Task method budgeting. A system of budget allocation which begins with a determination of goals and then goes on to specify the amount of investment needed to achieve them.

Test marketing. A process by which a new product is tried out in a limited area considered to be representative of the entire market. Information from the test can be extrapolated and projected to the entire market for planning purposes.

Time utility. Value which accrues to a product when it is available for sale at the precise time it is needed. Antifreeze sold in the summer has no time utility.

Trade discount. Money paid to a person or organization in the marketing channel for services that would ordinarily have to be performed by the manufacturer.

Trade show. A periodic show or convention where manufacturers in a single or closely related industries meet to exhibit their products to potential customers.

Trade-in. Money allowed when an old product is turned in on the sale of a new one. The trade-in allows the dealer some latitude in dealing without having to change the base price.

Trademark. A brand with the benefit of legal protection. A trademark includes graphic content as well as the brand name.

Trading stamps. Sales promotion devices used by some retailers. The stamps have a certain value, and the person who is given them when shopping at the store can turn them in for merchandise.

Truck jobber. A wholesaler who specializes in the marketing of perishable foods and makes regular deliveries to retail stores.

Truth-in-lending law. A federal statute which requires sellers to reveal annual interest rates to those who borrow money and buy on credit.

Tying contract. An agreement which states that an intermediary must carry other lines made by a company if he or she wishes to carry one specific line. Such agreements can be illegal if they restrict competitors from markets.

Undifferentiated marketing. A condition in which a firm produces one product and attempts to make it fit all potential markets with a single marketing mix.

Unit pricing. Items priced in terms of a standard unit of measure, e.g., pints, quarts, gallons, and pounds.

Utility. The value of a particular good or service to an individual.

Variable costs. Costs that change with varying production levels. See Fixed costs.

Vertical marketing system. Distribution systems that are professionally managed, centrally controlled, and created to attain operating economies that would be impossible on a catch-as-catch-can basis.

Warranty. A guarantee given to the buyer that covers a fixed period of time and insures that the manufacturer or the retailer will replace a product or provide a full refund if the product is defective, or fails to meet the conditions stated by the manufacturer.

Wholesaler. An intermediary who takes title to goods handled.

Wholesaling. The process of buying stock from a manufacturer, storing it, and selling and shipping it to either an industrial user or to a retail outlet, depending on the type of products.

Zone pricing. A system of uniform prices quoted on shipments anywhere within a given geographical area.

Index

Access, 13
Administrative vertical marketing, 60
Adoption process, 97–98, 136
Advertising, 2, 14, 35, 67, 68, 86, 100–112, 134
  cooperative, 49, 137
  defined, 101, 136, 139
  as marketing department function, 31–32
  situations benefiting most from, 111
  subliminal, 96, 142
  (See also Promotion)
Advertising department, 32
Advertising media, information from, 75
Age:
  in consumer markets, 15
  marketing strategy based on, 17
Agents, 62–63, 136
  (See also Manufacturers' agents; Selling
    agents)
Annual income, marketing based on, 17
Annual marketing plan, 82, 85
Anti-smoking campaigns, 95
Area samples, 79, 136
Attitudes, 94–96, 133–134, 136
Auction companies, 62, 136
Audits, marketing, 128–131, 135
Automated vending, 63, 65
Awareness, consumer, 97

Barriers, 80
Barter system, 45
Behavior, consumer, 90–99, 137
Behavioral psychology, 90
Bidding, 53
Biogenic motives, 92
Bottom liners, 8
Boycotts, 115
Brand(s), 136
  conditions for success of new, 43–44
Brand identification, 43
Brand insistence, 44, 136
Brand loyalty, 20, 95–96
Brand names, 43, 136
Brand preference, 44, 136
Brand recognition, 44, 136
Brand satisfaction, 43
Breakdown analysis, 82, 83
Broad product line, 40
Brokers, 62–63, 136
Budgets, 88–89, 123
  promotional, 102–103, 134
Build-up approach, 82, 83, 133
Business climate, distribution and, 58
Business environment:
  organization to suit, 22
  product managers and, 27–28

Buyers, department store, 63
Buying habits, 4, 57

Cash discounts, 49, 136
Cellar-Kefauver Act (1950), 113
Chain stores, 63, 64, 136
Circulation factors, 109
Clayton Act (1914), 113, 115
Cognitive dissonance, 98
Cognitive learning theories, 90–91
Collective demand, 12
Colleges and universities, information from, 75
Commission merchants, 62, 137
Communications process, 100, 137
  illustrated, 100
Company:
  distribution and nature of, 58, 60
  planning and position of, 82
Compatibility, product, 41
Competition, 2–3, 9
  pricing and, 50, 51
  unfair, 113–115
Computerized checkout system, 65
Computers in sales forecasting, 89
Concept testing, 40–41, 137
Confirmation, consumer, 98
Consultants, 3
Consumer behavior, 90–99, 137
Consumer climate, 4
Consumer education, 9
Consumer markets, 14, 15
Consumer products (goods), 2, 19, 106–107, 137
Consumer protection, 9
Consumer requirements, 1, 7
Consumer research, 73–74
Consumerism, 7, 9, 137
Consumption levels, 20
Contracts, 119–120
Contractual vertical marketing, 60
Controls, 8, 122–132, 135
  basics of, 122
Cooperative advertising, 49, 137
Copyright law, 117, 118
Corporate environment, organizing to suit, 22
Corporate marketing information systems, 74
Corporate vertical marketing, 60
Correlation statistics, 86
Cost analysis, 131–132
Cost plus profit method, 53–54, 137
Cost/volume analysis, 131, 132
Credit, retailer, 61
Culturally induced motives, 92
Customer requirements, 7
Customer wants, 1
Customers, 1

Customers (*Continued*)
 actual, 123
 buying habits of, 57
 potential, 123

Dealer promotion, 112
Decision(s):
 consumer, 98
 pricing, 50
 product planning, 42–43
Decline stage of product life cycle, 14, 36, 42
 advertising approach in, 106
Decoding, 100, 137
Demand, 12, 66, 102
Demand forecasting, 82–83, 85–87
Demarketing, 3, 137
Demographics, 18, 137
Department stores, 63, 64, 138
Departmental integration, 21
Departmentalized retail stores, 64
Differentiation, product, 12, 66, 102
Diffusion process, 39–40, 138
Diminishing returns, law of, 81
Direct mail advertising, 110–111
Direct mail sales, 63
Direct sales, 56
Discount stores, 64, 138
Discounts:
 cash, 49, 136
 trade, 49, 143
Discrimination, marketing and, against women,
  16–17
Distribution, 9, 68, 81
 choosing best channels of, 56–57
 defined, 2
 exclusive, 58, 138
 feedback, 122
 geographical factors in, 17–18, 57, 58
 market organization and, 22
 multiple channels of, 57
 pricing affected by, 47
 selective, 58, 142
 systems of, 55–68, 122
Distributors, 2, 56, 123, 138
Door-to-door (house-to-house) selling, 63–65
Drop shippers, 62, 138

Economic analysis, 13
Economic climate, 3–4
Economics in product planing, 42–43
Economy, 1
 of scale, 60
 trends in, in forecasting, 83
Ego enhancement, 98–99
Encoding, 100
Environmental Protection Agency (EPA), 5

Ethnic differences, 97
Ethnic segment marketing, 19
Evaluation, 98, 124
 market segment, 13
 of promotional effectiveness, 103
Exclusive distribution, 58, 138
Experimental research, 71
Experimentation, 77–78
External variables, 8

Fair Packing and Labeling Act (1966), 114, 134
Family relationships, 97
Federal Trade Commission Act (1914), 113
Feedback, 60, 100, 122, 138
Final examination, 133–135
Financial data in marketing system, 124
F.O.B. point-of-production, 52, 138
Food, Drug and Cosmetic Act (1938), 114, 138
Forecasting, 80, 82–83, 85–87, 133
 (*See also* Sales forecasting)
Formal research, 70
Frequency of sales calls, 31
Full-scale marketing, 42
Functional cost analysis, 131–132
Functionally integrated marketing operations,
  illustrated, 67
Functionally oriented marketing organizations,
  23
 illustrated, 24
Fur Products Labeling Act (1951), 114

General distribution, 58
Geographic factors in distribution, 17–18, 57, 58
Gestalt theory of learning, 91
Go-no-go point, 37
Goals:
 market share, to establish prices, 46–47
 marketing, 9–10, 122
 marketing audit and, 129–130
 media selection and advertising, 108–109
 planning and long-range, 82
 pricing, 45–46
 of promotional activity, 101–102, 124
Government controls (regulation), 8–9, 20
 (*See also specific acts*)
Government intervention, 8
Gross margin, 46
Growth stage of product life cycle, 14, 35–36
 advertising approach in, 106

Hazardous Substances Labeling Act (1960), 114,
  134
High prices, prestige and, 50, 51
Hiring from within or outside, 32–33
Horizontal marketing audits, 129

Hypothesis formation, 69
Hypothesis testing, 69

Impulse buying, 64, 99, 139
Incremental cost pricing, 54
Independent manufacturers' agents, 22
Index numbers:
    to analyze performance, 127–128
    tables, 128
Indirect selling, 2
Industrial advertising, 102
Industrial market research, 73–74
Industrial markets, 14
Industrial products (goods), 19, 20, 139
    distribution channels for, 61
    geographic concentration of markets for, 17–18
    promotion of, 107
Inflation, 4
Information sources, 75, 123
Informational advertising, 102
Institutional advertising, 107, 108, 139
Integration, departmental, 21–22
Intensive distribution, 58
Interest, consumer, 98
Interlocking directorates, 115
Internal variables, 8
Introductory stage of product life cycle, 14, 35
    advertising approach in, 68, 106
Inventory data in marketing reports, 124
Investigations, informal, 71

Jobbers, 56, 139

Learning theories of behavior, 90–92
Legal environment, 11, 113–121
Legal obligations, 119
Legal right, 119
Leverage, principle of, 61
Libraries, 75
Line acceptance, 124
List price, defined, 49, 139
Local advertising, 107–108
Long-range planning, 82
Loss-leader pricing, 51, 139

McGuire-Keogh Act (1952), 114
Magazine advertising, 109, 110
Mail interviews (see Surveys)
Mail order sales, 63, 65, 139
Management:
    market research and, 133
    marketing, 122–132
Manufacturers' agents (representatives), 22, 57,
    63, 68, 139

Marginal information, 124
Marginal utility, 81
Market(s), 12–20
    defined, 12
    ultimate, 20
Market advantage, 3
Market data in marketing reports, 124
Market demand forecasting, 82–83, 85–87
Market factor, 86
Market managers, 29–30
Market-oriented marketing organizations, 26
Market potential, 83
Market research, 69–79, 133, 135
    defined, 69, 139
    industrial, 73–74
Market segmentation, 66–67, 140
    characteristics of, 13–14
    ethnic and cultural, 19
    major ways of, 20
    product life cycle and, 14
Market share, 31, 83, 140
    goals of, to establish prices, 46–47
Market specialization, 31
Market variations, anticipating response to,
    80–81
Marketing concept, 1, 4–6, 8, 66, 139
Marketing control programs, 135
Marketing control report system, 123–124
Marketing departments, 21–33, 67
Marketing executives, 8
Marketing function, 1, 23
Marketing mixes, 2, 66, 139
    focusing on, 80
    planning based on composite of, 81
Marketing planning managers, job description
    for, 29–30
Marketing policy, 10
Marketing process, 1–11
Marketing report system, value of, 124
Marketing reports, 123–124
Marketing research (see Market research)
Marketing strategy, 139
    based on age or sex, 17, 19
    based on annual income, 17
Mark-on, defined, 54
Mark-up system, 51–52
    defined, 54, 140
    of products sold door-to-door, 65
Maturity stage of product life cycle, 14, 36
    advertising approach in, 106
Measurement, 13
Media selection, 108–110
Middleman (see Wholesaling)
Midterm examination, 66–68
Miller-Tydings Act (1937), 113
Monopolies, 113, 114, 140
Motivation, consumer, 4, 92, 96, 140

National advertising, 107–108
Need:
 defined, 12
 in product, defined, 34
Net sales, 131
New product development, 41, 140
 failure of, 37
 planning, 39–40
 stages in, 39
New products:
 ideas for, 40–41
 pricing of, 50–51
Newspaper advertising, 109–110
N.I.H. (Not Invented Here) Factor, 41

Observational research, 69–71, 77, 140
Odd pricing, 50, 140
O.E.M. (Original Equipment Market) products, 14
Operating statement, 131
Opinion leaders, 97, 140
Organizing for marketing, 21–33
Original Equipment Market (O.E.M.) products, 14
Out-of-home advertising, 110

Penetration pricing, 51, 140
Percentage of sales method, 88, 103
Perception, defined, 92, 140
Performance analysis of marketing program, 126–127
 tables, 126, 127
Person-to-person interviews (see Surveys)
Personal selling, 2, 100, 101, 111–112, 134, 140
Phaseout of product, 21
Place utility, 55–56, 68
Planned obsolescence, 44
Planning:
 management, control and, 122
 market, 9, 10, 70, 80–82, 122, 130
 of marketing organization, 23
 product (see Product planning)
 research project, 71
Population trends, 18
Positioning, product, 4, 140
Prediction of outcome, 69
Preliminary analysis, 70–71
Preliminary screening, 40
Prestige products pricing, 50, 51, 140
Pretesting of survey questionnaires, 78–79
Price(s):
 in buying decision, 98
 defined, 45
 discrimination in, 115
 levels of, 50

Price(s) (Continued)
 list, defined, 49
 reductions in, 52–53
Price/volume factor, 3, 46, 47
Pricing:
 decisions on, 50
 defined, 2, 50
 strategy for, 45–54, 122
Primary circulation, 109
Primary data, 71, 133, 141
Print medium, advertising in, 111
Product, defined, 1, 34
Product advertising, 107, 108
 (See also Advertising)
Product development, 10–11
 (See also New product development)
Product divisions, illustrated, 25
Product life cycle, 14, 67–68, 141
 advertising approach during, 106
 in marketing planning, 88
 practical applications of, 36–37
 price reductions in, 52–53
 stages of, 14, 35–36, 42
Product lines, 40, 141
Product managers, 25, 27–29, 141
 illustrated, 25
Product oriented marketing organizations, 24
 illustrated, 24
Product planning, 2, 34–44
 for branded products, 44
 decision to make or buy products in, 42–43
 defined, 2
Production capabilities, 10
Production of ideas, 40
Production orientation, 6–7, 24
Profit(s), 4, 8–10, 46
 as goal in pricing, 45–46
 market segmentation and, 13–14
 maximization of, 46, 68
 and plan implementation, 88
 pricing based on cost plus, 53–54, 137
Projective tests, 94
Promotion (advertising), 100–112
 of consumer market products, 106–107
 in marketing reports, 124
 under Robinson-Patman Act, 121
 (See also Advertising)
Promotion allowance, defined, 49, 141
Promotional activity, goals of, 101–102, 124
Promotional budgets, 102–103, 134
Promotional effectiveness, 103–104
Promotional mix, 100, 134
 establishing optimum, 101
Promotional strategy, defined, 2
Promotions (job), 32–33
Psychoanalytical theories of learning, 91–92
Psychogenic motives, 92

Public relations, 101, 141
Pulling strategy, 105–106, 141
Purchasing specialists, 19
Pure Food and Drug Act (1906), 113
Pushing marketing strategy, 106, 134, 141

Quota samples, 79

Random samples, 79
Receiver action, 100, 141
Reference groups, 96, 141
Research interpretation, 72
Research projects:
    carrying out, 72
    guidelines on cost of, 74
    planning, 71
Retailing, 2, 63–65, 123, 141
Return on investment (ROI), 88, 141
Risk in buying unknown products, 98
Robinson-Patman Act (1936), 113, 115, 121
ROI (return on investment), 88, 141
Role, defined, 96

Sales:
    advertising to stabilize, 102
    engineering features of, 123
    exceeding estimates, 122
    figures on, in marketing reports, 124
    materials requirements for, 123
    orientation of, 7
Sales activity in marketing reports, 22, 62, 81, 124
Sales approach, 1, 6
Sales branch, 63, 142
Sales budgets, 123
Sales departments, 30–31
Sales force, 1, 31, 67, 123, 126
    information from, 88, 133
Sales forecasting, 85, 87, 89, 123, 142
Sales jobs, 31
Sales office, 63, 142
Sales potential, 85
Sales promotion, 2, 100–112
    defined, 101, 142
    (See also Advertising)
Sales quotas, 123, 142
Sales territories, 31
Sales/volume analysis, 131, 132
Samples (sampling), 79, 86–87, 142
Saturation problem, 80–81
Scaling techniques, 94
Scientific method in marketing research, 69–72
Secondary data, 70, 133, 142
    sources for, 74–75
Segmentation, market (see Market segmentation)

Selective distribution, 58, 142
Self-image (self-concept), 4, 142
Selling (see Sales)
Selling agents, 62, 142
Senders, 100, 142
Sensation, defined, 92
Services, marketing, 19–20
Sex, marketing strategy based on, 17, 19
Sherman Antitrust Act (1890), 113–115
Shipping costs, 52
Short-range planning, 82
Single (limited-line) stores, 63
Situation analysis, 70–71
Skimming, 50–51
Social classes, 20, 97
Social responsibility, 4–5
Specialty stores, 63
Speculative production, 55
Staff acceptance, 124
Standard Industrial Classification (S.I.C.) codes, 18, 142
Status symbols, 96
Stimulus-response (S-R) theories, 90
Stockpiling materials, 123
Subliminal advertising, 96, 142
Submarkets, 13, 15
Supermarkets, 64, 142
Survey questionnaires, 78–79
Surveys, 75–77, 135, 142
    market demand, 86–87

Target return system, 46, 143
Task method, 89, 143
Technology, obsolescence and, 44
Telephone interviews (see Surveys)
Telephone sales, 63
Television advertising, 110
Television sales, 63
Test marketing, 37, 41–42, 87, 143
Testimonials, 102
Textile Fiber Products Identification Act (1958), 114
Time utility, 55, 68, 143
Total corporate planning, 82
Trade associations, 3, 75, 83
Trade discounts, 49, 143
Trade-in allowances, 49, 143
Trade magazines, 123
Trademarks, 117–119, 134, 143
Transmission system, 100
Trial period, 98
Truth in Lending Act (1968), 114, 143
Tying contracts, 115, 143

Uniform Commercial Code, 120
Uniform delivered pricing system, 52

Uniform Sales Act, 120
Unit pricing, 50, 68, 143
Universal Product Code, 65
Unprofitable products, 42
Utility, 1, 81, 143
    place, 55–56, 68
    time, 55, 68, 143

Variety, product, 81
Vending machine sales, 63, 65
Vendors, 20
Vertical marketing audits, 129
Vertical marketing systems, 60, 143
Volume, 68
    pricing and, 46, 47
Volume/cost analysis, 131, 132

Webb-Pomerene Act (1918), 113
Wheeler-Lea Act (1938), 114
Wholesaling (wholesalers), 2, 61, 123, 138, 143
    defined, 56
    full-function, 62
    promotion of, 107
Women, marketing program for, 16–17, 19
Wool Products Labeling Act (1939), 114

Youth market, 15

Zero Population Growth, 18
Zone-delivered pricing, 52, 143

Catalog

If you are interested in a list of SCHAUM'S
OUTLINE SERIES send your name
and address, requesting your free catalog, to:

SCHAUM'S OUTLINE SERIES, Dept. C
McGRAW-HILL BOOK COMPANY
1221 Avenue of Americas
New York, N.Y. 10020